WITHDRAWN

WHAT IS MUSIC?

What Is Music?

BY

John Erskine

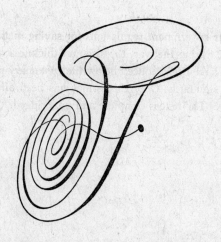

J. B. LIPPINCOTT COMPANY
PHILADELPHIA AND NEW YORK

Preface

The teaching of music in the last century has made brilliant advances so
far as concerns technique, but I am one of those who believe that otherwise it has settled into a rut. It is both too complicated and too narrow.
This book is an experiment by way of pointing out where simplification
and expansion are needed.

Musical theory begins to be a venerable subject, and from different
epochs it has collected rules which now appear to be barnacles. We know
they are barnacles, yet we preserve them to pad our textbooks. It would
be honest and intelligent to teach only the rules we use. In the first half
of this book I try to select the few essentials. My confidence in my choice
is not excessive, but I am rather pleased with myself for making the
attempt.

In the second half of the book I try to sketch the relation of music
and musicians to society. The curse of the art and profession at the present
moment is the tenacity with which otherwise first-rate musicians insist
on traditional ways of reaching their audience, in traditional programs
supported by traditional forms of patronage. Like most other vital things
at this moment music as art and as profession needs to break out of its
confining patterns. I try to indicate what those patterns are, and in what
respects they prove themselves too small. Our spiritual inheritance will
some day be shared and enjoyed in a society which is free and self-respect-
ing and humane. Perhaps even an outline or our present condition will
suggest where progress might begin at once.

John Erskine

Contents

PART ONE

PART TWO

Part One

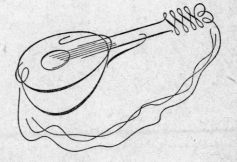

Chapter one:

THE PURPOSE OF THIS BOOK

1 THOSE WHO LOVE music ask certain questions about the art, questions which musicians seem unwilling or unable or too busy to answer. In this book I bring the questions together, and try my hand at solving them. I do not apologize for my audacity. I have sung a little and played a few instruments, and at intervals I have composed, though only as an amateur. These pages would be better if they were written by one whose equipment was professional and thorough. Yet in one respect I feel qualified to speak; I doubt if even master musicians love music more than I do. In a lifetime of devotion I have heard other music-lovers ask for light, but rarely have I seen frank recognition that music as we know it is the youngest of the arts and the least developed; that its development in the last century has been rapid and uneven; that among musicians themselves there is confusion as to the very nature of music, and violent difference of opinion as to what is good music; that the instruments on which music is produced have not been developed as fast as the scope of music has been extended, so that the composer, to say what is on his mind, now needs more instruments and more kinds of instruments than he once did; that the musical profession has become so highly specialized that the composer and the performer are nowadays quite different creatures; that in consequence of all this the art of music is undefined and disorganized, and the profession of music is unsatisfactory—surprisingly so when we consider how fast the love of music spreads and how willing man in general is to reward the artists who excel.

What I here write may seem discouraged and discouraging, unless the reader loves music and bears in mind that I love it too. Isn't it timid or stupid of us music-lovers to keep on praising our art, preaching the necessity of it for culture and civilization, if at the same time we continue to ignore, perhaps wilfully, the aspects of music which need definition or explanation or development or even reform? The whole picture should be studied. I here try to outline it. If I bring to it too little illumination, I comfort myself with the hope that wiser musicians will bring more. But someone must make a start.

Of course you can dispose of me in advance by saying that a genuine lover of music won't notice the undeveloped or unfinished condition of the art, will ask no questions, will be annoyed rather than assisted by the intrusion of the mind upon an experience which is chiefly emotional and should be entirely so. I confess I'm ready at all times to think well of music-lovers, even of the most headlong. To be so much in love that the mind passes out completely, is to be mad, and I follow Plato's doctrine that madness is an ingredient of poetry in all forms. Too many of us, though none too rich in common sense, are disproportionately sane. Yet the greatest music, I firmly believe, is yet to be composed. Before it can be created, our hearts must be larger, our souls must be nobler—and our intelligence must be employed, even in our adorations.

If a visitor from another planet, curious about our ways, should look in on a concert by one of our major orchestras, he would probably ask what in Heaven's name (or the equivalent) was going on there. I said, if he should look in on a concert. Though there would be sound in plenty, I assume that his attention would be claimed first by what he saw. On the platform he would see some eighty or ninety players, lugubriously garbed, rubbing, blowing or beating instruments of fantastic shapes. In the center of the platform, on the edge near the audience, he would notice a small square box, and on it a man dressed, like the players, in black, who sways in a slow dance, varied by spasms or contortions. The visitor might mistake him for a snake-charmer. The players face in his direction and watch his movements, fascinated. The audience too are under his spell, though he keeps his back turned to them. He will look around only if they clap their hands, which at intervals they do.

The audience pack themselves into narrow seats, fastened to the floor. There are more women than men. The men, like the players and the dancer, are costumed as if for a funeral, but the gowns of the women suggest a carnival or a masquerade.

The visitor could be pardoned if he thought he had before him a religious ceremony or rite. Before long he'll be told that it is costly, that it is maintained by voluntary offerings of the well-to-do and penitent, that no offerings so vast are made to other cults. But for the moment it's enough for him to exclaim, "What is this?"

"This," say we, "is music."

"But what is music?" says he.

We smile at his ignorance and hand him a history of the art, which is not what he asked for, but it's easier to tell how music began and how it grew up than to say what it is.

This book will try to define music, to describe its office in human society, to indicate its importance in the future development of mankind. History is valuable as history, but the past is not a definition of the present, though we try to make it so. The etymology of a word may furnish piquant contrasts to the present use of it. This book will attempt a strictly contemporary portrait of music today. If a precedent for such rashness is needed, I'll name Aristotle, who thousands of years ago gave an account of life in all phases as he saw it, and having described fish and politicians and other phenomena, reported on poetry and drama, on the conditions and the functions of the poetic arts. It may be said, in general, that later critics have not imitated him. Nor caught up with him.

If you ask a scholar to define music, he parries by giving you its history. If you ask a musician to define his art, he parries by giving a performance. After all, he argues, music is its own definition; if you would know what music is, I'll spread it out for you to examine. But he can play or sing only one example at a time, and the art is too immense and too varied for him ever to display it all. A Mozart sonata, however performed, does not define the art in which Debussy and Gershwin have their place, and Shostakovich and Chopin. And there can be no complete definition of music which doesn't consider the response of the audience.

This book pretends to aid performance as little as it contributes to history. It hopes merely to make the love of music to some degree more intelligent. I would not match myself against the musicologists, still less against the great artists of our day. But when it comes to defining music, nothing that musicians themselves have written or spoken reduces me to humility or awe. Musicians are notoriously inarticulate about what concerns them most. I tremble for their art whenever in writing or speech they defend it. Just now they are saying that music has special value in wartime, that it soothes the nerves, that it comforts in anxiety and consoles in bereavement, that it fortifies in danger and clarifies in perplexity —in short, that it props the public morale. No doubt it does, but the argument is a boomerang. Are the musicians describing the functions of an art, or advertising a tonic? The patient stops taking his tonic as soon as his health is restored. After the war, shall we put music aside?

In describing the material out of which music is made, I shall try to present harmony and counterpoint, not in their historical development, but as they are today. In art we sometimes blind ourselves with history, so that we waste time preaching theories which in practice we have, without realizing it, long since abandoned. Roofs were formerly supported by walls or columns, and therefore the architectural student must learn the difference between Ionic, Doric, and Corinthian columns, as though it were still important. The really important fact is that columns are no longer used, since most of our roofs are supported by steel frames. Where columns still appear they serve no purpose and are structural fakes; the steel frame goes up first, and on it we hang brick walls instead of glass, which would let in light, but in the past there were always brick walls; and on the suspended walls we sometimes hang a column which holds up nothing but must itself be held up.

So in music we still tell beginners to avoid consecutive fifths and fourths, once thought to be unpleasant sounds. They occurred frequently in great music; they were always present in the overtones of chiming bells. If the rule-makers could damn consecutive fourths and fifths and yet go sentimental over the sound of a carillon, it must have been because their ears weren't keen enough to detect all there was in a bell. Since music today is full of once forbidden things, in the present account they will not be listed as forbidden. Yet some consecutive fifths sound better than others. The reason for this difference is worth explaining.

It's a great pity that music is studied so much with the eye. The ear is in danger of atrophy, or at least of underdevelopment. Every art should be studied in terms of its medium, and of the effect of that medium on the audience. Music is an art of tones rather than of noises. This distinction is real, and I belong with those who think it should be made. The human ear discovers in tone two kinds of pleasure. In the first place, tones can be arranged in a scale, a ladder of regular intervals moving either up or down. A scale by itself gives pleasure. A succession of notes picked here and there from the scale may form a pattern which gives pleasure, provided that the skipping is not so violent as to break the sequence from note to note. Such a sequence we now call a melody. In the second place, each tone carries with it certain overtones or harmonics, which give pleasure if we can hear them. The ear is not very sensitive to these ghostly sounds, but with practice and training it may become so. To make it easier for us the musician accompanies a given note with other notes already sounded by the overtones. This is what we call harmony. A chord consists of a fundamental tone with its faint harmonics italicized, as it were.

It is a peculiarity of the human ear, as yet unexplained—a mysterious faculty, I should say, of the human brain—that we can hear different sounds simultaneously without getting them mixed up. We can hear them as separate tones or we can attend to the effect of them all together. We can, if we wish, shut out all the sounds except one. If you and I, walking in the country, notice the whisper or hum of roadside or woods, I can call your attention to a woodpecker, and you, with no effort at all, can listen exclusively to that bird. But you can also listen, if you wish, to more than one bird sound at a time. In music we enjoy a chord as a single mass of vibrations, or as a group of separate notes, and we derive a different pleasure from each possible arrangement of the notes. Through a succession of chords we follow the movement of the different parts, each of which becomes a melody to be enjoyed by itself or in conjunction with the others. Some chords and sequences of chords make upon us an unfinished impression—they ask a question. Other chords and cadences satisfy with an answer. Out of question and answer comes the subject matter of music, and also its language, and at last its form. When we know something of what music wants to say, and how it says it—what is its grammar and its rhetoric, and what form its total utterance is likely to take—then we are ready to tell the visitor from another planet what music is.

Since music is a language, let us remind ourselves of a certain handicap in using one language to define another. Human speech may have musical qualities, but it excels in the ability to state an intellectual concept and to present an argument. Music has intellectual elements, but its strength lies in its ability to express aspiration, yearning, spiritual upreaching. It speaks to our mind, but its eloquence rouses emotion and influences character. The best of every language, unfortunately, cannot be translated into other languages. The painter, the sculptor and the dancer can give partial versions of a story which has been told in words, but they can reproduce nothing which is in essence literary; they cannot, for example, convey a witty remark. And music is the art which is least translatable. It can be associated with other arts but it cannot by itself describe or reproduce them, and no other art can by itself reproduce music. Music can indeed mimic nature, it can imitate the cries of birds or animals, the sigh or roar of the wind, but such imitations must be enjoyed for themselves only. They are not the subject matter nor the language of music; they remain imitations.

With so many inadequacies in so many kinds of language, it is not surprising that so little has been told about the art of music. I dare not hope that this book will surmount all the difficulties. But if we try to define music instead of rewriting its history, perhaps even musicians will see further into its nature, and learning more of music, perhaps we may know more about ourselves, on whom music casts so mysterious and so binding a spell.

Chapter two:

HOW MANY KINDS OF MUSIC?

1 WE ARE NOT yet finished with that visitor from another planet. For a moment longer we would trace his advance in music appreciation from unprejudiced innocence toward perplexed culture. He began by using his eyes rather than his ears, taking in the appearance and behavior of orchestra, conductor and audience, but sooner or later he will notice the music. He may owe the awakening of his auditory interests, not to the players on the stage, but to the listeners out in front, who are provided, he will discover, with two commentaries on what they came to hear. These commentaries need not agree. Usually they contradict each other. The visitor may listen to the music, if for no other reason, to find out who is wrong.

The faces of these men and women, seated in formal rows, display one comment on the program. The music changes them. When the performance stops, each face reverts to itself, but while the music continues, the soul, off its guard, comes to the window and looks out. Each soul, it would seem, finds in the music a different message; some eyes are troubled, some are peaceful, some are bright with discovery, some remember what is gone. But at the end, when they applaud, they will all wear a smile, all the same smile, which is the curtain to a drama.

The visitor is observing the oldest thing known about music. How ancient instruments sounded or how they were played, can only be guessed at, and our guesses are influenced by all the later music we have heard, but two thousand years ago men observed and recorded this miracle of the listening moment, this involuntary revelation of the heart.

The painters of the Renaissance, that musical period, loved to portray intimate concert scenes—some enthusiast bending over a lute or singing, and someone listening. The listener's face made the picture, by supplying, as in modern concert halls, a commentary on the music. This sort of commentary, the natural and pure reaction to lovely sound, the poet Richard Watson Gilder described in a vivid sonnet—

> *"When late I heard the trembling 'cello play,*
> *In every face I read sad memories*
> *That from dark, secret chambers where they lay*
> *Rose, and looked forth from melancholy eyes . . ."*

The music evoked memories; since the tone of the 'cello is moving and tragic, the awakened memories were sad. The poet does not, however, tell us specifically what the memories were. He is describing absolute music and its effect, beauty of sound creating in the hearers beauty of mood.

The other kind of commentary is in the printed annotations which the modern symphony audience usually hold in their hands—what often amounts to a set of instructions not only as to when and how the music came to be written, but as to what feelings and ideas it is expected to call up.

When music is its own subject matter and its own language, needing no other commentator than the heart of the listener, it is called absolute or pure music. When critical annotations attempt to translate music into another language or to bring another medium to its aid, the result is called program music—not because the annotations are printed on concert programs, but because they are put first, so that the music becomes a running comment or illustration of a sequence or scheme which is already in the hearer's mind. Operatic music, for example, since it must accompany a pre-existing libretto, is program music.

Having used the lines from Gilder's sonnet to describe pure music, I am tempted to digress a moment to caution you against the musical observations of most literary folk. Poets were once supposed to sing and to accompany themselves on the lyre or harp. For this mythical reason, and for no better one, we who are guileless and easily deluded assume that the masters of lordly language have also a musical education. Sometimes they have and sometimes they haven't. But even though they are good musicians as well as good poets, it doesn't follow that they are good musicians while they are writing poetry. Robert Browning was a trained musician and he wrote a rather large number of fine poems which to the unwary seem to be about music—such poems as *Abt Vogler* and *A Toccata of Galuppi's*—but in one case the theme is a philosophy of life, and the interest of the other poem lies in the program it suggests, an old love-story.

On the other hand some of the profound things about music have been said by poets who were musically ignorant, in some instances tone deaf. I offer no explanation. Why the musical Browning should write unmusical verse, or why the unmusical Tennyson should write verse of liquid beauty, I can't say. In English poetry the clearest understanding of absolute music is shown, to my way of thinking, in William Wordsworth's poem, *The Education of Nature*. He portrays a child growing up in solitude; the music she hears is of nature—the sound of the waterfall, of the wind in the trees. But over her face the lovely sounds bring an answering expression, and the poet raises a question which a musician can understand—if the music of nature is ceaseless, may not the revelation called to the hearer's face remain there always, instead of vanishing when the concert is over?

> *"She shall lean her ear*
> *In many a secret place*
> *Where rivulets dance their wayward round,*
> *And beauty born of murmuring sound*
> *Shall pass into her face."*

So much for the poets as guides to music appreciation. Look to them, not for music, but for poetry. For an insight into music, let us return to the art itself.

As between absolute music and program music, which kind is better? In a moment I shall give my reasons for thinking the question intrinsically futile, but we can hardly refuse to consider it since it is raised in all the arts by artists, by some of the very persons who should know better. Painters and sculptors as well as architects and musicians like to tell us that their particular art should be enjoyed and interpreted in terms of its peculiar medium—that paintings should not convey a story but should speak to us through line, mass, and color—that music should rely on neither pictures nor words but should speak to us through tone, melody, harmony, counterpoint, rhythm. So the artists like to say, and periodically there is a movement toward pure poetry, pure music, pure what-not; on several occasions in my life I have even heard pure oratory, which charmed and persuaded without saying a thing. But pure music or pure poetry is for many people hard to understand. They like to have the meaning of a work of art detachable from the medium, so that they can take it out and examine it at their convenience. The language they know best is the language of words, and through words they try to connect the experience of art with some more usual or more familiar experience of life.

When I was eight or nine years old I heard an adverse comment on a painting I happened to admire. The painting was a landscape, with colorful meadows in the foreground, austere mountains in the distance. In the nearest meadow two men were working. The critic said the picture was inferior because its appeal was in the two men. I asked if the appeal should be in the meadows and the hills. The critic explained that a picture ought to be effective even if we turned it upside down; it should speak to us through its design or its color or through the other elements which are purely pictorial. This doctrine made on me a lasting impression. The two men in the meadow had excited my friendly interest, and I was sorry to learn they shouldn't have been there. In later years, if I could have found that critic, I would have asked whether the Mona Lisa and the portraits of Raphael and of Rembrandt are good pictures, and whether their excellence depends on their effectiveness when turned upside down. But at the time I recognized the force of a new idea, and I applied it to other arts. I applied it specifically to a piano piece called *Moonlight on the Hudson,* which I did not play but some of my friends did. Musically this piece was worth little, and I took pleasure in hinting to those who had practiced it for hours that it didn't sound like moonlight, still less like the Hudson. But my teasing brought a counter-attack; how about the *Moonlight Sonata* and the *Harmonious Blacksmith?*

It was comforting to learn before I was much older that Beethoven never called his sonata Moonlight, that Händel did not intend his delicate theme and variations to represent a blacksmith, harmonious or otherwise. Those unlucky titles were bestowed, when the composers could no longer protest, by misguided admirers of the music who thought they could help it out by hitching a program to it.

I was further comforted, still later, by a famous passage in Walter Pater's *Renaissance* which praises music for its ability to get on without a program. "All art," he says, "constantly aspires to the condition of music. For while it is possible in all other arts to distinguish the matter from the form, and the understanding can make this distinction, yet it is the constant effort of art to obliterate it. That the mere matter of a poem, for instance, its subject, namely, its given incidents or situation—that the mere matter of a picture, the actual circumstances of an event, the actual topography of a landscape—should be nothing without the form, the spirit, of the handling, that this form, this mode of handling, should become an end in itself, should penetrate every part of the matter: this is what every art constantly strives for, and achieves in different degrees."

In what sense is it true that all art aspires to the condition of music, in which the form and the matter are identical? Artists—we include musicians—are as reluctant as they ever were to let their medium do its work, without borrowed aid or supplement. Musicians agree in theory that music is a self-sufficient language, but they know that like any other language it has its limitations, and they are somewhat unwilling to respect those limitations and stay within them. On the other hand they pay tribute to absolute music by saying or implying that program music, the kind that attempts to tell a story or paint a picture, is old-fashioned and out of date—which it certainly is not. They will refer with a smile to Johann Kunau (1660-1722), a far from contemptible composer who wrote among other things some musical versions of Bible stories. Or they will mention charitably, to show their acquaintance with the literature, some notable cat-fugues, some hunting music which preserves the baying of the hounds, innumerable instances of bird songs and bird calls. They seem to imply that no one would now stoop so low. But we have, and enjoy, our musical portraits of Lincoln and Barnum, scored for full orchestra, and most of the romantic composers, however devoted to the strict medium of their art, have liked to give their pieces names which recall a literary theme, as in the case of Schumann's *Carnival* or his *Kreisleriana,* which owe something of their inspiration to the writings of Jean Paul Richter and E. T. A. Hoffmann. Yet the composers who choose for their work such titles or who annotate them in literary or pictorial terms, usually deny any intention of writing program music; they explain that they would merely evoke in the audience, by association of ideas, a mood sympathetic with what they are about to hear. Didn't Whistler call his paintings Nocturnes? And didn't Field and Chopin invent the name in order to indicate the twilight mood of certain short pieces?

The distinction, then, between absolute and program music seems to be not always clear to musicians themselves, and we need hardly take their word for it that absolute music is the better kind. But as I said a moment ago, the question seems to me rather silly. Obviously, not all music is pure music, but Pater was right—it tends toward the pure condition, if it has vitality enough to show any tendency. Much good music will continue to be written to a program, but because it is good music it will be enjoyed for itself and the program will be forgotten. The wretched librettos of well-known operas are just so much excess baggage, which the inspired music will throw overboard as soon as it can. Already the best of Richard Wagner is as much at home in concert halls as in opera houses, and it is not impossible that the imperishable things in *Tristan* and the *Ring* will survive longest in symphonic arrangements, since Wagner excelled in his use of the orchestra—as he did not excel in his employment of the human voice, or as a dramatist, or as a poet.

The same principle holds for music apparently less important—for songs and folk tunes; if the quality of the music is fine enough, it can best be enjoyed without the words or other program originally attached to it. The tune of *The Star Spangled Banner,* which once supported the words of a drinking song, happened to be floating around unencumbered when Francis Scott Key needed music for his flag poem. Today we all know the tune, but few of us know the words. So with the songs of Stephen Foster or the great Negro spirituals—so with a contemporary song like Jerome Kern's *Old Man River,* composed as it were only yesterday; in music the perfect things need no aid from another medium and will not long tolerate it. The composer may not have intended absolute music, but absolute it becomes. Moreover, the well-meaning folk who chide you and me for not remembering the words of our national anthem, are sounding off in a field where they are insufficiently instructed. The words are forgotten because the music is memorable. If the words were memorable they would be enjoyed for themselves, and the music would be forgotten. The songs of Burns, of Thomas Moore, of Beranger, were all written to music and were intended to be sung, not read; but against such literary power the music hadn't a chance.

This constant tendency toward the pure condition of music springs from the will of the audience, on whose faces as they listened the man from another planet saw revealing comments. The members of all audiences resent whatever limits their interpretations. If they like a work of art, it belongs to them and if it continues to enjoy their favor they may even remold it to suit themselves. They will at least leave out what they find superfluous. Since each hearer derives his personal meaning from great music, the words or other program contrived by another person are liable to get in his way. He ignores them, therefore, so that the music may come to him in a pure and unprejudiced condition.

2   IN EVERY EPOCH there is a phenomenon known as modern music. This must be so, since the human ear by much listening becomes more acute, learns to hear more of the harmonics which are always present in a tone, discovers a pleasure, therefore, in tone-combinations which formerly were ignored or disliked. But since not all ears acquire acuteness at the same rate of speed, the enjoyment of newly discovered harmonies is neither universal nor uniform. The path-makers in music as elsewhere must expect criticism or opposition. Not infrequently they comfort themselves by reflecting that Debussy was once considered too advanced, that the London Philharmonic refused to play Schubert's C major symphony when Mendelssohn tried to introduce it, that Chopin was condemned for the crudity of his harmonies and modulations.

But there are two kinds of modern composer, and only one kind has the right to assume that he is in the line of musical evolution, and that people on closer acquaintance will rise to the privilege of appreciating him. If the composer is writing pure or absolute music, he is likely to be in the line of evolution, and his work probably represents the normal growth of the art, leading but not out-distancing the more and more acute audience. But if the composer is writing program music, his innovations are not necessarily dictated by the essential structure of musical tone; they are more likely to be suggested by the program. It may even be that for a special effect he will provide not music but noise, as in the representation of a real blacksmith at work, or a boiler factory, or a battle. Program music has little to do with evolution or progress, since among the various programs a composer may choose for his texts there is no inevitable sequence, rarely even a connection.

So long as a composer respects the harmonics of a tone, he knows he is true to his medium, no matter how advanced he may seem. Historians say that the first recognized harmony was the octave—that when the monks in the abbeys chanted eight notes apart they felt that they were making a richer effect than when they chanted in unison. But we have illustrations nearer at hand than these medieval ghosts; many of our friends are at that stage of musical development where their utmost in part-singing consists in carrying the tune an octave above or below. If you sing middle C they can hit the same note higher or lower, according to the range of the voice, but they'd rather not join you on the same level.

As their ear becomes discriminating they may venture away from octaves and try thirds—that is, if you sing C, they will sound E above, or if that E is too high for them, they will drop it an octave. The interval of E above C is a third; the interval of C above E is a sixth. Play *Yankee Doodle* on your piano, starting the tune on C, with E above. Continue the upper interval throughout, as an accompaniment to the melody. Here you have the effect of consecutive thirds. Make the same experiment with consecutive sixths, starting the tune on C and the accompaniment on E below.

Examples:

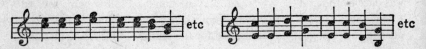

In both cases the effect is pleasing, but before long it becomes saccharine, at last cloying. When thirds and sixths were first introduced they may have caused distress by their audacious departure from simple, manly octaves.

As a matter of fact, musicians today are wary of thirds and sixths, not because they detect danger in those sweet intervals, but because they prefer a more powerful interval, the fifth. Of the three notes which form

the triad on C ♪♪ which two make a better combination, C and E

♪♪ or C and G? ♪♪ The musician would probably say, C and

G. In this triad C is the basic tone, or "tonic," and G is the fifth or "dominant." The tonic sets the chord or names it; the fifth dominates it, does so naturally, not by a man-made rule. If a triad is extended in a chord of four or more notes, the tonic, the third or the fifth must be doubled, but it is safer to double the tonic or the fifth than to double the third. By making the third too strong we are in danger of killing the dominance of the fifth, which musicians, except on rare occasions, for special effects, are reluctant to do. It usually seems desirable to preserve in the chord the relative strength of the notes in the triad, as the triad is first heard in the harmonics.

Where should we listen for harmonics? Once we have heard them, we can pick them out of any well-sounded note, whether of the human voice or of the various instruments, but it is most practical for the beginner to look for harmonics on the piano, the instrument which fortunately or unfortunately is for most of us the gateway to music. Press down, without striking, the notes of the triad C, E, G,  an octave above middle C. These notes, held down by the right hand, are silent. Now with the left hand strike sharply but do not hold, the C below middle C. In a second or two you will hear the tones of the triad vibrating under your right hand. By holding down the keys you have lifted the dampers off the notes of the triad, and the overtones of lower C have set the strings vibrating.

Notice that G, the fifth, is louder than E, the third. If you struck the triad with your hand the notes would sound nearly of the same strength, but in the harmonics, vibrating naturally, the fifth dominates. This is because we rearrange the harmonic triad on the piano so that the hand can play it, but in their natural position the harmonics are widely distributed, the fifth sounding an octave and five notes above the tonic, and the third sounding an octave and six notes above the fifth. Because the harmonic of the third vibrates so high, it is a weak sound, much weaker than the fifth.

Once the ear has become accustomed to this balance of strength, the same balance seems desirable when the harmonics are translated into notes to be played or sung. Harmony, as taught and practiced among us, is simply a record of what the ear has so far learned from harmonics. As fast as our ear gains in acuteness, we add new chords to our system. No doubt we shall appreciate some day the delicate quarter tones which orientals already enjoy. In comparison, our whole tones, even our half tones, are rough blocks of sound.

Yet to be aware of the triad, to hear the tonic, the third and the fifth separately even when they are sounded together, to hear them in different positions, with the third or the fifth at the bottom of the chord instead of the tonic—is to have made already very respectable progress toward an understanding of music. If we learn also to distinguish a major triad

from a minor —to feel, that is, the change of color

when the third is lowered half a tone—we shall then be able to recognize the harmonies used by Palestrina (1525-1594). In Palestrina's music there is more than harmony, but he was a master of chord-building, and since the natural harmonics do not change, he continues to seem modern, and in his economical and severe style he has as yet no rival.

To understand at least in outline the more elaborate and more complete chords, we should remember that not only the tonic of a triad but also the third and the fifth have each its own harmonic triad. The harmonics may set up further harmonics, even ghostlier than themselves, but we shall have our hands full if we consider here only the harmonics produced by tones actually played or sung. Whenever some composer has caught and written down harmonics previously not heard, he may be said to have enriched the science of harmony with a new chord, yet he has invented nothing—he has merely increased our awareness of those overtones without which the most musical note would be an impoverished noise. We cannot pay too great respect to harmonics, to overtones; unless they are developed in the human voice, the voice is flat and unpleasant; until radio engineers learned to capture them in the tone of a piano, the fact that pianos are percussion instruments was clearly demonstrated to all who listened in.

Let us consider for a moment what part the fifth or dominant plays in the development of new harmonies. The triad on C has G for its fifth

. When we play this fifth, however, we sound a second harmonic

triad , and when we play this triad we sound from its fifth a

third harmonic triad. This succession of fifths indicates a progress through all the keys, if we continue to sound harmonic triads and build on them.

But the thirds also sound their harmonic triads, with emphasis on the harmonic fifths. The tonic C sounds G, the third E sounds B. When we play the triad we are sounding the harmonic fifth on E, and we need only a keen ear to realize that we have the chord of the seventh, . We know this chord best, or perhaps we know it too well, in a modified form called the dominant seventh —in which the seventh is lowered a half tone.

The merit and also the blight of the dominant seventh is the ease with which it supplies a fool-proof exit from one key into another, so that unless some inward grace prevents you, you may parade from dominant seventh to dominant seventh through all the keys, or until you arrive wherever you yearn to be, which is the way with village organists and others who don't know how to modulate.

We achieved our chord of the seventh by hearing the harmonic fifth on E. If we now listen to the harmonic fifth on G, and add it to the chord of the seventh, we shall have the chord of the ninth . Nothing but the limitations of the ear need interrupt the indefinite extension of the first simple triad. But don't overlook this challenging fact, that in every additional tone you sound you find two more tones in the harmonics, and the more tones you add, the further you are from capturing in one chord all the potential harmonics. On the other hand, the harmonics, from phantom triad to phantom triad, are all implied in the first tonic, third and fifth. We may not notice them while they remain mere harmonics, but after we have heard them clearly articulated they are not likely to escape our attention again. That is perhaps the reason why composers of the most modern type sometimes revert to early or even primitive models; the simplest chords, skilfully used, give them rich effects. Less educated ears, however, continue to find in the primitive style only primitive values.

The fascination of the pure art of music lies precisely in this, that so long as we keep to the path of development indicated by the harmonics, we can create no world of sound which will not cause another world of sound to come into being. I do not refer now to the aura with which imagination encircles and glorifies every art; I speak of a physical fact, rooted in the nature of sound, and, as old philosophers believed, controlled by the rhythm of the universe. The art of pure music has more than once been said to partake of the mathematics of the heavens, and in moments of supreme beauty we recoil from the possibility that composer or performer was enjoying, just for those moments, a spurt of good luck; rather, we are convinced that all of us, audience as well as performer and composer, are exalted or intoxicated by our obedience, at least for that season, to a divine law.

We have glanced at the strong influence of the fifth of the triad in building up or uncovering new harmonies. The third of each triad has its own special mission, which, when we understand it, will explain why the third should be highly esteemed but used sparingly. The fifth, the stronger interval, outlines the structure of the expanding chord; the third contributes less to structure than to quality. The fifths dominate, but the thirds and their harmonics are also present, even though we try not to notice them. And we do make that attempt. To simplify the subject for ourselves it is customary to say, as I have said, that the chord of the seventh on C consists of the tones C, E, G, B . These are the only tones which in that chord we teach ourselves to hear. But harmonic triads are major triads, and if E is sounding its harmonic triad, the third is G♯, the fifth B, and in the chord of the seventh, therefore, we should hear a G♯ alongside the G♮ which is the fifth on C . The fifth will be stronger but the G♯ will be there; similarly, if we told the whole truth about the chord of the ninth we should have to say it contains the tones C, E, G, G♯, B, D, D♯ .

Every tone, then, contains discords in the harmonics, a kind of discord to which not even the conservative object—which is just as well, since nothing can be done about it. Though every tone produces in its harmonics a major triad, we may play a minor triad if we wish, but we must accept a faint major triad along with it. This is less evident on the piano than on a chime of bells, or any other instrument rich in harmonics and therefore not docile to our artificial scales. It is usual to say, for example, that if a triad is built on each note of a major scale, the triad on the tonic, on the fourth and on the fifth will be major, but the other triads will be minor, and the triad on the seventh will be diminished. But this result follows only if we assume that the triads will contain no tones which are not already in the given scale. In other words, we may build a triad on each note of the scale of C, using only the white notes of the piano. Here's the result:

There is no reason, of course, why we should not construct a series of triads on any scale we please, using exclusively the white keys or mixing in a few black ones. But we should give a correct account of the result. Our major and minor scales, like our method of tuning the piano, are ingenious expedients which compromise with the natural harmonics, even with the instincts of the average musical ear. A violinist or a singer is unlikely to sound the steps of a scale exactly as they are distributed on a piano. That is why the instrument, playing a concerto with the orchestra, establishes at once a contrast of tone rather than a blend. When we build our arbitrary series of triads, we must reckon with the fact that in spite of us each tone in the scale will persist in sounding the harmonics of a major triad. Not only the tonic and the fourth and the fifth, but the other tones as well, sound major triads. This is not an unpleasant effect; on the contrary, it often contributes great beauty. But we should not pretend the effect is otherwise.

The persistence of the major harmonic triad is easily observable in the tones of a carillon, but even on a piano the phenomenon can be studied. The C scale gives us this series of harmonic triads:

If we now play a series of triads strictly within the C scale—on the white keys—the result is complicated by the harmonic triads:

The principle here illustrated is of more value to the orchestra than to the piano. On the keyed instrument any notes which are played together will have approximately the same force, no matter how hard the fingers try to differentiate. One note played pianissimo in a chord which otherwise is forte, will be lost; we might as well not play it at all. But in the orchestra, where different instruments have their individual quality of tone, the notes representing harmonics can be so allotted that, although not loud, they will be heard above or through a mass of sound. In the orchestra, furthermore, it is easy to distribute widely the notes of a complicated chord, and the more widely a chord is extended, the more obvious become its harmonic values. Within the stretch of the hands, this principle can be illustrated on the piano. Play a dominant seventh chord with the ninth added, and the fifth above the ninth; then play the same chord more widely distributed; then bring the notes of the chord as close together as possible.

3 THE COMPOSER OF pure music, then, as he learns to hear more acutely, adds to his resources chords which we sometimes call new or modern, but he merely uses at last what was waiting to be used. Even if his harmonies astonish us, we are rash indeed to call them ugly. He seeks beautiful materials in order to create beauty, and there is no wiser path for him to follow than the laws of sound. But the composer of program music does not always wish to create beauty. His music interprets a variety of subjects, some of which are themselves ugly or terrible. He has at his command the same chords as the composer of pure music, but if he would represent the noise of cannon bombarding a city he may bring the notes of the chord close together, as in the above example.

I say, he may avail himself of a harsh sound for descriptive purposes, but he will not necessarily do so. Creative artists in all mediums disagree about the right way to imitate nature. Is it better to represent the reality or to reproduce it? Should the composer, if he is describing a battle scene, be content to excite in us some of the emotions proper to that subject, or should he use in his orchestral scoring a few machine-guns? The majority believe that the medium of any art should remain faithful to itself, that music should remain musical, that painting should remain pictorial, that sculpture should remain sculptural. But there is a minority who hold another opinion. This old question is not likely to be settled. There are paintings—I've seen at least one—which reproduce a beach by covering the canvas with glue and sifting real sand on it.

Yet even if we hold with those who think that program music should suggest life rather than reproduce the sounds of it, we must still reckon with those varieties of program music which are not primarily concerned with the creation of tonal beauty. In dance music the tune is secondary to the rhythm, and the purpose of the rhythm is to set the dancers in motion. For this, no other instrument is needed than a tom-tom. Even in the ballroom the essential part of the band are the traps, the battery of percussion instruments which excite the nerves and stir the blood without much aid from harmony or melody. The marches played by military bands are closely related to the most primitive type of dance music; their purpose is to rouse the hearers to action, and they could make their effect with nothing but a drum, or with a drum and a fife, or with a trumpet. The drum by itself can suggest tragedy, a catastrophe, a funeral march; certain harmonies sung by voices or played on the organ may prompt the mood of devotion, of prayer or praise. All these are traditional kinds of program music. An important modern innovation is the accompaniment to a motion picture, which not only reënforces or underscores or interprets the drama, but also performs the practical service of keeping the audience awake. In the days of silent pictures the alarm-clock music was supplied by pianist or organist. To watch a picture without music is an experience as sleep-inducing as driving a car on a long, straight, smooth road by night.

Whether any kind of program music should be beautiful is, in theory at least, not important so long as the composer knows clearly what his program is, and so long as his work unmistakably serves his purpose. Confusion in the program is by instinct resented. To set sacred words to a secular tune is an offense against rather elementary taste—unless the incongruity is deliberate, by way of derision, in which case even the sophisticated may be shocked. In some operas famous more for their music than for their dramatic sensitiveness, grief and tragedy are at times announced in coloratura passages. Most hearers understand without taking a course in esthetics that there is something inadequate in setting death to a trill.

Program music, it will be seen, has much to do with those functions of the art which the public find immediately serviceable, and for which they are ready to pay in advance. Absolute music, on the other hand, is the kind which the composer writes primarily to satisfy himself, and for which the audience, after they have heard it and only then, may or may not feel indebted. As an art music is more likely to develop in its pure state, but much that is created for a program is of a quality to be prized for itself, and therefore likely to be enjoyed after its immediate purpose is served. Good program music tends to become absolute music.

Pure art of any kind has the same importance for mankind as pure science, the same ultimate usefulness, beyond special satisfactions. The development of pure music, as I've tried to suggest, is made possible by increased ability to hear what is already in the universe, just as the expansion of the field of science is made possible by increased ability to see what was always spread before our eyes. There may be an apparent flaw in this parallel, since the musician's ear is cultivated with few mechanical aids, whereas the scientist helps himself out with the telescope or the microscope, but the difference is only relative; the musician has now-a-days his own mechanical aids for acoustical research, for establishing pitch, for standardizing tempos. Both art and science are advanced by keener observation, by bolder imagination, by sounder reasoning.

And when the arts and sciences advance, progress is likely to follow in decent living, in public and private justice, in all we like to include under the broad term, democracy. You may believe that I here mistake the order, that the humane conditions come first and that progress in arts and sciences is a result, not a cause, but if this is your philosophy of history, you and I don't agree. In placid stretches of time the conditions of society satisfy the majority, or if we suspect they are less than perfect, we do nothing to mend them. We are not necessarily smug, we may even say that the human brain has evolved as far as possible, and we cannot therefore imagine the next step. At those moments when the long up-climb of the race seems at a standstill or even seems to be set back, the arts may flourish in a sense; there may be a pious cherishing of masterpieces, with much echoing and copying, but there will be no progress. At such moments, I repeat, the defeatist wonders whether the dream of infinite progress is not an illusion, whether we are not as a matter of fact at the end of our rope. So men despaired in England on the threshold of the astounding Elizabethan age; they grieved that there would be no more literary genius, at the very moment when Shakespeare was dipping his pen in the ink, and they gave up hope for anything new in music, just before John Dowland (1563-1626) charmed not only England but the Continent with his lute-playing and with his exquisite songs.

At no time are we at the end of our rope; the rope can always be lengthened by sharpening our faculties, by stretching our capacity to hear and see, by giving ourselves broader bases for imagination. Because music is a popular and influential art, its service to the intellectual and spiritual education of mankind is great. If I now place absolute music above program music, it is for this reason, that in program music there is no necessary development of the medium; new program effects can be secured by combinations of old musical material. In pure music, however, we go forward only by rousing ourselves from our deafness, by using more of our faculties, by exercising some of those neglected powers which, once awakened, may take our world forward another stage.

The visitor from a strange planet, therefore, will see by the faces of the audience that the music says something to them. If he could look inside their minds he would know that it says to each something different. Those to whom music is a natural language or who have acquired command of it, find the message which is personal to them. Even those to whom it is a foreign tongue may enjoy the sound without knowing what is being said. For them a program serves as a translation, or at least they hope it does; if the annotations with which they are furnished announce that the music represents a place or an event, a mood or a line from a poem, they will try to discover a connection between the comment and what they are hearing. They will probably be disappointed, but in the effort they may perceive certain values which otherwise they would have overlooked. Program annotations are to this extent and in this roundabout way helpful, that though music cannot be translated, it can be paraphrased, and with time the willing and attentive listener may attach general meaning to fragments of the musical idiom. Large numbers of musical enthusiasts, the majority of concert goers, have progressed to this extent. They are in the condition of an intelligent dog who obeys accurately, guided by the tone of the voice and the sound of the total command, but with no conception of separate words, of grammar or of sentence structure. I offer this parallel in seriousness and with respect. The visitor from a strange planet should know that he will be doing well when he gets from music a message as clear as a fine dog gets from our communications.

But if the visitor is as keen as I have assumed, he may counter by asking whether the language of music, however untranslatable, cannot be described; he may challenge me to suggest the nature of its vocabulary and of its construction. Whether or not I succeed in answering his questions, he is now aiming at the heart of the matter. Like any other language music should be studied by the direct method, not through translation and not through paraphrase but through itself. To understand it we must pretend for a moment that we were born to this strange tongue, and that we can express ourselves through no other.

Chapter three:

WHAT IS MUSIC MADE OF?

1   THE PECULIARITY OF MUSIC, as Walter Pater said, is that we cannot separate what it says from the way it says it. When we speak of the language of music, therefore, we are talking about its content. This truth is hard to put into words but fortunately any music lover can understand it. If we keep it in mind, the inadequacy of words will not handicap us in this discussion.

In any language we communicate with each other by reminding ourselves of what we know already, or by restating experience so as to suggest new experience, or by asking questions. The discourse of music proceeds by complete statements, by unfinished or doubtful statements, and by outright questions. Here in essence is the grammar and the rhetoric of the art, for which the musician has his own terms, but it is an advantage at first to consider the language of music as an example of language in general.

Besides grammar and sentence structure, music has form, the beginning, middle and end which Aristotle started the literary folk talking about. Musical form, like literary form, is not a fixed and stationary pattern but a design in motion. It is like the series of toy blocks which children arrange, so that each block as it falls will communicate motion to the next. A question calls for an answer; if it is a true answer rather than a contradiction or a retort, it will suggest a further question, which will bring a further answer, and so on until the subject is exhausted.

There is a temptation here to encourage a parallel between groups of questions and paragraphs, between larger groups and chapters. This temptation should be resisted. It is a catastrophe for a musician, even more than for a writer, to imagine the structure of his composition as a frame which can be put together or taken apart, piece by piece. In any work of art which is an organic whole, stages of growth can be discerned, but it is not for us to determine the importance or the place of any one section removed from its context. We hear a piece of music as an extended performance, not as a frozen design. If we stopped at any moment the effect of what we hear might be incomplete, but it still could be divided into a beginning, a middle and an end, very much as a growing tree has always a bottom and a top, and a section in between. The beginning of a piece of music, like the bottom of a tree, will remain the point of departure, but the middle and the end will not be determined until music or tree has its full growth. The composer, like the writer, attends to the sequence of question and answer, making sure that they unfold inevitably in a straight line, so that the composition begins with the question which really should come first, and stops when there is nothing more to say. What we mean by form is the movement which gives life to the piece between the point from which it started and the period in which it ends.

There is a further temptation, to which we occasionally yield, to think of musical structure in terms of superficial patterns like sonatas, or suites. I call these patterns superficial because they are imposed on musical subject matter, not evolved out of it. They have their origin in social or economic conditions, in some program for which the composer labored as an assistant. A court fiddler or bandmaster would compose dance music to grace a special occasion; knowing which dances the guests might call for, he prepared music for every kind, and if the separate pieces were good enough he played them even when there was no dancing. In what order the dances were performed during the evening, we can't be sure, but when the composer published his music he alternated slow dances with livelier ones, so that when performed as a group they would not be monotonous. Dances arranged in such a pattern were called a Suite. The first and the last dance were usually in quick tempo, so that the beginning and the end might be cheerful.

This is structure of a sort. But just as true structure of composition in words lies in a continuity from the first question to the final answer, so the essence of musical discourse is an unbroken progression. Either the various movements of a Suite are artificial divisions, or they are separate pieces organically unrelated.

It is by the alternation of question and answer that the musician recognizes organic continuity. If he asks very simple questions and answers them quickly, the result is a structure of small importance. But if he asks elaborate questions, which will need an entire movement or section for adequate answer, the answer will prompt another large question, which can be dealt with only in another movement, and out of this second question and answer may come a third movement. Any account of the sonata form is likely to tell you that it often or usually contains four movements, the characteristic opening, the slow lyrical section, the scherzo (these two often in reverse order), and the final movement. But if the account of the sonata is accurate, it will warn you that there may be only three movements, or only two, or the entire sonata may be in one long movement. The structure is determined by the inner progress of question and answer.

The simplest form of question in music is the dominant seventh chord; the most complete answer is the major triad. If we sound the chord of G major, for example, the ear feels no need of a further musical statement; on this triad we can rest. If, however, we lower the octave G to the diminished seventh F we feel the need of the chord of C major, . Whether or not the listener knows the name of the notes or the nature of harmonies, he will feel that this sequence is natural and inevitable. On the other hand, if in the chord of D major, we lower the octave D to a diminished seventh, we should expect the F sharp to go up to G .

Why does the F, when it is diminished or lowered to F natural, go down to E? Why, when it remains an undiminished seventh, does it go up to G? We can find the answer by playing the chord of the undiminished seventh on G and the chord of the dominant seventh . It is natural for the chord of the seventh to return immediately to G, and for the dominant seventh to resolve itself into the chord of

C major . If you will look at your piano you will see that

F natural is closer to E than to G, but F sharp is closer to G than to E.

When we listen to music our ear exerts a certain will-power. It prefers one progression rather than another. Its usual impulse is to resolve a chord into whatever sounds are nearest. In any melody the composer can count on the natural willingness of his audience to hear the sequence which is smoothest, least violent.

The composer not only can count on this form of coöperation from his hearers, but he knows that if he has established a key or tonality in their minds, he can interest them by departing from it. They will be curious to learn how soon he will get back. Children and mature folk who play by ear, in technical ignorance of the language they are using, invariably discover certain combinations of chords whose chief interest is that they are departures from or returnings to the original key.

More often than not they find they can go from one chord to the other with an adequate sense of logic, provided the chords have one note in common. You don't need the diminished seventh for your modulation. Later on, considerably later, the improvisers discover that not even one note in common is necessary. We can leap boldly from key to key provided the change suggests a pattern.

There seem to be two ways of asking and answering questions; we may begin with the question, or we may make a preliminary statement of the key, the question being indicated later by departures from it. But for any musical discourse some key or tonality, some standard of reference, must be established, even in the music which tries to avoid the restrictions of tonality. Perhaps to sound the first note is to set up a standard of reference, since the note will carry in its harmonics or overtones the suggestion of a chord. But when you begin with the dominant seventh, a question or incomplete statement, you hear simultaneously the sounds from which it came, and the sounds to which it is going. The composer need not, however, give the implied answer. When the dominant seventh on G is sounded, you are led to expect the chord on C.

This answer to this question is in music a platitude. So long as musicians could think of nothing after a dominant seventh except the natural resolution, the dominant seventh was fated to be always the chord next to the last. It served notice that the piece was over. But those who have something to say besides platitudes will remember what the ear expects and give us something else. Since we can modulate directly from any chord to any other chord, especially when they have one tone in common, there is no reason at all why the dominant seventh on G should lead into the chord of C major. It might very well lead directly to B major.

In the discourse of music, as in the discourse of words, a distinction should be made between a question and an unfinished statement. The question needs an answer; the unfinished statement may be left hanging in the air, often more effective in that condition than if it were complete. For an absolute answer the final chord, whether major or minor, should rest on its tonic, its key tone, and this note should be heard not only at the bottom of the chord but at the top. The plain triad, with the fifth as the top note, sounds less conclusive than the full chord with its octave. If the third were the top note instead of the fifth, the effect likewise would be somewhat tentative. Composers, aware of this fact, create expectancy by closing a phrase of the melody on the third or the fifth rather than on the tonic.

Similarly, the chord of the triad may rest on the third or on the fifth . In neither case will the chord sound conclusive.

It contains no dominant seventh but it lacks the tonic for its foundation note. In ordinary speech we hold the attention of the audience by the inflection of our voice; from something other than the structure of our sentences, our hearers know that we have something more to say. The musician gets this effect by the position of the triad, and by the absence of the tonic octave.

I am describing not rules set down by theorists, but habits of the human ear. The study of harmony out of books has, I repeat, this danger in it, that unless we are careful we begin to define music in terms of the eye. Music cannot be seen. The printed page is not music; it is a printed page. For this reason I stress the fact that music is a form of discourse, of expression in motion, proceeding by question and answer from what we have heard to what we expect to hear. It is a misfortune that children learning to play are told that a dot in a semi-circle, placed above a note, means that that note or chord should be "held." The child gets the idea that when this symbol is reached the fingers must be held down on the keys to rein in the music or hold it stationary. If the child listened to the sound without being misled by an awkward way of representing music in print, he would know that the music at this place, instead of being stopped, is encouraged to sound on.

Harmony in books defines questions and answers as dissonances and consonances. Dissonance is an unlucky word; it seems to describe something unpleasant. A dissonance is only a chord which must move on to another chord. In other words, a dissonance is a question. A consonance is a chord which demands nothing after it; it satisfies by itself. It is what I have called the answer to a question. Since all chords must move on unless the music is to stop, there is no essential difference between a so-called dissonance and a so-called consonance.

This nomenclature is harmless once we have learned what the terms mean, though it is a pity that any chords should be handicapped by the name of dissonance. But there is room for considerable objection to the statement, quite orthodox among those who write harmony for the eye,

that F and C sharp is a dissonance, but F and D flat

is a consonance. Play these two chords on the piano and see if you can tell any difference between them. The theorist will come back at me sharply with the argument that our method of tuning the piano obliterates the difference between C sharp and D flat, but the difference exists. There may be some esoteric truth in this statement, but the difference, if it could be established, would have little to do with what the theorist is talking about. His mistake is in writing for the eye and not for the ear, and he wants us to determine whether a chord is a dissonance or a consonance merely by whether the half-tone above C is printed as C sharp or D flat.

What he means is that the full triad on F becomes a dissonance if we raise the dominant of that chord to C sharp. The ear then expects the chord of D minor, or B flat. It isn't the F and the C sharp which make the chord a dissonance, but the combination of those two tones with A. Undoubtedly the theorist had the A in mind, but he forgot to tell us about it. Had he given us the whole triad, we should have understood without any instruction from him that it was an unfinished chord, a sound in transition, a question. Unless he tells us, we are likely to hear not A but A flat, a major triad, quite properly called a consonance, if you like big and unwieldy names.

The point is that sounds are lettered and carry the labels of sharp and flat only in books. To the ear they are sounds.

2   HARMONY IS CONCERNED with tones played simultaneously in a chord, but since one chord is followed by another, harmony is concerned also with the succession of the different notes in the chords. If you're accustomed to think, as most singers do, in terms of human voices, a chord probably means to you four notes sung by soprano, alto, tenor, and bass. Each of these parts sings a note in the chord, but as the music progresses, each part becomes a melody. In good part-writing these melodies are almost equally important. No matter how many notes there may be in the harmonies, whether the music is written for voices or for the full orchestra, a succession of chords is a succession of melodies evolving together. The relation of these simultaneous voices is called counterpoint. For convenience we may consider harmony as the perpendicular aspect of music, and counterpoint the horizontal. By these terms we seem to make a distinction, but when we deal with more than one chord we involve ourselves in counterpoint, and

the language of music, from the musician's point of view, is never exclusively harmony or counterpoint, but both together.

One melody played alone carries with it the implications of harmony. I do not refer to those harmonics or overtones already described; I mean that the average person with an ear for music, hearing a simple melody, will understand certain chords as an accompaniment. The chords usually understood are the tonic triad—the chord of the dominant, or the triad on the fifth—and the chord of the sub-dominant, or the triad on the fourth. In C major the tonic triad is ♪ . The chord of the dominant is ♪ . The chord of the sub-dominant is ♪ . The merest piano-thumper, needing an accompaniment for *Yankee Doodle*, will guess from the melody which of these chords to use and at what points. For example:

Any melody, of course, can be harmonized in several ways, and a good musician, like a good writer, avoids the obvious and the threadbare. But these musical platitudes have become platitudes because they are implied by the melody.

The simplest form of melody is the scale, of which the commonest varieties are the major and the minor.

Major

Minor - various forms

In the minor scale E, the third, is flat. Playing the scale you may feel the need of flatting also the A. The minor triad on C suggests the chord of A flat. The minor scale can of course be played in various ways, the only essential being the diminished third. The A is usually flat. If it is played as A natural in the ascending scale, it is often diminished in the descending.

The next most familiar scale is the chromatic, in which all notes are used.

There is also the whole-tone scale, which you can pick out on your piano by playing every other note on the keyboard.

If you want to, you can construct a scale in which the notes are separated by the interval of a tone and a half. The word scale means a ladder. If the rungs of the ladder are spaced too far apart, the ladder is of course hard to use, and if you over-exaggerate the distance between the rungs, you will have not a ladder but a picture frame. Your natural or acquired taste is your only guide—and it may be added, the hearer's only protection.

Singers and instrumentalists practice scales for technical facility, but also, and perhaps even more, to train the ear in the different ladders of sound. The composer may ask a performer at some point in the music to run off a scale, up or down, much as scales are climbed or descended in practice, but in general he makes a more profound use of the scale to create expectancy in the hearer. If we know the particular steps of sound which he is using, we know also which steps he is not using; in the whole-tone scale, for example, we don't expect half-tones. Once the scale is established, therefore, the attention of the hearer is focused on the sounds from which the next notes will logically be chosen. The hearer's expectations will be to a certain extent conscious if he is a trained musician, but it is extraordinary how quickly the ear, even of the untrained, accepts a scale and instinctively expects the tones which belong to it.

On the other hand the composer, having established one scale, may surprise us by shifting to another. The commonest illustration is the shift from major to minor, or from minor to major. If a piece starts in the major and stays in that scale for a while, then changes to a minor and later returns to the major, the listener has the double pleasure of surprise and recognition; or it is better to say he has the pleasure of surprise when the scale is changed, and the pleasure of mingled surprise and recognition when the original scale is restored.

This, of course, is a form of question and answer. The alteration of the major scale into the minor sets up the question; the return to the major provides the answer—and something more. Any musical effect, when repeated, is a different effect; the repetition changes it. Strictly speaking there is no such thing as repetition, for the second time a melody is heard it either wears thin or seems richer. This principle, of course, applies to more than music. Even the theme which gains by repetition will be worn out at last if it is repeated too often. But though it is impossible to reproduce an effect unchanged, yet since music is a time art, and since it must be performed always from beginning to end, the composer relies on repetition to remind us from time to time of what he has previously said. A repetition in music, therefore, is a summing up, and the summary is more often emotional than intellectual.

The repetitions, however, need not be literal. We can repeat a theme note for note, or we can repeat the pattern of that theme approximately so that it is recognizable as a summary and yet may differ from what it summarizes. This sort of variation is usually called "development." What is developed is the possibility of extending the question or asking a new one.

These observations can readily be illustrated. In the folk melody associated with the words *Au Claire de la Lune,* the scale and the pattern of the tune are established in the first section.

In order to fix this pattern in our minds, the section is repeated. Even within this brief section a question has been asked and answered.

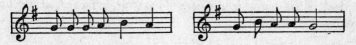

But the whole section together, when it is repeated, sets up a larger expectancy, a larger question. We can't sing or play the little theme twice without creating the impression that the tune is unfinished and more is coming. In the third section the key is changed and perhaps also the scale; the instinct of the ear may be to supply minor harmonies or major.

In either case we arrive on the dominant of the original key, and with great satisfaction to the ear repeat the original theme.

A more subtle yet still simple illustration, a repetition is found in the old chorale, familiar to hymn singers:

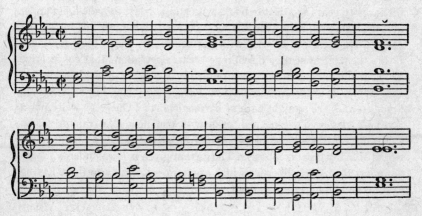

The first section asks a question by ending, where it started, on the tonic triad, but with the third of the triad in the melody. The second section takes the melody with some boldness much higher in the scale, apparently deserting the original theme, yet the very notes of the original theme are implied in the new pattern, as we can ascertain by ourselves by singing the melodic stretches together.

The second section, however, ends on the triad of the dominant. The third section takes the melody back to the high note of the second section, repeating and varying the effect but again ending on the triad of the dominant. The composer stated his musical question three ways. The fourth section of the melody returns to the tonic, in fact sounds the tonic twice to make sure of it.

3   I HAVE ALREADY reminded the reader of the fact that music is a time art, and therefore the composer repeats his material in order to keep it fresh in our minds. In painting, a space art, the artist need state a theme only once, since if his statement is powerful enough our eye will be attracted to the part of the canvas on which it appears, and we can look at it as often as we please. But in a constant stream of sound a pattern would be forgotten unless it were repeated many times and in many ways. In this element of repetition harmony and counterpoint fuse; in repetition also lies the secret of musical form.

At the risk of laboring the point I offer some elementary illustrations, using first the powerful interval of the dominant and the rule for avoiding consecutive fifths—a rule which still embarrasses the theorists. Even today there is still much shaking of heads and of fingers over these terrible fifths. Fifty years ago the textbooks with a light heart forbade them under all circumstances. Now even the most conservative musicians know that consecutive fifths can be used with excellent effect, but if they don't still forbid them, at least they discourage them. They admit that consecutive fifths, like consecutive octaves, frequently sound surprisingly well, but they advise us not to contaminate ourselves; the young in particular are urged to walk the straight path of harmonic virtue. One very well-known textbook, deservedly esteemed, asks with commendable frankness why consecutive fifths should be prohibited although they are found in the works of many great composers. The answer given is that students should not allow themselves liberties which are permissible only to those having experience and mature judgment.

Pedagogy could hardly sink lower. If consecutive fifths or any other musical resources are used by the masters, then the sooner we learn to use them, the better. If, however, they sometimes sound well and at other times do not, we shan't know how to use them unless we discover, or someone tells us, what makes them at one moment pleasant and at another moment unpleasant. It would seem to be the function of a textbook to explain this mystery; if the book, however, can't explain or is unwilling to make the attempt, nothing is accomplished by advising us to stay off consecutive fifths altogether.

I believe the theorists get into difficulties because they deal with music so much through the eye and so little through the ear. They make rules which seem reasonable on the page but often become insignificant when translated into sound. The composer with a strong natural talent, trusting his ear, gets along nicely without the visual rules.

The interval of the fifth is the most powerful of those produced by natural harmonics. Many of us find pleasure in the austere sound, others prefer to soften it by adding the third. When we make a four-note chord out of a triad, we must double one of the original three tones, but we usually double the tonic; to double the third would kill the rugged dominant effect of the fifth. Just how dominant you wish your consecutive fifths to be is a matter of taste, but the rule for softening up is simple— add the third, and if that doesn't satisfy you, double the third.

Here are some consecutive fifths:

Here are the same fifths sweetened for those who don't like harsh flavors:

Here are the same fifths sweetened as much as possible:

You will notice that though the fifths remain consecutive, they are no longer conspicuous when the third is added or when the third is doubled. The third may be major or minor. In the illustration here given, the first chord is minor, the second major, the third minor, the fourth minor. Suppose we make them all major.

At one spot in this sequence the effect, as most ears would agree, is bad. I should call it startling but no worse than that. The F in the second chord is F natural; in the third chord we have two F sharps. When a note of one chord is raised or lowered half a tone in the next chord, but not in the same voice, we have what is called a cross or false relation. Whether such an effect is bad remains, like consecutive fifths, a matter of taste. The effect is undoubtedly harsh in various degrees, depending on the quickness with which one chord follows the other. If the original tone is still fresh in mind the change may shock. Within the same part, or voice, the raising or lowering of a note by a half-tone causes no inconvenience whatever. The objection to the change in different voices is not logical; the hearer should be able to follow the harmonic development no matter in what position the chords occur. Most of us, however, listen to one voice at a time, and find it difficult to follow when they skip around.

The repetition of chords or patterns of chords has given occasion, therefore, for rules and regulations, about the value of which we do not all agree. As we practice the art of music today, any sequence in the pattern of the chords, any repetition or variation of the chord sequence, is acceptable if the repetition is recognizable and if it sounds well. These two conditions cannot be fixed rules, for our ability to remember what has gone before and to recognize it when we hear it again varies greatly, and whether harmonic progressions sound well depends upon the extent to which our ear recognizes and likes the natural harmonics of a musical tone. If our taste in chords and chord sequences is narrow, the reason probably is that our ear has been trained only in music written before composers knew or accepted all the legitimate possibilities of harmony.

When melodies or melodic themes are repeated, certain natural effects are inevitably reached; they did not need to be discovered, since music could hardly avoid stumbling on them. But the theorists soon had their rules ready to complicate these effects and make them seem difficult. Composers today disregard these formulas, and hope merely to address listeners who through musical experience have become discriminating.

The simplest form of melodic repetition is, of course, repetition without change or development or adornment. This bare kind of repetition persists in folk songs and in religious hymns, where the tune is sung over and over again. We should tire of it if we paid close attention, but since it is not absolute or pure music, our attention is diverted to the dance or the words which it accompanies. The tune of a Virginia reel bores nobody so long as the dance goes on.

As soon, however, as the tune is heard for its own sake or with more attention than is given to the words, the stark repetition becomes un-pleasing or even painful, like the dropping of water on the skull. The most primitive musician probably devised ways of altering the tune, or of repeating it from an angle which would give the effect of alteration. Some ancient examples of this tendency we still enjoy in the kind of repetition which is called a "round." One of the finest rounds, perhaps the most famous, is the setting of the medieval song, *Sumer Is Icumen In.* This lovely music is published complete in modern notation in *Grove's Dictionary,* in an article under the title of the words. But we all know much simpler rounds; most of us indeed have sung them. Perhaps the best known is *Three Blind Mice.* One group of singers starts the song; the next group begins at the end of the first phrase and repeats the tune literally; when the second group reaches the end of the first phrase, a third group begins. Since they all begin on the same tone, there is hardly room for a fourth group. If the round is properly constructed, the three groups sound the notes of a triad. A fourth group would merely get in the way.

If each group sings the melody to its conclusion and there stops, the voices will drop from three to two, and from two to one, just as they grew up at the beginning from one voice to two, and from two to three. If the voices repeat without pause, they can go on indefinitely, but when they stop at last it is the mark of the true round that the part which was first to start should be the first to stop. Those who have amused themselves singing rounds know that voices keep sounding the tonic triad. The harmonic effect of a round, therefore, is of one prolonged chord. The composer takes care that the accented notes are chosen from the tones of the persisting triad. If we write out "Three Blind Mice" as it is sung in a round, these observations become clear.

Obviously a round cannot be an elaborate structure melodically, since the melody is repeated without change; nor harmonically, since it is limited to one tonic triad with excursions into the dominant or the dominant seventh. A more highly developed kind of repetition is the "canon," so called from a Greek word meaning law or rule. A canon, like a round, sends the melody off in one voice, giving it, as it were, a handicap, and then starts a second or pursuing voice, carrying the same melody. But the voices in a canon need not always begin on the same tone; the pursuing voice may start an octave above or below. This difference of pitch gives variety in addition to the mere repetition. A canon may be of two voices or three or four; the two voices may sound alone; any number of voices singing in canon may be accompanied by still other voices which avoid the melody and supply richness to the harmony. *Sumer Is Icumen In* is a canon rather than a round. It is written for six voices, only four of which repeat the melody. At the conclusion the voices do not drop out one by one, but sum up the piece in firm chords.

From the round to the canon is one step in the development of musical repetition. The next step is the "fugue." The word means flight; in a fugue, as in a canon or a round, the voices pursue each other, but whereas the pursuit in a canon or round begins the identical melody on the tone with which the announcement was first made, or on the octave of that tone, in a fugue the second or pursuing voice begins the melodic pattern four notes below or five notes above—in other words on the dominant. If there is a third voice, it begins the melodic pattern on the same tone as the first voice, and a fourth voice would begin, like the second voice, on the dominant.

In a fugue the repetition of a melodic pattern is not literal; to secure variety and smoothness of harmonic effect, the theme is altered where necessary, its pattern is developed and transformed, the only requirement being that even in its most completely altered condition the pattern should be still recognizable. When all the voices of a fugue have been fully extended and developed the composer modulates into the dominant and begins over again, leading off now with voice Number Two, following with voice Number One, Number Four, and Number Three in the order named, and repeating the notes which each voice originally sang. Once more the themes are extended and developed. The fugue is then closed in any way that suits the composer, but usually in some effect of massive climax, as though the voices threw themselves, triumphant or panting, across the goal line.

We no longer compose fugues, canons, and rounds, not at least in their classic form. Bach and Händel enjoy an enormous popularity in this kind of writing, but contemporary musicians are not disposed to imitate them. The method, however, of introducing and re-introducing a theme—what is called the fugal entrance—and the method of varying and echoing a theme, are incorporated in the language of music today.

Out of the most natural kind of repetition developed what is called the sonata form, the structure of the first movement in the traditional sonata, of the first movement also in the traditional symphony. Our sonatas, as we noticed before, usually are in several sections, which follow somewhat the plan of the old suites. That is, they get variety from the alternation of fast and slow movements. The tendency, however, is to think of the sonata as a single composition, and though the alternations of fast and slow continue, many sonatas are now divided into few movements, or they are imagined as a single movement. This evolution commends itself to musicians for the good reason suggested earlier, that the question and answer of musical discourse should continue unbroken; when there is a break, we understand that the subject is exhausted.

The name sonata, however, was first applied only to the repetition pattern in the first section. The pleasure derived from it is illustrated in its most rudimentary forms, in the old tune which we have already noticed, *Au Claire de la Lune*. The theme of this song, you remember, is stated, then repeated. The statement and the repetition may be considered as filling up two lines of a quatrain, or two sides of a square. The third line, or the third side, is a departure from the original theme, a development of it. The original theme is then repeated, to furnish the fourth line, or the fourth side of the square.

This AABA pattern is fundamental in musical rhetoric. Music repeats its themes to fix them in our memory, to make sure we've grasped them sufficiently to recognize them when they return later. Any departure from the theme or any development of it must be fairly short, or at least not so long as to drive the original theme out of our head. The final section brings back something for us to recognize, and recognizing that with which we started, we know we have completed the circle, and have come to the end.

There are some simple truths about repetition, whether in music or in literature, which it might be helpful here to recall. In a poem where every stanza ends with the same phrase, this refrain will be tedious if it is not properly employed, but very effective if the poet knows what to say between the recurrences of the refrain. Since the words of the refrain remain unchanged, its meaning can be altered only by what is said in the preceding stanza. If the poet knows his business, the stanza content will always give the refrain a fresh meaning. Perhaps you are familiar with the poem, *Batuschka,* by Thomas Bailey Aldrich, written in the last century but prophetic of what happened in the first world war. The first stanza of the poem gives a picture of the Russian capital in the old days, with the people praying, "God save the Czar." The second stanza describes political prisoners hearing from their dungeon the petition, "God save the Czar." In the Red palace the Czar himself joins in the prayer, "God save the Czar." But some day, comments the poet, when the people can endure no longer, "God save the Czar!"

In music the final return of the theme in the AABA pattern should give us this sort of surprise, an unveiling of new significance in what we have already heard. Perhaps even the original repetition of a theme in the AA part of the pattern, has a novelty of its own; nothing heard twice is quite the same as when heard only once. But from what we have noticed about the use of a refrain, we can understand that the effect of the final A depends on what is said in B, the third part of the pattern, what is called the development section of the sonata form. This is the section which young amateurs usually dislike, and therefore shirk as much as they can. Once the first section is mastered, the second and the fourth section are things to thank Heaven for, since they repeat the first, but that disagreeable third section demands extra study, obviously a waste of effort since the section is brief and will not return.

For purposes of definition I have made the sonata form a little simpler than it is. I have spoken of the A section, which is repeated immediately and later repeated again, as if it contained only one theme. In practice it contains at least two themes, and sometimes more. Two, however, is the usual number. If the first theme is brilliant, the second will be calm; if the first is stately, the second will be lighter. The sonata form, therefore, uses all the obvious resources of musical rhetoric, contrasts of theme, contrasts of mood, the contrasts which are secured by repetition, and finally the contrasts of key. In order that the discourse may continue unbroken in a series of questions and answers, the A section with its two themes ends in the chord of the dominant or in some other chord not the tonic. Coming back to this chord, whatever it is, with the repetition, the discourse proceeds through the development section to another chord based on the dominant, or on anything but the tonic. The A section then repeats for the second and last time, but it finishes by maneuvering to the tonic triad, or to whatever harmonic combination the exploring composer may select to convey the sense of finality.

4   WHEN WE CONSIDER different keys, we are face to face with the subject of modulation. Modulation is the passage from one key to another by logical harmonic sequences. In its simplest form modulation is the change from the chord

of the tonic to the chord of the dominant. In any triad the dominant, as you remember, is the forceful tone. When you hear a chord, you hear prominently its fifth, and if you sound the triad built on that fifth, the sequence seems natural, because the two chords are bound together by a strong continuing tone. The sequence from the chord of its dominant, back to the chord of the tonic, is called a perfect cadence.

Here we have been reckoning the fifth in the usual order, from the tonic upward. Reckoning upward from the dominant to the tonic again, we have the interval of the fourth. The sequence of the chord of the fourth, or sub-dominant, back to the chord of the tonic, is called a plagal cadence.

If we were to continue indefinitely from tonic chord to dominant chord, and from that chord to its dominant chord, we should run through all the keys. We should reach the same conclusion in reverse order if we proceeded from the chord of the tonic to the chord of the fourth or sub-dominant, and from that chord to the chord of its sub-dominant, etc. This is modulation in its most elementary form, but also in its most elaborate. To run through all the keys in order to get from one place to another, is the longest way round.

The shortest way would be to go directly wherever you wish, with no modulation at all. You can play a tune, with or without its harmonies, in the key of F, and you can repeat it immediately in the key of F sharp or A flat or what you will. The police won't stop you, and there's no reason why they should. The difference between a change of key through modulation and a change of key without modulation is a difference, not of correctness, but of effect. At different times composers feel the need of one effect rather than the other. Play *My Country, 'Tis of Thee* in the key of G; play it again in A; play it again in B. With each step up you get a mild excitement, a heightening of effect which comes partly from the shock of the change, and partly from the quicker vibrations as you go up the scale. The vibrations would be the same even if you modulated into the higher scale, but the modulation would kill the effect of surprise.

If you wish to modulate, learn first of all to respect the dominants and the sub-dominants, and train yourself to avoid as much as possible the dominant seventh, which, as we presumed before to say, is much overworked and has become a musical platitude. You can modulate directly from any chord into any other, provided they have a single note in common. The diminished seventh is almost as much overworked as the dominant seventh. It is the dominant seventh in which the third and the fifth are lowered or diminished half a tone, and the seventh half a tone further. From that crowded stance it can shoot in any direction, like a spider.

The essential principles of modulation, then are these.

FIRST: The most natural sequence for the ear is from the chord of the dominant to the chord of the tonic, or from the chord of the sub-dominant to the chord of the tonic.

SECOND: Any two chords are sufficiently related if they have a single note in common.

THIRD: To pass from one chord to another no bridge at all is needed except good taste.

FOURTH: Good taste suggests that it's not enough to change the key at random; it is well to know in advance the effect we wish to create. A leap from one key to another is mere restlessness, unless it has a purpose. If we know what our purpose is, it will be clear in the musical effect.

5 THE DIFFERENCE IN QUALITY between keys, and between the same keys in different octaves, is a rich resource in the language of music. As we go up the scale, each tone is produced by an increasing number of vibrations per second. The octave above Middle C therefore, or the octave below it, though they are the same tone, are not of the same quality. A composer chooses a key as the painter chooses a color; the primary colors are few, like the tones in the scale, but every color has a variety of shades. A tune played in the middle of the piano would in one sense be still the same tune if played an octave higher, but in another sense it would be radically changed.

This change is felt by all listeners, but it can be described only very roughly in words. A melody repeated in a higher octave suggests a change of expression, as though a speaker repeated a remark with a smile, or sarcastically, or more nervously; a melody repeated an octave below suggests other changes of expression—greater solemnity, perhaps, or discouragement, or despair, or insistence.

This difference between various positions, high or low, is called a difference of pitch. If we couldn't tell whether the scale were moving up or down, we should be badly off musically, but not necessarily in a hopeless condition; our ear would be defective, but it could be trained. Yet even those who can follow the direction in which the tune moves, even those who can judge accurately the intervals between notes, may have only what is called relative pitch; they may not be able to whistle accurately on request the A to which the orchestra tunes, they may not be able to tell merely by listening to a piece of music what key it is in. If they can tell, they have absolute pitch.

There is no mystery about absolute pitch. The natural possession of it is evidence of no miracle, merely of extraordinary memory in one field. Some people can remember colors with the same sureness, can go downtown and buy a piece of goods to match something they have left at home. Few of us have absolute pitch without training. Or perhaps training is too big a word. We can cultivate absolute color sense or absolute pitch only by giving to colors or tones our repeated and close attention. But it is easier to give close attention to the gradations of the scale, once we have noticed the quite different effects which different vibration-numbers produce.

The number of vibrations to each tone are determined by nature, but the particular tone which serves as a standard starting point for the scale is determined arbitrarily by the musical profession. The earliest standard pitch was fixed by a French committee in 1859; having been endorsed by later committees, it became known as the international pitch. By the present definition of international pitch, A above Middle C is the sound produced by 440 vibrations a second.

Whether a note is higher or lower, whether the vibrations are more numerous or fewer, depends upon several factors, all of which affect the quality of tone and present special problems for the different instruments, including the voice. If you divide in the middle a vibrating string, you raise the tone by an octave. This method, however, would give your piano such a shape that you probably couldn't get it into your house, and it would give you a violin which you couldn't hold. By making the low strings thicker than the high, you bring a number of octaves within easy reach. You also lower the tone by diminishing the tension of the string. It is because of the strain on the high or E string of the violin that a post is placed on the right side of the bridge, inside the instrument, to keep it from collapsing. So far so good. But strings of different thickness stretched with a difference of tension may sound as though they belonged to separate instruments. It is always a problem in the production of music to keep the scale consistent and even throughout, and here no instrument offers greater problems than the human voice. It is not hard to sing low and sound like a bass, nor to sing high and sound like a soprano; the difficulty is to sing both high and low and sound like yourself.

Inseparable from pitch is temperament or tuning. Once the standard A is established at 440, or at any other number of vibrations per second, it might seem easy to tune the rest of the scale, but as a matter of fact it isn't easy at all; a method altogether satisfactory has not yet been found. To understand the problem completely we should consult the article on Temperament in Grove's *Dictionary,* or some other account which is both historical and scientific. Here only the outlines need be given.

If you divide a vibrating string in the middle, each half will sound the octave of the tone produced by the whole string. If you divide the string into thirds, the longer fragment, two-thirds, will sound the fifth of the original tone. We can get at the natural or harmonic fifth another way, also at the natural major third. We can play the tonic and the dominant together, and since any note sounds its harmonic triad, if the dominant agrees completely with the harmonic fifth there will be no clash of wave-beats, but a perfect consonance. The same is true of the major third.

Here we deal with acoustical facts. But these facts lead straight to an acoustical paradox which, if a solution were not found, would put a stop to music as we know it. If we play C with its fifth, G, in perfect tune, G and its fifth, D, in perfect tune, D and A, A and E, etc., we eventually get back to C again, but this will not be the same tone as the C from which we started. If we start with C and its major third, E, perfectly tuned, and then build a series of perfect fifths on C until E is reached again—C, G, D, A, E—the two E's will not be in tune. Nature here seems determined to drive us mad. One consonance, the octave, the ear insists on, but if the octaves are in tune, obviously some or all of the smaller intervals must be tempered or shrunk. It would be theoretically pleasant to keep the harmonic triad always in tune, and to shrink the other notes, but this is impossible for the reason noticed above, that a series of perfectly tuned fifths would ultimately put the octaves out of tune. We might do pretty well by the white keys and tune the black keys unevenly, but this method would confine us to the key of C. In any system of uneven tuning—and until fairly modern times there was no other kind—some keys are more nearly in tune than others, and some chords produce a clash of wave-beats so unpleasant that when prolonged, as on an organ, it long ago was described as a wolf-howl. To suppress the "wolf" is still the problem of tuning.

Sebastian Bach wrote his *Well-Tempered Clavier* to illustrate the system of tuning which we now follow for the piano and organ. It provides with approximate perfection the same distribution of wave-beats for all the scales, so that modulation is as easy between any two keys as between any two others. The tuner tempers the fifth from perfect consonance until he can hear the clash of the proper number of wave-beats per second. He tempers the major third also until he hears the clash of the proper number of wave-beats. We tune our pianos, actually, by putting the notes of the triad to a very precise degree out of tune.

The voice, of course, tunes itself, from note to note. It has no single fixed tone to start from. Violinists tune their strings, and each string, therefore, provides one fixed tone, but all other tones they find, as the singer does, by ear. The better a musician's ear, the more likely he is to reach for the perfectly tuned third and fifth. When singers or violinists perform with a piano they temper their tuning in unison on octave passages, but otherwise they like to go their own way. Most of the time they and the piano are slightly but not disagreeably at odds. The pianist, even when he plays alone, is conscious that his well-tuned instrument is, except for the octaves, a little flat.

6   AMONG ALL THE RESOURCES of the musical language, none is more important than rhythm, nor, we may add, more frequently misunderstood. There not only can be no music without rhythm, but rhythm can at times stand by itself as an adequate language, though whether it should then be called a musical language, most of us would dispute. The beat of tom-toms illustrates in the most obvious way the peculiar language of rhythm when it speaks alone. Tom-tom effects can be reproduced with full orchestra or on the piano, even though no drum is used; chord masses or single notes repeated

unmercifully can wear down the nerves and drive us into action of some sort.

Tom-tom music is perhaps a branch of program music, or perhaps we should consider it an illustration of that incantation or spell or enchantment which among primitive people a bard is supposed to exercise. Orpheus with his lute made trees move around, and at Alexander's feast the inconsiderate but technically prodigious minstrel, by the motivating influence of his art, persuaded the audience to burn the palace down. These effects, assuming that they occurred, must have been the product of rhythm.

What is rhythm? Since the word is used in many ways, a satisfactory definition must give the sense which is implicit in all the uses. We see rhythm in a painting or in a building, in the swaying of tree boughs or the heaving of sea waves; we hear it in verse and also in prose, in the rattle of car wheels and in music. If we are hasty we conclude that the root idea of rhythm is repetition, the repetition of a sound or of a color, of design or of structure. Yet the ticking of a clock, though it is repetitious, lacks the chief characteristic of rhythm; it doesn't in the slightest rouse our interest or produce excitement. On the contrary, it puts us to sleep.

The repetition which may be called rhythmic is not too regular, it is not mechanical, and it excites us by fixing our attention not on what is past, but on what is to come. A color rhythm in a painting sends the eye searching the canvas. Having seen the same color or the same pattern at least twice, we conclude that it may occur in a third time, and we look for it. No rhythmic pattern is completely fixed, but it must have in it such a degree of regularity that we expect it to recur. Whether it does indeed recur is of small importance so long as we expect it.

By no other definition can we say that the swaying of tree tops or the breaking of waves on the shore is rhythmic. The branches make us expect a continued swaying, and at about the same velocity, but when we beat strict time it is clear that the tree hasn't its eye on the conductor, nor has the breaking wave. In music itself the conductor does not wave his stick with the precision or the monotony of the clock, not unless he is leading a military band on the march or is otherwise producing the motivating tom-tom kind of music. The military band, once started, can continue without a leader. The conductor of the symphonic orchestra is needed, not to keep time, but to hold the players together when they vary the tempo.

In the swaying of the tree branches, many rhythms are present simultaneously. The larger branches sway more slowly than the small, and each leaf flutters by a system of its own. Something almost as complex can be observed in well-imagined music. There are recurring patterns in the large accents, and other patterns in the less important accents; each musical phrase, though only a few notes long, has its rhythm; by the employment of rests or pauses the composer can hold up for a moment the swaying of whichever rhythmic branch he pleases, or he can startle us with masses, so to speak, of silence by stopping all the branches at once.

So much has been said about rhythm that most of us think it is present everywhere in life and is therefore inescapable; without the proper rhythm in ourselves, we cannot enjoy health nor even perhaps life. But there is much self-flattery in these ideas. Rhythm is indeed present in the universe, but for the most part it escapes our attention, unless it hits us in some of its cruder forms. Our Western music is still rhythmically crude—there is no other word for it. A large part of our interest in ragtime, jazz or swing, is in the energetic rhythms. I don't mean that jazz is not at times very beautiful in every musical sense; there is no reason why it shouldn't be so always. But we need to remind ourselves more often than we do that though jazz rhythms are not the most subtle in the world, they are on the whole more subtle than those we usually notice. Even the jazz which musically is very bad, may legitimately attract through its rhythmic power.

Again I would not be misunderstood; I am not saying that subtle rhythms are absent from the works of those composers whom we call great. I do say, however, that some of us play great music and practically all of us still listen to it, as though it contained no other rhythms than those indicated by the number of beats in the bar. The rhythms of Sebastian Bach are so comprehensive that by a little search we can find in his pages even our own patterns of jazz rhythm, just as we can find prophetic flashes of the most modern harmonies. The rhythms in a Chopin mazurka are incredibly subtle. Most amateurs, however, and altogether too many professionals reduce Bach to a sturdy wooden utterance, and aside from an occasional accelerando or retard, they iron out Chopin into something that can be practiced with the metronome. The give and take of true rhythm is still an ideal. Perhaps the morning stars had it when they sang together. I am reluctant to believe they beat three to the bar, or even four or five.

The modern system of dividing music rigidly into bars or measures, with the number of beats fixed in advance or announced from bar to bar, is something that the devil himself might have thought of. It is perhaps convenient for a bad music teacher or an incompetent conductor, but it has little to do with music as it should be performed, and it compels the unfortunate student, by which I mean all students, first to learn how to count out his notes by the bushel or peck, than to spend the rest of his life getting these pitiful gauges out of his head.

The first beat in every bar, we are taught, is the main beat and should have a heavy accent. The third beat should have a light accent. If we play something in ¾-time, we are taught to emphasize the first beat and to a lesser degree the last. When we play in 4/4 or common time, we must emphasize alternate beats, with more attention to the first. If there are five beats to the bar, we separate them into groups of three and two or two and three, putting the main accent of course at the beginning of the first group, and a lighter accent at the beginning of the second. But how often do we find a musical phrase which is one bar long and no longer? Even if it is the right length, how often will it be moulded to a rhythmic pattern which fits those heavy and light accents? If it runs over into a second or a third bar, how likely is it to call for those heavy accents just where each bar begins?

Once the tempo is established, the competent musician forgets the bar lines entirely and phrases the music for its sense, putting the accents wherever the meaning requires. In other words, he reads his music just as we read a printed page, raising or lowering the voice and accenting the syllables for no other purpose than to bring out the thought. We often wish we had graphic symbols to show the reader more accurately what the author means. If music had any such helpful devices, we would appropriate them for our printed page. But of what assistance would it be to the reader to mark the sentences off in time periods, with an inflexible alternation of accents?

Music was not always set down in this absurd fashion. The medieval and renaissance composers used no bars, but trusted their clients to come at the proper phrasing through an understanding of the musical discourse. To perform music properly, we must still think of it in terms of itself, with no artificial lattice-work superimposed.

A moment ago I said that the musician forgets the bars as soon as the tempo is established. How does he know what tempo the composer wished? He is guided by the directions which the composer drops along the way, to indicate various gradations of fast or slow. But more precisely he is guided by the metronome, a time-beating machine which was developed in the eighteenth century, and perfected by Johann Nepomuk Maelzel early in the nineteenth. Maelzel's metronome is immortalized in the symbol MM. followed by a musical note and a number. This means that if you adjust the pendulum on your Maelzel metronome, the machine will beat out that number of that kind of note a minute. Composers tell us the tempo they want by writing the Maelzel marks at the beginning of the score. By the same method editors indicate the tempo the dead and helpless masters would have indicated if they had had a metronome, and the same taste as the editors.

A metronome, remember, indicates no rhythms, nothing but tempo. It's as regular as a clock. The moment you have learned the tempo, you'd better shut off the machine. If you let it keep on beating while you practice, you'll play like a metronome.

7 I HAVE TRIED to describe, at least in its elements, the language of music. But what is the subject matter which this language conveys? When Walter Pater described the condition of music as envied by the other arts, he implied that the language and the content of music are identical, that the note to which we listen is a word, but it also is the idea which that word expresses. This description is to a degree helpful, but after our discussion here of rhythm, pitch, and the other matters which belong to the language of music, perhaps we may attempt to define music's subject matter apart from the language which expresses it.

All other arts—literature, painting, sculpture, architecture—record literal experience. To deserve the name of art, however, they must, in addition to the literal record, suggest something over and above, something *plus*. This something *plus* is appreciated by the imagination and by the emotions rather than by the mind. The poet writing of the *Charge of the Light Brigade* records the carrying out of a mistaken order; the something *plus* which the lines convey is a response to abstract heroism, to a vision far more universal than the specific incident. The architect may build only a literal home, a roof to cover us, or he may suggest the abstract desirability of home in general. Any art, we may say, whatever else it accomplishes, expresses in addition that longing, that aspiration, which Plato called the growing pains of the wings of the soul.

But other arts convey this ideal longing as linked to a precise message.

Music alone expresses longing in an isolated state. The painter, before he can stir our aspirations, must show us the face of Mona Lisa. The musician expresses the longing which we would have if we had seen the Mona Lisa, but he omits the picture, and the aspiration which he rouses is entirely detached; we can tie it up with any form of beauty our personal experience has discovered.

This distinction between music and the other arts is fundamental and should be maintained, even though the other arts have in some cases taken Pater's hint and have tried to be, like music, abstract. To some extent they succeed. A sculptor may give us a solid three-dimensional form called *Flight,* or *A Bird in Flight,* and we may understand the idea of universal flight, but the title of his piece has helped him out amazingly. Perhaps he has achieved program sculpture rather than absolute sculpture. To whatever degree he has been successful, the musician has a better language for that kind of subject. Music can express flight by rousing the aspiration for wings.

It is easy to see why a Greek who followed Plato's philosophy would praise music above all other arts. The Platonic fable described the gods as living by the contemplation of Ideas. An Idea was the reality, of which human qualities are but shadows and recollections. Here in this life, said Plato, we see a strong bridge, or a strong horse, or a strong man; but in the heavenly ride the gods contemplate Strength, not a quality attached to one thing or another, but an essence complete in itself. Here we see beautiful landscapes, beautiful actions, beautiful men and women; there the gods contemplate Beauty, not a quality added to a person or thing, but a universal and eternal essence.

The subject matter of music is longing and aspiration in the abstract or, as Plato would have said, in reality. It is the very nature of music to be absolute. In so far as it adds itself to any program, it must to some extent come down to earth. The result may be, for the uninitiated or unmusical, entirely satisfying, but it will not be music at its best.

$\mathcal{C}$hapter four:

MUSICAL NOTATION

1   THE VISITOR from another planet, attending a symphonic performance, might ask what those pages are which the musicians arrange in front of them on frail metal desks an arm's reach away, and which they turn from time to time. If we answered, That's the music, the visitor might protest that he had been listening to the music, and according to the assurances we had given him, music is for the ear, not the eye. We'd be patient with him, of course; we'd explain that even a composition which addresses itself to the ear must be recorded in some permanent form, elaborate compositions especially, since they are not easy to remember. We might add that it's just as sensible to print music as it is to print a literary work; in both cases the composition gains not only in permanence but in facility of distribution. But the planetary visitor, if he were as intelligent as we have assumed, would then retort that our parallel holds good for printed dramas but not for printed novels or essays, since these latter are not recited but are read in silence. Why not admit they are composed for the eye?

Unfortunately he would have a point. There was a time when narratives were written in verse and recited, like lyric poems—chanted is perhaps the better word; and what we would now call an essay was in the past delivered as an oration or a lecture. There were many books and much written music before the invention of printing, but until speech was recorded in letters there was strictly speaking no literature. We lack a special name for the glorious compositions, the masterpieces of man's early days, which were handed on by oral tradition.

The moment literature was printed, writers began to neglect the appeal to the ear. No noble style is possible unless the prose man as well as the verse man composes with the cadence of the sentence in mind. We are deluged with prose which has no style at all, setting forth the thoughts of the stylistically deaf and dumb. The same calamity sometimes occurs in music. It is uncomfortably possible to approach music as a problem in acoustics, or in mathematics, in either case a problem which can be worked out on paper in dead silence.

On the other hand, if a subtle or complicated book were not printed, it could not be remembered at all. The ancient masterpieces which were transmitted by ear from memory had to rely on certain aids, stock phrases, what we should call clichés, no more pleasant then perhaps than now. The music to which the visitor from another planet has been listening is more complicated than any literary composition, since it is produced by instruments differing from each other in tone and performing simultaneously different tone-patterns. To make this clear to the visitor, we could show him the pages on the desk of the first violin, those on the desk of the 'cello and those on the desk of the kettledrum. He would see a resemblance in the horizontal lines and in the bars, but the melodic design of the notes would not be the same, nor the markings of the clefs. He might conclude as most of us do on our first sight of printed music that it is hard to read. We should tell him that this impression though common is not correct. Words are difficult, but notes are astonishingly simple.

Musical notation can be expounded by tracing its historical evolution, or better still, we can build up for ourselves hypothetically the system on which it is based, telescoping for convenience the historical development. Let us imagine that we know the tune of the song but we fear we may forget it. Why not invent a memory aid? Why not draw a picture of the tune? Here's a graph of *The Star Spangled Banner,* for example.

In the first phrase of the song, the graph turns down a short distance and rises sharply for a longer distance. In the second phrase it comes down again almost to its previous low point, then makes a brief upturn. In the third phrase the tune starts again where it left off, jumps to the highest note previously sung, then descends a little way. In the fourth phrase it rises slightly, then climbs down the scale which in the first phrase it climbed up.

This up-and-down graph might serve as a general memory-nudger, but it has two defects; it doesn't tell us on what note to start the tune, and it doesn't indicate accurately the intervals between the different notes. We could make shift to get on without knowing the precise pitch, but the distance between the high and low notes can't be measured by guessing. Why not draw a straight line horizontally through the graph? Such a line would help to estimate the height of the jumps. No matter where this line might be placed, if we wrote at the beginning of it the name of one note in the scale, we could measure with fair accuracy how far at any point the graph was from that note. If we mark the line with a capital G, we mean that whenever the graph crosses it, we are to sing the G above middle C. In time the music copyists will turn the G into a decorative symbol to designate the G or treble clef.

But even with this line much of the graph would still be vague. We could read it accurately whenever it crossed the G line, but at other times we couldn't be sure. Why not have more lines? Why not have a line for alternate tones in the scale, it being understood that the spaces in between would represent the intervening tones? Music for average voices would lie between high G and the G two octaves below. We already have the line with the letter to designate the octave below high G. Why not draw above it three more lines? That's all we should need at the top. Let's draw three lines below it. It's fairly easy to read the notes on three unlettered lines, but for a larger number the eye would be glad to have guidance. The fourth line below our G line is F. This F becomes in time the symbol of our bass clef. If below the F line we draw three more lines, we have an accurate scale or ladder large enough to hold three octaves of notes.

The lines, or rungs of our ladder, you observe, number eleven. They make an impressive pattern, perhaps unnecessarily impressive. The line in the center is middle C. We shan't need to write it all the time. We notice that it comes two lines below G and two lines above F. Why not omit it until it is needed? We can always draw it through the note. When the note is silent, an empty space on the paper will separate the upper group of five lines from the lower. If the notes in the upper group want to come down, they can find middle C by drawing in the short line—musicians call it a ledger line. If the notes in the F clef wish to rise, they can draw the ledger line above them.

This scheme makes possible an accurate record of the notes within the part of the scale represented by these lines, and once having discovered the principle of the ledger line for middle C, we can use the device above or below any clef in order to write extra high notes or extra low. The more ledger lines there are, however, the harder it is, as every beginner knows, to read the notes at sight. We wish there were guiding letters in the extreme spots. If we use notes more than an octave above or below the clefs, we write them within easy reading distance, and mark them with the number 8, to show that they must be played as octaves.

And finally, instead of using ledger lines we can, if we wish, change the marking of a clef. If, for example, the notes lie below G rather than above it, the clef mark can be moved up to one of the higher lines. The notes then will lie on the staff. This device is used for some of the orchestral instruments, notably for the 'cello. We shall discuss movable clefs more fully a few pages later.

The notes, placed on the lines or between them, indicate not only the elevation or pitch of the tone, but its duration. Quite simply, almost too simply, our system of notation assumes that the length of any tone can be cut in half, the halves can be cut in quarters, the quarters into eighths, etc. A half-note followed by two quarter-notes, we say, is equivalent to a whole-note, and a whole-note theoretically should occupy the time elapsing between two bars.

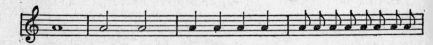

If we wish to prolong a half-note by the length of a quarter, we add a dot.

Of course, a system so simple must also be equally rigid. Music expresses rhythms as free as the swaying of branches in the wind, but our system of notation assumes that the branches sway in a jerky fashion, and that every movement divides precisely into halves or quarters or eighths. It is true that we can print three notes to be played in the time usually occupied by two; we represent the triplet pattern by an arch binding the three notes, with the number three added to make the device fool-proof. The effect of three notes played against two is pleasant, and if our rhythmic perceptions are not acute, we may imagine in it a certain freedom. Actually, however, we are still dividing the notes mathematically. To play three against two, we multiply the three by two and the two by three, so that there will be six beats in each pattern. In one pattern we accent every second beat, in the other every third beat.

Our notation permits only two methods of dealing with an absolutely free rhythm. Either we maintain a fairly constant tempo with one hand, and with the other bring along as large a number of notes as we please, or we abandon altogether the attempt to mark the tempo, and treat the melody as a free cadenza.

(Chopin: Nocturne, Op. 9, No. 1)

(Rimsky-Korsakoff: *Scheherazade,* Op. 35)

We have said enough already to indicate the general play of musical notation. The lines of the staff help us to see how high the note is or how low, the shape of the note shows us how long it should be held, the letter at the beginning of the clef fixes the pitch. From the numbers or from the letter C at the beginning of the clef, we learn how many beats there are to a bar, and what is the length of the note on each beat. With these principles in mind, we can read music—if we don't care what key it is in.

The key is indicated by the symbols for sharps or flats, the black keys needed for each scale. The key of G major needs F sharp. D major, the key of its dominant, needs an F sharp and a C sharp. F sharp is printed always before C sharp, since it is by the addition of C sharp that we modulate into D major. To reach the next related key, A major, again the chord of the dominant, we need G sharp and to get into E major we need D sharp. So long as the sharps and flats are properly printed, we don't need to look at them too closely; it's enough to see how many they are. One sharp denotes the key of G, three sharps the key of A, five sharps the key of B, etc.

If we start from C major, the one key which needs no sharps or flats—

we call them accidentals—the key five tones above calls for one sharp, and the key five notes below calls for one flat. So long as the keys rise on successive fifths, sharps are added. In general we write flats when we are going down, as in a chromatic scale, and sharps when we are coming up. There is otherwise no difference between sharps and flats, since they both designate the same black keys, but we often make a distinction for the sake of common sense or convenience. The key of D flat and the key of C sharp are to the ear identical; so are the key of G flat and the key of F sharp. Which key the composer chooses, will depend upon the modulations he wishes to make in the course of the music. On the other hand, though it would be possible to treat the key of B major as the key of C flat major, the result would be such an orgy of accidentals as to discourage once for all any idiot who tried it.

To read music is simple, but it's another thing to perform it properly. Just because the notation is over-simple and over-rigid, the artist accepts it merely as a general guide to the composer's intention. In performance, the quarter-notes are rarely precisely or invariably one half the length of the half-note: the dot hasn't always the same value; the bars, as we said before, are as much as possible ignored. Our way of printing music represents a reaction from older and more complicated systems at which we might well glance a moment, since they persist in fragmentary fashion on our modern pages.

2 THE ANCIENT GREEKS designated the notes of their scales entirely by the letters of the alphabet. Our modern scale is still lettered from A to G, but to write music we use musical symbols. A melody, of course, can be recorded by letters, otherwise the Greeks could not have managed it, but they must have performed their music at a slow pace. With letters the up and down movement of a tune cannot be shown graphically, and music cannot be read with speed if every note must be examined with care, to calculate its position in the scale.

Jean Jacques Rousseau, good musician though he was, once proposed to revive all the inconvenience of an alphabetical notation by substituting numerical figures for letters. He tells about it in the *Confessions*. The tonic would be represented by the figure 1, the third by the figure 3, etc.; chords would be indicated by figures placed above each other. His system is explained at length in the essay called the *Dissertation on*

Modern Music, now included in his complete works. In 1742 he expounded his idea to a committee of the Academy of Sciences, and during several meetings with these gentlemen he answered their objections, which were strong. Apparently they criticized him less for musical heresy than for lack of originality; they told him he wasn't the first to propose a numerical system. No criticism could have offended him more. But the composer Rameau laid his finger convincingly on the weakness of the system by saying that music written in numbers would be almost impossible to read. Rousseau tells the story at his own expense by way of illustrating the superiority of experience over theory.

The origin of our notes seems to lie in the accents which the Greeks used to guide readers of words as well as readers of music. The acute accent, the grave and the circumflex, the exclamation mark and the question mark, are the only survivors in modern printing of these enormously useful guides to expression. Why words must now be printed with so little aid to correct inflection, is a mystery we needn't go into here. Fortunately the ancient signs or neumes survive, much developed, in music.

The grave accent, (\) a slanting mark from the upper left hand to the lower right hand, became in the twelfth century a lozenge-shaped point (♦) which a hundred years later was written on a staff line (-♦-). This lozenge-shaped mark was solid black, like the head of a quarter-note but without a tail. The acute accent (/), from the upper right-hand corner to the lower left hand, became the tail of the quarter-note. The combination of the grave and the acute, the curved line which gives us a circumflex accent (∧), became the binding mark which holds several notes together (♩♪).

It is obvious that the method of lettering the scale is not essentially different from any systems which name the notes, call them A B C, or do, re, mi. By the eleventh or twelfth century the first seven letters of the alphabet were in common use, as were various forms of the staff and various neumes or note signs, indicating the tone by their position on or between the lines. The scale beginning on A, a minor scale without G sharp, the augmented seventh, still seemed most important, as it had seemed to the ancient Greeks. Our modern preference for the major has shifted emphasis to the scale of C, the other white note scale, with which we usually begin our study of music. From our point of view the lettering should start here; C ought to be A. But it's just as well to leave the lettering undisturbed, since our taste may change again, and in time we may hear in the old A minor something fundamental which now we neglect.

From reproductions of medieval manuscript music, most of us know in what chief respects the notation has changed. It is natural for us, accustomed to our own habits and exploring backwards, to feel that the ancients did the changing. We represent a whole-note by the outline of an oval figure without a stem. The whole-note has the value, naturally, of four quarter-notes. The half-note is represented by the outline of an oval with a stem, a quarter-note is the solid oval with a stem; an eighth-note is a quarter-note with an angular stroke at the end of the stem. From there on we represent subdivisions of time by adding these angular strokes.

The medieval notes were written usually in black. The longa or whole-note was a black square with a stem on it. The brevis or half-note was a black square without a stem. The semi-brevis or quarter-note, was a black square placed lozenge-fashion.

More subtle variations of note-value were indicated by red ink instead of black, but in the early fourteenth century the humane principle was announced that wherever the scribe ran out of red ink, he could indicate the effect by leaving the notes open. By the time Shakespeare was writing his early plays, musical notes were written generally in this form. We no longer use the longa or the long; the breve is the ancestor of our double-note; the semi-breve of our whole-note.

Toward the middle of the seventeenth century, about the time that Cromwell was maneuvering the head off Charles I, certain guides to expression were introduced by the Italians and adopted throughout Europe—the words piano, forte, presto, adagio, and the symbol for crescendo and diminuendo. Couperin, Sebastian Bach and Rameau, somewhat later, used a dot as a staccato sign.

The clefs which we know best are the treble or G clef and the F or bass clef. The C clef, once a favorite for vocal music, is now employed chiefly for certain instruments, such as the viola and the bassoon. It was and still is a movable clef. When placed on the lowest line it is called the soprano clef; when on the second line, the mezzo-soprano clef; when on the middle line, the alto clef; when on the fourth line, the tenor clef. For each of these voices the position of a clef made it possible to write music without ledger lines.

In our music today we are accustomed to the G clef and the F clef, because they are used for the notes of the right and the left hand in piano music. Our staff has five lines, and though we may have heard of smaller or larger staves, few of us have seen them. The five-line staff has been standard for voices since Shakespeare's time or a little earlier. Until 1800, however, instrumental music was frequently written on staves of six lines, of eight, or even of as many as eleven. This fact should be borne in mind when we consider the key signatures.

In early music, even on the five-line staff, the F sharp to indicate the key of G major was often written on the lowest space as well as on the top line. So long as the staff had many lines, it was important to mark the sharps and flats on all lines and spaces. Our present method of giving the sharps or flats in each key is convenient though not scientifically accurate. We never mix sharps and flats in a signature, though G minor, for example, contains not only a B flat and an E flat but also an F sharp.

There is dispute among musicians today whether our method of marking the key signature at the beginning of the piece and repeating it at the commencement of each line is either intelligent or convenient. A competent musician knows the key from the sound of the notes, and it makes little difference to him whether the sharps and flats are written once for all at the left-hand end of the staves, or are inserted when needed. Some composers, therefore, write their scores without sharps or flats, inserting those marks when they need them, but otherwise understanding that the note should be played natural. In our present method a sharp or a flat which is not in the key signature is called an accidental, and when it occurs in any bar we understand that if repeated within the same bar it will remain sharp or flat. In the following bar, however, it reverts to its original value. The modern reformers say it is much simpler to understand that notes are always natural unless they are marked otherwise. To remember the original signature and to revert to it after a bar full of accidentals, is not always easy. Moreover, we cannot quote a chord from a page of music without marking the sharps or flats in that chord. Key signatures, and sharps and flats in general, probably constitute the greatest difficulty in reading music.

Since the adoption of modern tuning and the consequent ease of modulation, the necessity arose for a sign to mark the double sharp ✖ , which means that the note is to be raised not one but two half tones. A double flat is marked by two flats placed side by side ♭♭. The natural sign ♮ is used to contradict an accidental sharp or an accidental flat. Before the eighteenth century, it was the custom to contradict a flat with the natural sign, but to correct a sharp by the flat sign. Some acquaintance with all these notations is useful today, since the interest in old music is lively, and singers, instrumentalists, and conductors have constant occasion to consult old scores either in manuscript or in reproduction.

At the beginning of a piece the clef sign comes first, then the key signature, then the indication of the time. The symbol C 𝄴 marks common time, or four quarter-notes to the bar. Other times are represented by fractions—three over two, three over four, six over eight, and so on, the numerator indicating the number of beats, the denominator showing the length of the note on each beat. With the time marks is associated, of course, the bar, a vertical line dividing the music into equal lengths. The principal accent is supposed to fall, and in many cases does fall, on the first beat after the bar. The time may change from bar to bar; with every change there must be a new time signal. At the end of the section or of the whole piece, there is a double bar,‖ , to show that the conclusion has been reached.

The bar began to appear in music early in the sixteenth century, in manuscripts in which a single staff of ten lines was employed. No doubt the purpose was to guide the eye in associating so many notes on so many lines, but with the accurate printing of music nowadays this usefulness diminishes fast, and, as we said before, an invariable accent on the first beat contributes the most objectionable kind of monotony.

The merits and handicaps of the bar are paralleled in the use of capital letters for writing and printing. It is well, of course, to end a sentence with a period and to begin the following sentence with a capital—if we have no other means of knowing when a sentence starts and when it stops. If, however, we have progressed so far in literacy that we can measure the sentence by the sense, neither period nor capital is necessary. In English we begin every line of verse with a capital, whether or not the first word in the line begins a sentence. It is extremely hard to convince immature readers that the capitalized first word should not enjoy an unnatural emphasis, and should not be preceded by a meaningless pause.

In ways similarly unfortunate the bar hypnotizes all but the best musicians. It tends to break up long phrases and to induce a uniformity of rhythm which the composer, perhaps, did not intend. Unfortunate children are encouraged to count out loud while they play. The scars of that counting, or vestiges of the scars, may be discerned in their playing to the end of their days. Even conductors are found who in the same way, if not to the same degree, are hypnotized by the bar, but the conductor has an excuse; the men in the orchestra must on occasion remain silent for many bars, they must count the silent bars, and they count from the first beat of each bar. The orchestra, therefore, must have a clear first beat. If the conductor is not a master of his craft, he may yield to the temptation of accenting the first beat in order to make it doubly clear. A great conductor, however, will get this clarity without emphasis. To those who watch from the audience, he may even seem not to mark the first beat at all, so preoccupied is he in molding the phrases, which seldom correspond exactly with the bar lines.

3   MUSICAL NOTATION is problem enough for the singer or the violinist who has only a melody to read, one stream of notes upon which the attention can be concentrated. The pianist must read the notes on two clefs, often several notes on each clef simultaneously. He may be reading the notes of successive chords, or he may be following, as in contrapuntal music, different melodies. He wants a text which offers the fewest possible problems. In musical notation, therefore, other kinds of logic yield to his convenience. Since a whole-note is prolonged through an entire bar, it has on occasion been equally spaced from each other, but this practice is tabu; the musician written in the middle of the bar, with quarter-notes scattered around it, reading the score for the first time wants to see the notes at the spot where they are to be played. His eye can't leap ahead to the middle of the bar and select a note to be played earlier. Musical notation, in other words, keeps its first and primary value as a graph; when once the musician has learned the music, the script will serve him merely as a reminder. Yet as the art progresses the convenience of a first reading increases in importance. The soloist who plays or sings without notes may study the text repeatedly. Orchestral players, however, are expected to read the music at sight—not only music already famous but scores they have neither seen nor heard before. As the wages of the orchestral players mount, the ability to read at sight becomes more essential. Every minute

of rehearsal time is costly. If the orchestra plays over·the radio, the cost of rehearsal time is prohibitive, and the men must be able to read any music set before them. The notation, therefore, must take the form which is most saving of time.

If the piano accompanies a voice or is associated with some instrument, the solo staff is placed above the two piano clefs. In organ music there is an extra bass clef on which the notes for the pedals are written. Whether the extra clef is for the pedals or for the voice, the player must read all three clefs at once. Here the practical advantage of the bar begins to show; the vertical lines aid the player to keep his place in the music.

If there are more instruments, each will have its separate staff. In a piano quartet (piano with three other instruments) the pianist must follow the music on five staves. In a string quartet the composer writes his music on four staves, the first violin on the top, the second violin, viola, and 'cello beneath. It would be expensive, however to print for each instrument all the notes in a piano quartet or a string quartet, and it's superfluous since each instrument does not necessarily play all the time. The piano, when associated with other instruments in chamber music, plays from the full score, but each of the other instruments reads from its separate part. As a matter of fact, all the artists, when studying their parts, will look at the full score, and before they come to performance they will have in their head those sections of the music which they don't play, and which are not before their eyes. In a string quartet all four instruments play from parts, and nobody uses the full score.

Obviously the score expands and becomes more complicated as more instruments are added, until the dimensions of the full orchestral score are reached. The conductor with an orchestral score before him has plenty of notes to look at simultaneously. Incredible though it may seem to the uninitiated, he can read at sight even the most elaborate scores, but no conductor does this from choice; he gives to the music profound and long preliminary study, so that at the first rehearsal he frequently knows every note by heart. It is not unusual for a conductor with a phenomenal memory to rehearse without the music, yet hear and correct errors as they are made. It is almost a fad nowadays for conductors to dispense with a score in concert performance. The players of some veteran orchestras, though they are accustomed only to their separate parts, acquire such a knowledge of the music as a whole that they know when to enter after a long silence, even without a signal. I once was in the audience at the Paris opera when all the electricity in that quarter of the city was cut off and the house was plunged into darkness. The performance continued without a pause, until after a minute and a half the lights were turned on again. The orchestra and the singers had kept together perfectly in the dark, without the conductor's help. It is fair to add that the opera in question was Gounod's *Faust,* which I suppose that orchestra could play backwards, standing on their heads.

4   THE ORDER in which the music for the various instruments appears on the full orchestral score records to some extent the steps by which the orchestra developed. On the five staves at the bottom of the page is written the music for double bass, 'cello, viola, second violin, and first violin. The string section is the oldest and most characteristic part of the orchestra. It does most of the work and usually is seated well forward on the stage, so that its tone, none too powerful at best, can be heard to advantage. If the double basses are ranged along the wall in the rear of the orchestra with the tympani and the larger brass instruments, it's only because they take up too much room to be stationed elsewhere.

Above the staves for the violin the composer writes the music for the brasses—for the tuba, trombones, trumpets, and the horns. In a group of staves at the top of the page he writes the music for the woodwinds— the bassoons, the clarinets, the oboes, the flutes, and the small flute or piccolo. The flute is so ancient an instrument and its tone is so readily mated with that of the violin that we might expect to find it placed next above the strings, but the trumpet and the horn also have claims on antiquity. The conductor, looking down at his score, or looking out at his players on the platform, thinks of the orchestra as three choirs, the string, the brass, and the woodwind, each with its special kind of tone color, each capable of producing unique effects.

The function of the conductor is of course to establish the tempo and the rhythm, but even more, it is to mix the characteristic tone of these three choirs as a painter mixes his color. The notes for all instruments are of the same size when printed on the score; in the combining of the tones the conductor is not guided by his eye. That the instruments differ enormously in tone quality is indicated by the fact that there may be fifteen or more first violins in the band as against two flutes, two oboes, two trombones. The tone of woodwinds is penetrating; that of brasses is strong. If the conductor so wishes, he can overwhelm the violins with these other choirs.

Two instruments, the drum and the harp, may date from a more remote epoch than the trumpet. The drums, or tympani, appear in practically every score. The music they play is printed on a line between the strings and the brasses. If there is a harp, its music is printed between that of the strings and the drums.

Our friend from Mars, on his first visit to one of our concert halls, will probably not notice the score on the conductor's desk, not even if the conductor uses a score. The elaborate page of music which we have just considered preserves the composer's text from performance to performance. It facilitates the preparation of accurate rehearsals. Yet in the long run the interpretation of the music is decided by the soloists, among whom the conductor is reckoned. There might seem to be an exception in the case of chamber music, but even a string quartet playing with apparent spontaneity and in complete agreement accepts the interpretation of a leader, usually the first violin. The soloists and the conductors have studied the notes, but equally they have studied tradition. The arias in an opera are sung in imitation of earlier performances, which imitated performances still earlier, and so on back to a notable performance under the composer's direction, or marked permanently by the genius of some great artist. Conductors and soloists sometimes break the tradition deliberately, but even then they are conscious of what they are doing, and they count on critics and general audience to recognize an innovation. In general, however, they accept and continue the tradition, knowing that their personality will be revealed most clearly when measured against a well-known standard.

This tradition has an obvious effect. The number of fine artists who give superb interpretations of old works is fairly large; their own personal ideas have been enriched by the studies of all their predecessors. On the other hand, few artists can establish a tradition, can perform a new work for the first time so that others will not wish to interpret it differently. Many great opera singers, for example, have created rôles, but it is hard to name in a century another Mary Garden who specialized in creating roles and in fixing them once for all in an interpretation which remains the despair of her successors. When you hear a performance of *Pelléas and Mélisande,* of *Louise,* of *Le Jongleur de Notre Dame,* you see an imitation of Mary Garden, or if you don't, you read next morning the lamentations of the critics that Mary Garden can't be successfully imitated. It would be an exciting and perhaps profitable experience to hear Chopin's Nocturnes, for another example, performed by a good pianist who had never heard them performed by anyone else. Perhaps he might find in the printed notes a reason for adopting the tradition which had otherwise been concealed from him, but perhaps he would hit on another reading and perhaps we should find it worthwhile.

The man from Mars will begin to see why it is difficult to say in a few words what music is. Our methods of recording musical sound for the aid of memory are crude. The instruments we employ, with one or two exceptions, are not entirely satisfying; we know where they might be improved. Though we are accustomed to our musical scale, we are conscious that it has certain limitations and absurdities, and not all our instruments can tune themselves to it. Yet we create for ourselves, through imperfect methods and instruments, an experience either of compelling beauty or of hypnotic fascination. This experience cannot be described in general terms; each person in the audience must speak for himself. Since he is not likely to be articulate on the subject, the best we can do is to watch the changing mood on his face as he listens.

Chapter five:

MUSICAL INSTRUMENTS

1   IF THE VISITOR from Mars has not yet heard enough about music, he may ask about the instruments in the orchestra or about other instruments encountered now and then in concert halls. He may go to church and hear an organ, or to a dance and hear a jazz band, and in these two directions if he so desires he may pursue us with hard questions which we might as well anticipate, so far as we can.

Since the visitor from Mars is by definition alert, he may observe that in orchestral concerts he rarely hears a human voice. At long intervals a singer appears, accompanied by the ninety or so instruments, and at intervals slightly less long there may be a chorus on the platform, but in general the orchestra does very well by itself.

Our visitor has really noticed something! Our music has developed faster than any single instrument. No instrument unaided can produce in its full range and power and color the music which we compose. Only three instruments, the organ, the piano, the harp, can be enjoyed alone.

The range of most instruments is limited, each commanding a section of the scale. Other instruments of approximately the same quality are called upon to fill out. The violin, the viola, the violoncello, and the bass violin, for example, are all the same kind of instrument in different registers. Together they cover, for practical purposes, the complete scale, yet no one of these instruments is exactly like another. The tone of the viola differs from that of the violin and from that of the 'cello. In the woodwinds the flute is supplemented or pieced out by the piccolo above, and by the bassoon beneath—also by the clarinet and bass clarinet, but here the differences in quality are very great, since the tone of the clarinets and the bassoon is produced by one method and the tone of the flute by another.

The human voice shares some points of resemblance with the stringed instruments and some with the woodwinds. Soprano, contralto, tenor, and bass, when they supplement each other, cover a large scale, though not so large as the strings. The quality of these high and low voices in women and men may vary as sharply as the quality of a flute and that of an English horn. Each type of human voice by itself has a very limited range.

THE VOICE

SINCE THE VOICE is the instrument most readily accessible to all of us, those who are curious about music should know in general what the voice is, how it is used, what are its possibilities and its limitations.

The voice has this immense superiority over other musical instruments, that it is part of ourselves and therefore saturated with the human personality. We judge character by the sounds we make, and the most attractive aspects of human nature are revealed or suggested by our singing tones. Is it ungracious to speak at all of our vocal limitations? Unless we are wilfully obtuse, we must admit that the largest part of our greatest music is independent of the voice. Beethoven's sonatas, his string quartets, his symphonies, the music of Chopin, the rhapsodies and the symphonic poems of Liszt, the best of Schumann and Tchaikowsky, and whatever later instances you care to add, indicate that our progress in music has been progress in instrumental music. This is true even of Wagner. We sometimes omit the voices and perform the orchestral accompaniment on the concert stage. If we omitted the orchestra, there'd be nothing left.

It should be as easy and natural to sing as to speak, since in both cases the same vocal machinery is employed. The muscles of the diaphragm help us to fill our lungs with air, the breath comes up from the lungs through the windpipe to the vocal cords, and those cords, set in vibration by the breath, produce the sound which comes out of the mouth. In ordinary conversation we breathe unconsciously, we open the mouth more or less according to our personal instincts, and the friends to whom we talk are satisfied with our elocution, unless our speech is too loud or too soft. I describe normal conversation, where the audience is small.

If, however, we speak to a large audience in a spacious hall, we must send the voice farther, which probably means we must use more breath. Also—and here is the great difficulty of human speech as of human song—we must call into use unaccustomed muscles without becoming self-conscious. Few of us find this achievement easy or natural. Trying to speak louder we tighten our throats, we put a dangerous tension on the vocal cords, and in a few moments we become hoarse and inaudible.

We have the same experience in singing. Most people can sing at least as well as they can talk. When we sing to ourselves without thought of an audience, we breathe naturally, we don't force the tones, we are not likely to spoil our voices. When we sing in a large chorus, however, or alone before a large audience, the fear of being inaudible causes us to tighten the throat, to blow instead of breathe, to make a noise instead of projecting a tone. The discipline of the singer's art has this one purpose, to make song as natural as speech should be.

I say should be, because in our ordinary talk we rarely do as well as we could. Most of us breathe with only the top of the lung, content with a partial use of the human bellows and wind chest. The sound can't come out unless we open the mouth, but most of us speak with the mouth half-closed. Unless we are under some obligation to make ourselves heard at a distance, we care little whether our voice is resonant, and still less whether our words are distinct. Not only is the mouth closed but our lips don't move.

I remind you of these facts to explain why the voice, which at one time seemed the greatest of musical instruments, today occupies a humbler rank. Even if we used it properly its range would be limited, but so few of us understand how to use it even in speaking that the singer, unlike any other musician, must first make over or reconstruct the instrument before he can learn how to perform on it. A considerable number of singers must put so much attention on the conditioning of their voice that they never get to the study of music.

The most serious handicap of the voice as a musical instrument is the fact that we expect all singers to pronounce words. Without words singers are practically of no use. Some attempts have been made to use voices in chorus as though they were instruments, enunciating a tone without the addition of speech, but the success of these experiments is more than doubtful, since we can't sing a tone without pronouncing a vowel. Prolonged vocalizing on the sound *ah* is monotonous, but the effect isn't improved greatly by an occasional shift to the sound *ee*. When words are joined to music, the flow of tone is broken by the consonants, and the quality of the tone is impoverished by some of the vowels.

Yet the popularity of song lies precisely in this, that the hearer who can't enjoy music alone is at least entertained by the words. Whenever a famous folk song, like *Sally in Our Alley*, or a famous spiritual, like *Deep River*, is praised as a musical masterpiece, consider what impression the tune would make were it not the setting for a highly lyrical or dramatic text.

For the reasons here suggested, the art of the singer is less important to music than it used to be—that is, less important relatively. Modern harmonies are rendered more easily by instruments than by voices. To a great extent the development of musical forms has been achieved by instruments. Though the voice is supposed to have its great opportunity in oratorio and opera, oratorio is out of fashion, and the tendency in opera is to relegate the music to the orchestra, and to write for the voices, as in *Pelléas and Mélisande*, phrases which are as close as possible to the accents of speech. The same tendency is obvious in a good deal of modern poetry, which substitutes for the minstrel tradition of song an art emotionally relaxed, a mood in which the bard drops into an easy chair beside you for a little chat.

The range of the human voice is more limited than it seems. A good soprano can reach high C, two octaves above middle C. A good bass should, and often does, reach low C, two octaves below middle C. Exceptional voices go beyond these extremes, but for practical purposes, it's fair to say that all types of human voice operate within the range of only four octaves. Yet the variety of types gives the impression of rich resources. No two voices, even in the same range, are exactly alike. There are heavy basses and lighter basses, grading up into baritones; there are baritones which merge into tenors; there are robust tenors and lyric tenors, and extra high voices of the kind which used to be called alto; there are deep contraltos, and mezzo-contraltos, and mezzo-sopranos, dramatic sopranos, lyric sopranos, and high voices of the coloratura type. Whatever notes the composer sets down in his score, the impression of the music will change with the voices which sing it. Yet there is only one proper way to use the voice, and many effects are denied to the singer which are possible for the instrumentalist.

All musical tones are produced either by setting in vibration a cord or flat surface, which in turn causes a column of air to vibrate, or by setting the column of air in vibration directly. The initial vibration is caused either by a single blow or by continued pressure. The single blow is called percussion. Drums and piano are percussion instruments. The strings of the harp are plucked rather than struck, but for practical purposes the harp too is a percussion instrument. It resembles the drum and the piano in the essential fact that its tone begins loud and immediately diminishes. The voice and the violin are string instruments; the vocal cords are set in motion, and kept in motion, by the pressure of the breath, the strings of the violin are made to vibrate by the pull and push of the bow. In all these instruments—drum, piano, harp, voice, violin—there is a resonance chamber or sounding board against which the vibrations started by blow or by pressure, reinforce and prolong themselves by setting more air in vibration.

Such instruments as the clarinet, the oboe, the bassoon, cause a column of air to vibrate in a tube by the motion, not of a string, but of a flat surface called a reed. In instruments like the flute and the recorder, instruments of the whistle type, the vibrations are started by the breath, striking on a sharp edge without the intermediary action of a string or a reed.

Musicians try to make every instrument transcend its limitations. Piano-makers and pianists cultivate a singing quality; by the use of pedals, and still more by the reinforcing of harmonics (holding down notes to prolong the vibrations), they would conceal the fact that the piano is a percussion instrument. Yet at times, of course, they frankly use drum effects. The violin becomes a percussion instrument when the strings are plucked, as in pizzicato, or struck with the back of the bow.

But the voice can't be anything else than what it is. It is not a percussion instrument. The vocal cords, unless they are breathed on gently, produce no musical sound, only a rasping cough or bark.

THE VIOLIN

THE VIOLIN, the viola, the violoncello, and the double bass, belong to one family. They differ in size, in pitch, and in the quality of the tone, but in construction they follow the same pattern, and they are played by the same method. Since the violin is the most brilliant member of the family, we are inclined to think of it as setting the standard from which the others vary. But the name violin means "small viol." The standard viol is the viola. The violin is a variation in the higher register, as the violoncello and the double bass are variations in the lower.

In all instruments of this type the body constitutes a powerful resonance chamber. Over this resonance chamber four strings are stretched. The vibrations are set in motion by a rosined bow wielded by the right arm. To alter the pitch of the strings, the fingers of the left hand shorten them by pressing firmly on a finger board, or by touching the string lightly at certain points without pressing it all the way down. By the first method the notes of the normal scale are produced, the quality remaining of the kind we associate with strings. By the second method the player sounds the harmonics of the note to which the string is tuned. Since these harmonics are very high, they greatly increase the upper range of the violin, but in quality they suggest a flute rather than a string instrument.

The four strings of the violin are tuned in fifths, the lowest string sounding the G below middle C, the next string sounding D above middle C, the next string sounding A, and the top string sounding E. The E string is stretched to a greater tension than the others, and to secure rapid vibrations it is made quite thin. The G string is stretched with least tension, and to secure slow vibrations it is made quite thick. There is a marked difference in quality, therefore, between the notes of the lower strings and those of the higher. To prevent the violin box from collapsing under a one-sided tension, a sound post is fixed inside the box between the upper surface and the lower, directly under the right side of the bridge where the strain of the E string is supported. The left side of the violin, therefore, the part over which the lower strings play, vibrates more loosely.

The viola is tuned, like the violin, in fifths, but the lower string sounds the octave below middle C; in other words, the viola is tuned a fifth below the violin. The 'cello is tuned in fifths an octave below the viola. The double bass is tuned in fourths. Its lowest string sounds E, the sixth below the lowest string of the 'cello. The compass of the whole viol family, therefore, is nearly as great as that of the piano—for practical purposes quite as great.

As we noticed in a previous chapter, if we followed the simple acoustic principle of doubling the length of the vibrating string in order to sound the octave below, our pianos and our violins would at once become unmanageable. The instruments of the violin family, tuned to successively lower portions of the scale, secure depth by stretching the strings with less tension and by using heavier strings. Even so, the distance between the notes of the scale on the viola finger-board is greater than on the violin, and of course still greater on the 'cello, and very much greater on the double bass. The human arm can't manage a finger-board longer than that of the viola. The 'cello, therefore, is played upright, resting on the floor, and the necessary reaching is divided between the player's two arms, the right arm reaching down with the bow, and the left arm moving up and down for the widely distributed notes. Because the finger-board intervals are so large on the double bass, the left hand can conveniently reach only four whole notes on each string. That is why the strings are tuned in fourths.

The variation in tone quality between the high and low notes of any member of the violin family is marked, but perhaps not more so than the variation between the high and low registers of the human voice. When we praise a singer for uniform quality of tone throughout the scale, we really mean that the difference in quality is evenly distributed. Whether a composer is writing for the violin or for the voice, he can express a dark sombre mood on the lower strings, and emotions more brilliant or more startling on the higher.

The relation between the voice and the violin has always been close. Three or four centuries ago viol or violin players had at their command what we should now consider only an elementary technique. The human voice could match or surpass them. Singing was usually accompanied, therefore, by string instruments, the voice doing most of the work and probably making the louder noise. Gradually the violin was improved, until it was brought to its present perfection at Cremona in the seventeenth century by the Amatis, by Stradivarius, and by Guarnarius. Since that time musicians have generally agreed that the violin, unique among instruments, has realized its utmost possibilities and is not likely to be developed further. No essential change has been made in it for over two hundred years.

With the development of the instrument came an enormous extension of the technique needed to play it. In the hands of the modern virtuoso, the violin is capable of fantastic pyrotechnics, profound emotional depth, and wide variety of color. The violinist, since he played the most effective instrument, became naturally the leader of the earliest orchestras, and even in our orchestras today the first violinist, though he no longer conducts, is, as it were, second in command, and is called the concert master. The importance of the viol family should be explained, however, less by the historical development of the orchestra than by the essential advantages of the instruments. Players of woodwinds or brass must stop occasionally to breathe, and must pause for longer periods to rest. Since the left hand and right arm of the violinist can sustain unusual effort longer than the human lungs, the orchestra depends chiefly on the violins for lyrical or singing effects.

For the last century the string instruments have taken from the human voice the dominating place in music. In the orchestra they furnish a constant body of tone, and are called upon to announce or emphasize most of the themes. Today, however, this predominance is challenged. The woodwinds, and especially the brass, are attaining a degree of virtuosity which fifty years ago would have been thought impossible. This development has been brought about by jazz and swing bands, which need for dance purposes every degree of beauty or excitement which can be extracted from trumpets, trombones, clarinets, and saxophones. It is now a truism that a first-rate trumpeter or trombonist looks for a place in one of the leading symphonic orchestras, but a super-excellent player on these instruments hopes for a place in a jazz band. A small group of brass and woodwinds can play louder than the same number of strings; they also can play just as soft, and they can imitate most of the string effects.

Since the violin long ago was brought to its present perfection, and since there seems no great likelihood that it will develop further, it serves to measure the change in the other instruments. In general, their capacity for loudness increases, and when brought together in the modern orchestra they can make a lot of noise. The violin is essentially a musical instrument, and its subtleties cannot be fully appreciated when overwhelmed in the general din. It is true that composers, even those who wrote exquisitely for small orchestras, kindled easily to the dream of larger ones to write for, yet the music of Haydn and Mozart is not improved by doubling the size of the band. On the contrary.

In the cult of loudness now in vogue, the violin is for the moment losing something of its prestige. Fewer youngsters wish to play it, fewer audiences understand its musical potentialities, few composers entrust to it their best ideas. When it performs as a solo instrument, it fares well only when accompanied by a small string group; the modern piano is much too loud for it, and so is the modern orchestra. String quartets, in which the whole viol family can display fully their remarkable qualities, are not popular; on many of us, accustomed to sounds more highly spiced, they leave an impression of tameness and monotony. Much of the beautiful music composed at a time when instruments of the violin family were supreme, is now rarely heard in its original form, and there is small cause for gratitude to the arrangers who occasionally recall some of it for the modern large orchestra. Theoretically it would seem reasonable that symphonic orchestration should vary with the musical subject; certain material suggests a large band, other material quite as clearly needs more delicate treatment. There is no logical reason why all opera should be scored for full orchestra. If these theoretical arguments prevailed, the violin would occasionally come once more into its own, but they don't prevail. Most symphonies continue to be heavily scored, and modern operas, in spite of mounting costs, must have all the instruments and a regiment of players. Against this tendency the violin cannot protect itself.

But no instrument or group of instruments, however loud, will seem loud permanently. If the audiences of our time want noise, their search for it will eventually be baffled by the limitations of the human ear drum. Already in the dance halls the blare begins to be painful, and even in concert halls during the performance of the newer symphonies the membranes of the ear protest. Will there be a reaction? Shall we rediscover the musical fact that loud and soft are merely effects in contrast, and that a massive fortissimo can be achieved on a very modest instrument if the contrasting pianissimo is sufficiently delicate? At the present moment no signs as yet promise this return to musical sanity. Until it occurs, we might as well be frankly aware of what we are doing when we line the violins across the front of the platform and pack in the brasses and the woodwinds behind them to drown them out.

THE FLUTE

CHILDREN discover that by blowing across the top of a bottle, or tube, or pipe of any kind, a sound can be produced. The breath, striking the edge of the bottle or pipe at just the right angle, sets the chamber or column of air in vibration. The proper angle is determined, as the children can tell us, by trial and error. The quality of tone thus produced is quite unlike any other. It is ghostly and hollow, it is soft if we don't breathe too hard, and it is penetrating. The children discover also that by blowing violently they can raise the tone an octave and make it very shrill, perhaps painfully so.

Bottles of different size, or tubes of different length, yield different tones. If we selected a sufficient number of bottles, each sounding a note in the scale, we could play a tune on them. Tubes of varied length are more convenient for this experiment than bottles. Primitive man tied together graduated reeds and produced Pan-pipes. The Pan-pipe principle survives in the pipes of the organ.

There were two disadvantages about Pan-pipes, eventually cured by two solutions. In the first place, only one note could be sounded at a time. If the player's mouth were large enough, he could blow into several pipes at once, but only into consecutive pipes, producing adjacent notes of the scale. Human lips couldn't blow, as it were, sectionally, picking out separated notes to form a chord. The organ was invented to blow several notes at once, however far apart in the scale.

In the second place, the Pan-pipe artist had reason to observe that fingers are more agile than lips. A scale of notes can indeed be blown rapidly by sliding a series of reeds across the mouth, but there would be obvious advantages in holding one reed steady and altering the pitch by the fingers. Before they could make a set of Pan-pipes, men must have known that a shorter reed sounds a higher note than a long one, but since nature wills us all to be conservative, it probably took several hundred years to discover that a reed can be shortened and afterwards restored to its original length, for all necessary musical purposes, without the use of knife or glue. A hole in the side of a reed or hollow tube fixes the length of the sound wave at that point. A finger pressed on the hole restores the sound wave to the full length of the reed, or as far as the next hole. With this discovery the flute was born—a single reed, blown into at one end, with eight holes along the top sides, stopped by the four available fingers of each hand. In time, delicate mechanical levers were added, by the aid of which the fingers could manipulate more than the original eight holes, and the tone of the flute was reinforced by closing the end at which the blowing was done, and by opening a blow-hole a short distance from that end. Henceforth the flute was to be played sideways, the player raising his eyebrows and squinting off toward the left, the fingers twiddling away toward the right.

The usual compass of the flute is three octaves, from middle C up. As on most wood instruments, a skilful flute player can blow at least one half-tone lower and several tones higher, but this is the range for which composers write, unless they are careless or optimistic. The lowest tones are mournful and haunting, the higher become gradually intense and piercing, but the flute when in good hands yields nothing but beautiful sounds. Two flutes are enough for a large orchestra. The quality rather than the strength of the tone carries through extraordinary masses of sound.

The instrument of which we have been speaking is the standard concert-flute, but there is a variety of flute which extends the scale downward, and another variety which extends it upward. The flute family is less numerous than the violin group, but it illustrates in a parallel way the inadequacy of most musical instruments when played one at a time, and their expanded usefulness when used with instruments of lower and higher compass and of the same tone. In the concert-flute the tone of the low notes is weak but rich. This richness is magnified in the bass flute, the compass of which extends down to below middle C. The high notes of the concert-flute lack richness, but they are brilliant. In the piccolo this brilliance is extended upward to B flat, one tone short of two octaves above high C. The piccolo is small, not quite half the length of the concert-flute. Its pitch is an octave higher, and its lowest note is D, not C. Its tone, of course, is shrill, but it is used with great effect either in unison with the flute or by itself.

Whatever the limitations of the flute, its musical importance is great. The method used in producing its tone is one of the oldest known to man, and the quality of that tone, especially in the lower register, gives the pipe organ its character. The flute doesn't sing. Though it blends well with the human voice, it has few vocal qualities, or none. The voice is more closely related to the violin.

Like all the instruments of the woodwind family, the flute, though dating from antiquity, has been slow to reach its present perfection. Perhaps it is rash to suggest that even now its possibilities have been realized. An instrument which changes its tone by opening or closing apertures at various distances along a pipe is limited to the number of apertures the fingers can cover, unless some mechanical device adds artificial fingers. All the half-tones must be playable before modulation is possible. The earliest woodwinds had to stick to their key. Before the invention of mechanical fingers, the usual scale for the flute was D major. It was not until the nineteenth century that an adequate mechanism was devised by Theobold Boehm, a distinguished flute player of Munich (1794-1881). Boehm's invention has been adapted to the other woodwind instruments. Yet even with this important aid, a woodwind player does not find the various keys equally easy. With some instruments, like the clarinet, the difficulty is solved by transposing—by altering the length of the pipe to change the pitch, and by writing the notes in the key easiest to finger. This is as though an incomplete piano player bothered by a piece in C sharp could tune his instrument half a tone higher and play the composition on the white keys of C natural.

The woodwind player in the present condition of his instrument must reckon with difficulties inherent in the very mechanism which has helped him out. Thanks to Boehm, it is now possible to bore on the side of the flute, not eight, but eleven holes, and these openings can be spaced at the distances acoustically desirable, without regard to the convenience of the human hand. The mechanism may be described roughly as padded keys which stop the openings unless they are lifted by delicate trackers. These trackers run along the pipe until they reach the fingers. The player need not make violent lunges up and down the instrument; within a limited area he manipulates a kind of keyboard.

But these trackers, terminating in one area, are not a keyboard. Notes brought by the mechanism within reach of the hands are still, for some purposes, rather far apart. A violin can play a trill on any two notes which lie on the same string, the piano can trill on any adjacent notes, but only with great difficulty can the woodwinds play trills on certain notes, no matter how near they lie in the scale. The composer must know his instruments, and have a heart, and not ask for feats too acrobatic.

Great music, let us repeat, is nowadays producible only by many instruments, no one of which can contribute more than a small part of the total effect. The point cannot be made too often or too strongly. The subject matter of music, both language and content, expands fast, but musical instruments develop slowly. To be a musician, and to be a player of some one instrument, are not necessarily the same thing. You may have studied the piano and acquired considerable technique without asking yourself what music is, what is its nature, where is it going—and meanwhile, what is its present condition.

Before we leave the flute we should notice one acoustical trait of all wood instruments. The player can extend their range by blowing harder. When the flute has played one octave by normal breath-pressure, it sounds the next octave with the same fingering by "over-blowing." The over-blown notes in the flute are exactly an octave higher because the pipe of the flute is bored conically rather than cylindrically—that is, the diameter of the pipe at the end into which the player blows is larger than at the other end. If the pipe were cylindrical, of the same diameter throughout, the over-blown notes would be a twelfth higher instead of an octave. In other words, the woodwind player's art sometimes involves a good deal of mental arithmetic.

There is another important difference between a conical and a cylindrical pipe. In the cylindrical pipe the sound waves go to the farther end and return to where they started; in the conical pipe they stop at the farther end. A sound wave, therefore, is twice as long in the cylindrical pipe as in the conical, and cylindrical wood instruments can play an octave lower.

THE CLARINET

THE CLARINET belongs to that class of woodwinds in which the tone is produced by the vibration of a reed. A reed is a flat tongue or strip of cane, wood or metal fixed at one end and adjusted over an aperture, so that when blown upon it will close the opening and then, by its resiliency, spring back. These alternate pulsations produce the sound. We are familiar with the principle of the reed in the common mouth organ, where narrow strips of metal vibrate in a slot or groove.

The woodwinds now commonly used in the orchestra are, with the exception of the flute, reed instruments. They are divided into two families, those in which a single reed vibrates against the mouthpiece, and those in which two reeds extend from the top of the instrument and vibrate against each other. The clarinet belongs to the single-reed family. On the modern clarinet the player, without using mechanical keys, can play the octave from G below middle C to G above. The F is natural; the octave sounds in the key of C major. By mechanical devices the compass is extended down to E below middle C, and a chromatic scale can be played to B flat above middle C. To raise the pitch further the player must over-blow.

It was long ago found advisable to use the clarinet as a transposing instrument—that is, for the sake of easy fingering the notes are written in one key but they sound in another. Until a century ago there were three clarinets in general use, the clarinet in C, the clarinet in B flat, and the clarinet in A. We now use only the clarinet in A and the clarinet in B flat. The clarinet in B flat transposes down a whole tone; to get from it the key of D major, the composer writes in the key of E major. The clarinet in A transposes down a minor third; to get from it the key of D major, the composer writes in the key of F major.

There is supposed to be a difference in tone between these two instruments, but many experienced musicians with sensitive ears are more than skeptical. If the B flat clarinet is used instead of the A, or vice versa, it's because the composer believes the fingering will be easier for the key in which he intends to write. In all woodwinds the fingering remains an awkward problem, but as mechanisms are perfected and players become more expert, the awkwardness becomes a matter only of degree. First-rate players can manage all the keys, and it need be only a question of time before the woodwinds cease to be treated as transposing instruments. But they will probably stay as they are, since many players, conservative like other human beings, will cling to the transposing difficulties as a beautiful or even essential part of their tradition.

The tone of any reed instrument is easily recognizable; it is incisive and at the same time plaintive. It also is remarkably flexible, almost as much so as the tone of the violin. In this respect it differs widely from the tone of the flute. The clarinet, having a lower range than the flute, produces deep tones of considerable power. When flute and clarinet are combined in the same melody, the mixture of tone is rich. Other effects, not always so rich but invariably challenging, are achieved by using the flute with the oboe, or with any reed instrument. In fact, the woodwind family give the composer a palette of colors more varied than he can get from the violin family or, until recent times, from the brass. For the orchestra during the last seventy-five years, roughly speaking, the strings supplied song, the brass furnished drama, and the woodwinds contributed color.

There are other types or variations of the clarinet, in fact a little family, all important, though for different purposes. Military clarinets are high, brilliant, and loud, though as in other members of the family their flexibility is great and they are capable of remarkable crescendos and diminuendos. The bass-clarinet is invaluable for orchestral composers, who use it not only for its characteristic color but also as a sort of pinch-hitter for the bassoon, where stronger tone is desired than the bassoon can produce. The bass-clarinet plays an octave below the clarinet proper, of which it is merely an enlarged example, but it doesn't look like a clarinet. It is not straight throughout its entire length, and the player seems to blow it sideways instead of directly into the top. The flare or bell at the lower end is turned up and outward, away from the player as he holds the instrument, and the upper end is turned down toward the player, carrying to him the mouthpiece containing the reed. These two angles make it possible to play an instrument which otherwise would be too long. Thanks to the bend at the top the player can hold the bass-clarinet at the distance most convenient for manipulation, and the upward bend of the flare or bell prevents the bass-clarinet from hitting the floor.

THE OBOE

INSTRUMENTS of the double-reed family are bored conically; they therefore produce a sound wave of only half the length produced in a cylindrical pipe. Putting it another way, to match the pitch of the cylindrical pipe, a double-reed instrument must be twice as long. To secure the necessary length of sound wave in the bass instruments, the inner tube or wind chamber is folded back upon itself.

The double-reed family consists of the oboe, the English horn, the bassoon, and the double bassoon. The oboe, familiar to us in Elizabethan literature as the *hautbois,* was originally notable for loudness. It has been developed and refined, but it is still an instrument of the upper registers, as the old name "high wood" implied; and its tone still has considerable carrying power. Its range is from middle C upward, with a possible half-tone or whole tone below middle C.

The mordant quality of the oboe distinguishes it sharply from the flute, and except in parts of the scale it is easily distinguished from the clarinet. It is used like the clarinet to sound by itself a sustained theme or melody, or to combine with other instruments for the same purpose. But it has special characteristics which suggest humor or satire. Like other double reeds it can sound an amazing staccato, evoking a range of effects from mystery and terror to ridicule. When the composer wishes to convey the idea that an operatic character is becoming absurd, he is likely to call on the oboe, or the English horn, or the bassoon, for squeaks or grunts.

The oboe excels in melodic lines which are sustained, serious, and noble. In the middle of its compass the tone takes on a naive quality which no other instrument can equal. Gluck made frequent use of this happy resource, as in the Andante of *Orfeo,* in the scene of the departed spirits. Modern composers follow Gluck in using the oboe for smooth, lyrical effects, always in the middle register, but where a dramatic purpose calls for satire or humor, they exploit to the full the instrument's less song-like resources.

THE ENGLISH HORN

THIS BEAUTIFUL instrument with the strange name sounds one-fifth below the oboe, to which it is often compared as though it were a first cousin, but from which it differs essentially. Its tone is not mordant or mocking. Its lowest notes are extremely grave, in its middle register it has a contralto quality, haunting and melancholy.

The origin of its name is not known. Since it is a long instrument, the reed is usually bent inward toward the player's lips in order to make the fingering more convenient, and it has been suggested that this setting of the reed at an angle gave the name *cor anglé,* angled horn, the term being promptly and universally misunderstood as *cor Anglais,* English horn, to match the French horn. The main value of this hypothesis, however, seems to be that it fixes in memory the characteristic shape of the instrument. We still don't know why, under any circumstances, it is called a horn. The best guess is perhaps the most obvious, that the melancholy, poetic beauty of its tone suggests the true horn.

In early examples the entire neck of the English horn was bent, somewhat as in the bass-clarinet. Now only the mouthpiece, holding the double reed, is set at a slight angle. The flare, or bell, is straight as in the clarinet, not bent upward as in the bass-clarinet.

Most concert-goers, and most American children who play in the school orchestra, know well the tone of the English horn as it sounds the famous theme of the largo in Dvořák's *New World Symphony.*

THE BASSOON

THE BASSOON is the bass instrument of the double-reed family. It has a wide compass, from B flat, a whole tone beneath low C, to the upper E flat of the treble clef. The highest octave is too weak to be of much use, but even so, the bassoon has a remarkable range, and its peculiar hollow sound, apparently soft, carries far.

It is easy to identify the bassoon by its unique shape and by the way it is held, diagonally across the body. The bell, or mouthpiece, points outward above the player's left shoulder, but since there is no flare, the long dark instrument seems to be of the same diameter throughout. The windpipe reaches down to the bottom of the instrument, folds sharply back, and comes up again to the top. A short distance from the top a metal extension of the windpipe, approximately at a right angle with the instrument, brings the reed to the player's lips. He seems to be sucking the reed, the mouth of the bassoon sticking up above his head.

The tone of the bassoon, like other tones, is indescribable. Perhaps we only fancy that the sonorous name of the instrument describes it. When played slowly legato, the bassoon suggests a baritone voice. When played staccato, it excels other double reeds in weird effects of humor, or fantasy, or grimness. A good player, of course, knows in advance what effects he will produce; the rank amateur is liable to mix effects by sheer bad luck. Most of us recall the passage in *The Rhyme of the Ancient Mariner* where the wedding guest, unwillingly detained by the mariner, catches fragments of the wedding music—

> *"Higher and higher every day,*
> *Till over the mast at noon—"*
> *The Wedding-Guest here beat his breast,*
> *For he heard the loud bassoon.*

Coleridge wrote these lines, it is said, after attending a village church where the choir in the gallery sang with the aid of a pitch-pipe, a few violins, and, for better or worse, a bassoon. Coleridge never got that particular bassoon out of his memory. Assuming in charity, however, that it was fairly well played, we can understand why the poet invoked its other-worldly tone to set the atmosphere of his ghost story.

The double-bassoon needs only a brief description. It bears the same relation to the bassoon as does the double-bass-viol to the 'cello. It supplies an extension of the compass into the lowest register. The pipe is over sixteen feet long, and is doubled back on itself several times. Its compass reaches from something more than an octave below low C, to something more than an octave above low C.

THE TRUMPET

ALL THE INSTRUMENTS in the brass choir are sounded by the same principle. They consist of a metal tube with a mouthpiece at one end. The player, by blowing, makes his lips vibrate across this mouthpiece, and the vibration starts sound waves inside the tube. The tube may be bent or twisted, it may have a mouthpiece of one form or another, the player may adjust his lips or his cheeks, or may blow hard or soft, but in every case he produces the tone by lips against a mouthpiece at the end of a tube.

The brass instruments force upon our attention once more the phenomenon of harmonics. A tube of any given length will sound a fundamental tone, the tonic of a scale, and other notes of that scale, but not all. The tonic and its octave are possible, the fifth above the octave, the second octave above the tonic, the third and fifth above that, the diminished seventh, the third octave of the tonic, and a further series becoming closer together as they ascend. These possible intervals are the same for a tube of any length; difference of length changes nothing but the key. Bugle calls, confined to the notes of the major chord, illustrate the limited powers of every brass instrument in its primitive state.

If a difference of tube length will raise or lower the key, the obvious way of supplying the notes lacking in the series of harmonics is to change the length of the tube. This was done in the trumpet, and in other instruments with variations not worth mentioning here, by providing a series of crooks or extensions, each of which tuned the trumpet to a given key. A trumpet could play in the key of E because the crook raised it to that pitch. The value of this improvement was great, but the handicap remained that though the trumpet in E could play other notes than the trumpet in B flat, it could play no more notes, and it had the same relative gaps in its scale. Composers could ask the trumpet, at that stage in its development, to play in any key they wished, but they could ask of it only certain notes.

By partially closing the flare or bell of the trumpet, a note can be lowered and the quality of the tone changed. In the course of time the alteration of pitch secured by "stopping," was achieved more satisfactorily by inserting short tube extensions controlled by three valves, each valve lowering the pitch half a tone, two valves lowering it a whole tone, and three valves a tone and a half. The quality of the tone is unchanged. With the valves the vacant intervals can be filled in any harmonic scale.

But brass instruments, even with valves, can sound only their harmonic notes; the method of tempering, which is used in tuning the piano, is for them extremely difficult, in some cases impossible. There is a difference of pitch also in the instrument when it is cold and when it is warmed up. Brass instruments, therefore, in some of their notes seem— and are—out of tune with the rest of the orchestra. You may consider this part of their charm, but the phenomenon deserves to be looked at from another angle; it's a large example of nature's reluctance to accommodate herself to the music man hears in imagination, and tries, if only approximately and by an assortment of means, to produce.

The trumpet is a cylindrical instrument, but the end which contains the joint is for quite a distance conical. The mouthpiece is cup-shaped, a matter of great importance to the tone.

That tone hardly needs describing. From the earliest history of man it has been associated with calls to arms, with triumphal processions, with magnificent ceremonies. It is clear and brilliant. If the trumpet were reserved for such effects, it would be heard rarely in the orchestra. But the crooks which are now used in this instrument give it a variety of color, especially in the low registers, and some of its piano or pianissimo effects are extremely beautiful. As a matter of fact, the trumpet is used more and more for effects far from what we would call trumpet-like. When a "mute" is employed, a pear-shaped stopper which fits into the bell, the tone is altered almost beyond recognition. It becomes a thin eerie sound, pleasant at its softest, rather cutting at its loudest. Though the use of the muted trumpet is favored by all contemporary composers for jazz bands and symphonic orchestras, many musicians, unable to share the composer's delight in a new resource, wonder if the trumpet is not losing some of its musical value in the popularity of its falsetto, untrumpet-like possibilities.

The crooks now in use give us the trumpet in C, the trumpet in B flat, and the trumpet in A—that is, the trumpet which sounds the note as it is written, the trumpet which sounds a whole tone below the written note, and the trumpet which sounds a tone and a half below the written note. The C trumpet has a compass from the F sharp below middle C to two octaves above middle C. The B flat trumpet has the same range but a whole tone lower, the A trumpet the same range a tone and a half lower.

THE HORN (*French Horn*)

THE DIFFERENCE between the tone quality of the trumpet and that of the horn is partly explained by the shape of the mouthpiece, which in the trumpet is a shallow cup, but in the horn a funnel. Both instruments now are made with valves and are capable of chromatic passages.

We are all familiar, at least by sight, with that early variety known as the hunting horn, the long tube coiled in a circle so that the huntsman, riding through the forest, could hang it across his body from shoulder to waist. The hunting horn was so coiled that the large bell pointed in the same direction as the mouthpiece. The modern horn still keeps this shape, but it is coiled within a small space, and in the center of the circle lengths of tubing are placed as well as the mechanism of the valves. The written compass of the horn is from an octave below middle C to two octaves above. These notes when played sound a fifth lower. The horn uses an F crook.

Since the bell of the horn points, like the mouthpiece, toward the player, and since it lies in a position accessible to the player's right hand, it was long ago discovered that by inserting the hand in various ways, the pitch or the tone quality could be altered. Curious effects peculiar to the horn are obtained by this method of hand-stopping. The horn also, like the trumpet, uses a mute, which suggests distance.

The characteristic tone of this instrument is dark and melancholy. Most listeners would describe it as haunting. In the orchestra it serves not only to sound a theme or melody, but to bind or glaze a whole passage where all the instruments are in use.

THE TROMBONE

THE TROMBONE ("big trumpet") is shaped like a trumpet, but it has no valve mechanism. It makes its changes of pitch by sliding out its tubing to the length needed. The left hand of the player holds the instrument to the lips, the right hand effects the slide.

There are two familiar types, the tenor or B flat trombone, and the bass or G trombone. Wagner and a few later composers have used the double-bass trombone, but the B flat and G varieties are the members of the trombone family now generally employed.

The compass of the B flat trombone is from B flat above middle C to A flat, three octaves and one whole tone below. The lowest notes are not particularly secure or pleasant. The effective compass is from B flat above middle C to E natural, two octaves and four whole tones below.

The trombone is one of the most musical of instruments; it challenges and rewards the player's skill to a degree that the uninitiated listener may not suspect. The sight of a player moving the slide up and down suggests athletic vigor rather than a sensitive ear, yet the trombonist, like the violinist, fixes the pitch of each note as he plays, and the perfect tuning of a first-rate virtuoso is a delight. The trombone, like the trumpet, may sound a military call or blare, but in the hands of a fine technician who can manage the leaps from one harmonic position to another, it is capable of surprising legatos, pianissimos, crescendos and diminuendos.

The Bass or G trombone has a compass from G above middle C to low C sharp—two octaves and three whole tones. Except for the difference of pitch, the Bass and Tenor trombone are alike.

The double-bass trombone has a compass from D above middle C to E below low C—two octaves and five whole tones. This instrument is employed to get a trombone tone in a register where otherwise the tuba must be used.

THE TUBA

TUBAS ARE brass instruments of wide bore which, because of the large air column, sound a heavy bass note. They are the pedal pipes to the organ, easily recognizable in the orchestra by eye and ear, their great size preparing us for their great tone. Like the trumpet, they are equipped with valves.

The three kinds of tuba in general use are the tenor tuba, with a compass from B flat below middle C to the upper F of the treble clef; the bass tuba, from low B flat to G above middle C; and the contra-bass tuba from E flat below low C to E flat above middle C.

In the descriptions which we have here given of the chief orchestral instruments, our friend the man from Mars may be pardoned if he has lost sight of our main point, that the material of great music today has increased faster than the capacity of any single instrument to produce it, rapid though the development of the instruments has been. If we consider the orchestra as a unity, a single instrument for the composer to play on, we must again remind the man from Mars that our orchestra is changing fast. The violins which only yesterday were the very heart of it, sounding most of the thematic material, furnishing most of the singing quality, and supplying the characteristic color, are now rivaled more and more closely by the woodwinds and the brass. New uses and new techniques for trumpet and trombone are discovered and perfected by jazz bands, which, as we have suggested before, do an extraordinary amount of exploratory work for the symphonic orchestra.

Because tradition is strong upon us, and because the great composers of the nineteenth century wrote for the kind of orchestra they did, we shall probably continue the composition of symphonies and operas requiring for their performance some ninety or a hundred players. But a jazz band far less numerous can produce as much sound and an even greater variety of sound-color. With the addition of a small string section, the concentrated instrumentation of the jazz composers could perhaps articulate more nearly the music toward which our imagination now reaches.

THE SAXOPHONE

FOR SOME OF US of course the mere mention of the word jazz is as a red flag, "jazz band" is a term of insult, and "saxophone" suggests the most detestable of noises. In my opinion this prejudice against the characteristic tendency of music today, and against the one instrument which we have most successfully developed, is nothing but a snobbish pose. When jazz bands play for dances in a large hall they often play too loud, but that fault has been shared by other kinds of dance band, since the moment when dancers began to talk while dancing. If it had been necessary to play minuets so that the music could be heard above animated conversation, minuets would have been played loud indeed. But the best jazz bands have opportunities to perform on the concert platform as well as on the dance floor, and to pretend that they are always and necessarily noisy, is absurd.

The hostility against which the saxophone still has to make headway does credit neither to our common sense nor to our sincerity. The tone of the instrument when well played is very lovely, and we invariably like it, provided we don't know it's a saxophone that we are listening to. If sometimes it is not well played, the same misfortune occurs to other instruments, notably to the piano and the violin, neither of which the musically fastidious propose to abolish.

The saxophone has been described as a conical tube of metal pierced by holes, with a single-beating reed at the smaller end. The instrument is furnished with mechanical keys, and there is a twist at each end of the tube to make playing more convenient—at the upper end a bend toward the player's lips, at the lower end a flare upward and outward. Technically the instrument is easy to play, and its tone is naturally flexible. It was invented by Antoine Joseph Sax, known as Adolph Sax, born at Dinant, November 6, 1814, the son of a celebrated Belgian musical instrument maker. Adolph Sax became an excellent clarinetist, and in the course of experiments to improve that instrument he invented in 1840 something with a new quality of tone, to which he gave his name. The saxophone was introduced officially into French Army bands in 1845, and for fifty or sixty years its value was appreciated only for outdoor music. With the coming of ragtime and jazz, however, players improved their technique, and the lyrical as well as the exciting possibilities of the saxophone were explored.

Since the saxophone is made of metal yet produces its tone by means of a reed, it resembles both the brass and the woodwinds. In quality it suggests at times a horn or a clarinet. When several saxophones are used together they can indicate the effect of violas and 'cellos, at times even of organ diapasons. To say the least, the saxophone is a versatile instrument, agreeable when heard in a solo passage, full and rich when used for background effects.

PERCUSSION INSTRUMENTS

WE HAVE SPOKEN of the string choir, the class of instruments which derive their tone from the tightly stretched string set in vibration by a bow—and of the woodwinds, in which the tone is produced by blowing. Simpler in principle and more ancient in origin are the instruments in which the sound is produced by striking on a resonant surface.

The percussion instruments now in use are more numerous than most of us realize. They are usually divided into those which suggest or stimulate rhythm without making a musical sound, and those which, though serving the same purpose of rhythmic excitement, produce tones of a recognizable pitch. In the first class are the side drum, the bass drum, certain other varieties of non-tuning drum, the tambourine, the triangle, the cymbals, the gong, the castanets, and devices for producing special effects such as the rattle and the wind machine. Chief among the musical percussion instruments are the kettledrums. Less essential to orchestral effects but still important are the celesta, the bells, the glockenspiel, the dulcetone, and the xylophone.

The habitual attendant at symphonic concerts probably knows by sight as well as by ear the triangle, the cymbals, and the kettledrums. The celesta may be familiar to the ear, but the listener perhaps does not recognize it on the platform nor understand its construction.

Even the simplest of these percussion instruments, the triangle, can be played in a number of ways to produce a variety of effects. The triangle is a steel bar bent as its name implies. It is struck with a metal stick. It must be large enough to make a sound which is not ridiculous, small enough to avoid giving out a tone of recognizable pitch.

It is used chiefly to mark rhythms, and to enforce crescendos by a tremolo (performed by beating alternately on two sides of the triangle), but it can produce extraordinary effects when played pianissimo with other instruments, and by a single note dropped in the middle of a pause it can give dramatic value to the silence.

The cymbals are two large round brass plates shaped like saucers. When they are brought together their edges meet. On the outer or convex side of the saucer, a leather strap is fixed by which the player holds the instrument—one cymbal in each hand. The strap is used also to hang the cymbal up when the player wishes to strike it with drum sticks. Cymbals are played chiefly in these ways: They are struck together with a sliding motion to produce a loud clang; this effect is used to mark the climax of great crescendos. The player may strike the edge of a cymbal with the stick of a side drum, to produce a startling sound, or he may use the stick of a kettledrum to get the effect of a deep gong, pianissimo. A long roll can be produced by rattling together the edges of the cymbals. On one cymbal, hung up by the leather strap, a roll can be played with two kettledrum sticks, or the same effect can be somewhat lazily indicated by holding the cymbal in one hand and rattling the drum stick on it with the other.

The bass drum, the side drum, and the other non-musical instruments are familiar or easy to identify. They hardly need comment here.

THE KETTLEDRUM

THE KETTLEDRUM is a large metal basin or bowl over which a leather skin is stretched. It is played with two sticks padded at the end. In its original condition it was imported from the East, where it was usually small so that it could be carried on the neck of a horse and furnish music to the cavalry. In its modern development it is large, and it rests on a frame supported by three legs. It is used in sets of three, each tunable to the chromatic compass of a perfect fifth. The smallest drum can play from B flat up to F in the bass clef, the medium drum from A up to E, or from G up to D, in the same clef, and the large drum a whole tone lower, from F up to C. There is no reason, of course, why kettledrums should not be made in other registers, if a composer insists, but the three drums described usually satisfy all ambitions.

Around the edge of the drumhead are handles for stretching the skin tighter or for loosening it. By twisting these handles one way or the other, the player tunes his instrument. The composer in other days expected him merely to sound the tonic and the dominant of whatever key the composition at the moment happened to be in, but we now ask for other intervals of the scale, and the necessity for constant tuning while the performance is in progress makes the manipulation of kettledrums a fine art. The player, knowing the key of the next passage in which he will be called on, and the particular notes which are expected of him, must tune to those notes even while the orchestra is deafening him in an unrelated key. When you see him leaning his ear to the drums, touching them ever so lightly and screwing away frantically at the mechanisms around the drum rim, you know he is tuning up.

Since modern kettledrums can be tuned mechanically by a system of pedals, it is now possible for them to sound an accurate but leisurely scale, if any such performance were desirable. Their function, however, remains rhythmic rather than melodic. Like any other kind of drum they are used to announce rhythmic patterns or to underline climaxes, or, when played piano or pianissimo, to suggest sombre or tragic moods. The double roll producible with the two padded sticks, swells or shrinks into remarkable crescendos or diminuendos. No one who has heard it forgets the tide of sound rolled up on the kettledrums, and pointed at the climax with a terrific thump.

But what sets this kind of drum apart from all others is that the sound produced is musical, of a recognizable pitch and in tune with the other instruments of the orchestra.

The kettledrummer, though he plays what may seem a limited instrument, makes a large contribution. He supplies that element of music which we refer to as incantation, the primitive influence that incites to action rather than to meditation. He plays the most "stirring" of instruments. And he ministers to this effect of incantation in its most subtle form. He must be an excellent musician; obviously he couldn't succeed in his tuning if he didn't know at all times what his colleagues were playing, and he couldn't supplement massive crescendos or underline delicate diminuendos unless he measured accurately the amount of drum tone the other instruments can stand.

The kettledrummer must have, in addition to sensitiveness of ear and musical training in general, great agility in the manipulation of the sticks. It is not easy to indicate every nuance of rhythm as he is expected to do, nor to execute the various crescendos and diminuendos. He needs almost as good a wrist as a piano virtuoso, but pianists do not necessarily make good drummers; the wrist is not used in the same way, and different muscles are called for.

THE CELESTA

IN THE OTHER musical percussion instruments, the celesta, the bells, the glockenspiel, the dulcetone, and the xylophone, the pitch is fixed so that no tuning is necessary. In all of them the tone is produced by striking a hard surface of metal or wood. Of all of them, therefore, the quality is in various degrees bell-like. Some of them are struck by hand with a stick or hammer. In the celesta, the glockenspiel, and the dulcetone there is a keyboard mechanism.

The bells used in orchestral music are tubular. They are hung from a frame, and the player stands up to strike them.

The xylophone, familiar to us all from the musical toys made on the same principle, consists of twenty-seven slabs of hard wood resting lightly on soft material which permits the slabs to vibrate when struck. The tone is strengthened by resonators. There are two "beaters" or playing sticks, either spoon-shaped at the end or globular.

The glockenspiel in its present form resembles the xylophone, but its tones are produced on steel plates instead of wooden slabs, and the player strikes with wooden hammers. The effect suggests a carillon.

The dulcetone is a small keyboard instrument in which steel tuning forks are struck by pianoforte action.

The celesta produces its tones by a series of steel bars or plates struck by hammers controlled by a keyboard. The compass is four octaves from middle C up. Under each steel plate or bar there is a wooden resonator which reinforces and modifies the tone. As on the piano, there is a pedal which to some extent prolongs the vibrations. But the celesta remains a percussion instrument, and its notes are loudest immediately after they are struck. The silvery loveliness of its tone explains its popularity with orchestral composers today, but curiously enough it is not effective when used alone, nor does it sound well in a small room, or with a small group of instruments. It is essentially an adjunct to the full orchestra.

THE HARP

THE INSTRUMENTS so far considered are usually played in various combinations with each other. Though they can be used separately, their solo repertory is small, and by themselves they do not satisfy our modern ears. It is well to consider once more the fact that with such a large variety of instruments there are only three, the harp, the organ, and the piano, which to any extent are what might be called self-sufficient. Neither the harp nor the organ is usually found in the home. The actual study and production of music, therefore, means for most human beings piano playing. This phenomenon deserves more thought than it usually receives. Though the piano is a noble instrument, and some of the greatest music has been written for it, its resources differ essentially from those of the voice, of string instruments, of woodwinds and brass. It has little in common with the organ, and it now preserves only a far-off relation to the harp. The modern composer studies the piano with the rest of us, but too rarely does he play the orchestral instruments for which he probably wishes to write, and still more rarely does he train his voice. It is not surprising that he writes few songs, or that if he writes them they are left unsung.

The organ is now firmly established as the instrument for liturgical music. It is sometimes called on to reënforce the orchestra, but in general we may say it is heard only in churches. The machines called organs which produce noise with the intention to entertain in large auditoriums or motion picture houses, are constructed and played to sound most un-organlike.

The harp has so old a history, and it has been puffed up for so many centuries by the poets, that hardly anyone speaks of it now without calling it a beautiful instrument. Its gilded frame is certainly graceful, and ladies with shapely arms like to pluck its colored strings. Let it be added for the record that some of its most enthusiastic advocates and defenders are men, whose arms may be graceful but whose harp-passion is disinterested, since they are expected to keep their coats on.

I make no bones of my opinion that the harp is an overrated instrument, limited and monotonous. I need little courage to say this, since most people, in spite of conventional praise, care no more for the harp than I do. Few children are taught to play it. Its size and weight are sometimes offered as explanation for its neglect; why learn to play an instrument which you can't carry around except in a moving van? But of course the same argument could be used against the piano. The fact is, that though some gifted musicians devote themselves to the harp and play it so as to command respect, its prestige is shrunk until it is no longer a solo instrument but a member of the orchestra, along with the triangle and the tuba.

Yet it can adapt to its own idiom much of the music written for the piano; it has a considerable repertory of its own; it can be played in different styles and in different moods. In other words, nothing prevents it from giving pleasure in a long solo program except the sleep-inducing monotony of its tone.

The modern concert harp is the descendant of the instrument which minstrels of old carried around with them and twanged as they recited. On the operatic stage poets like Orpheus and other inspired wanderers still pluck in pantomime while the orchestral accompaniment thunders along. It's well that they pluck in silence, for the chance is great that their harps wouldn't be in tune. An ancient harp could play in only one key, and even in that key its compass was extremely limited. The modern pedal harp, with a device for playing in different keys, was not invented until the end of the eighteenth century. Around the bottom of the instrument are seven pedals, one for each note of the scale. If the pedal is pushed down and slipped into a notch, the note which it serves is raised a half-tone—but simultaneously the same note in every octave is raised a half-tone. If F is raised to F sharp, then we can play in G major. If we need another sharp we must put down another pedal. This improvement had to be carried further, before we could play more than simple harmonies, a few chords and arpeggios.

The harp is played either by plucking, which is the same thing as a perpetual pizzicato, or by running the fingers up and down the string in a glissando. The plucking was the technique of ancient harps, which had few strings and those far apart. The glissando is more natural for the modern instrument, which has many strings very close together. But the early pedal harps could play in a glissando nothing but scales. The modern harp has the advantage of double action. This term means that each pedal can be set down either one notch or two. A single notch raises the string a half-tone, two notches raise it a whole tone. A curious and highly useful result is that several adjacent strings can be tuned alike, therefore can be taken out of the scale. If B is raised half a tone it sounds the same note as C. If B flat is raised a whole tone, it also sounds the same note as C. When this process is carried far enough, the harp strings, when played glissando, can sound a chord.

If the modern harp is employed considerately by the composer, it acquits itself creditably in orchestral music, but if it is played in a small room, the audience soon understands its handicaps and imperfections. It can sweep an effective arpeggio, but it can't play a chromatic scale. The seven pedals are there, but alas, the player has only two feet, and if the music should become excited, even so small a number of feet, frantically hopping and reaching, may get in each other's way. The pedals must not only be set in the notches, they must also at the proper time be released, and they are likely to come up with a thud.

It's a question how long the harp will remain even in the orchestra. The celesta with its keyboard can do all the harp can and more, with the additional advantage that it remains in tune. If a keyboard instrument were invented which imitated a tone plucked from strings, it would probably push the harp into the museum, along with the legendary minstrels.

THE ORGAN

THE ORGAN, complicated instrument though it seems, is in principle only our old friend the Pan-pipes with a mechanical system of blowing. The earliest organs inserted the graduated row of pipes into holes cut in a wind-chest; the chest was supplied with wind by a bellows; the opening into each pipe was closed by a strip of wood; the strip of wood was attached to the keyboard by a lever. If the key were pressed down, the strip of wood was moved to a point where it no longer obstructed the wind, and the pipe then sounded. Either the strip of wood was so short that it could be drawn out of the way, or there was a hole cut in it which would come precisely under the pipe.

In principle the pipe organ today still resembles its earliest ancestor. There must be a bellows to fill the wind-chest, and a wind-chest to supply the pipes. Each pipe is closed mechanically until it is needed; by a mechanism operated from a keyboard the player releases the wind from the chest into the pipe.

Pan-pipes had a flute-like tone. The fundamental quality of the organ is that of a flute, no matter how deep and massive the sound. Organ tone is of course capable of variation, but to retain its character, it must preserve some resemblance to the flute.

Variations of tone quality are secured by the use of "stops." So long as only one quality was desired, one set of pipes constituted an organ, and the instrument could be played as soon as wind was pumped into it and a key pressed down. Later it was discovered that if the bellows and wind-chest were sufficiently capacious, more than one row of pipes could be blown at once. If each row were of a distinct quality, it might be desirable to play them separately as well as together. To these several rows of pipes we give the name of stops. We also give this name to the handle or knob placed above the keyboard or on the side and operating a mechanism for bringing into play a whole row of pipes.

We now have a slide worked by a keyboard to make each note sound, no matter what stops are pulled out; and we have another slide operated by handles or knobs to turn the wind pressure into each pipe-row. Obviously the organ even in its simplest form was on its way toward its present distinction, as the most mechanically elaborate of all musical instruments.

With many stops to operate, many slides to pull out or push in, the organist had more physical exercise than he could enjoy. Furthermore, since the organ builders were of necessity mechanical-minded, they proceeded to supply additional conveniences, at the price of additional efforts. They invented octave couplers, by means of which any note was paired with the same note above, so that the player could produce octaves at dazzling speed simply by running a scale, or could strike a chord of six notes simply by pressing down three. But the more notes he pressed down, the harder it was on his fingers—and also on the wretch who somewhere inside the organ worked the bellows. The mechanical action of the old organs was at last displaced by a pneumatic action, and this in turn by electric action, which enables the player to manipulate and combine his stops with fantastic ease, and which substitutes a dynamo for the human organ blower.

But we are dealing with a far more complicated instrument than this description so far indicates. There are several keyboards for the hands to play on, and there is a pedal keyboard for the feet. The manuals should number at least three; very large organs have four or even five, but three are necessary to give any organ its complete character. The lowest controls the pipes in what is called the choir organ, the next higher—the middle keyboard in a three-manual instrument—plays what is called the great organ, the top manual plays the swell organ. If there is a fourth manual it is called the solo organ. The fifth manual, in the rare instances where it occurs, plays the echo organ.

It is clear, perhaps, why the organ was once spoken of in the plural as "organs." It is a set of instruments which, if properly built, should be clearly distinct from each other. For this reason they used to be enclosed in massive and towering cases, placed in the church or hall wherever there was most room. In these formidable cases, fastened high above the floor, in a gallery or over a choir screen, the large pipes of the great organ were accommodated in the lowest part, the lighter stops of the choir organ occupied a section above, and the stops of the swell organ were enclosed in a sound-proof chamber with shutters opening on one side. These shutters were operated by the swell pedal placed to the right of the pedal keyboard or over the center of it.

If possible, the organ case was boldly divided so that the pipes of the choir organ and the swell organ could be at some distance from each other, and from the pipes of the great organ. The sound would then come from different parts of the church, with an effect which, wherever the acoustics had been carefully studied, was very fine. But an instrument so scattered was hard to construct, so long as the action was mechanical, and it was also hard to play, since human fingers had to set in motion the multitude of wooden trackers which connected the keyboard with the distant pipes. The central wind-chest was stretched by flues into subsidiary wind-chests. The set of keyboards—what is called the console—was usually joined to the great organ, though it might be built into the choir or the swell, but wherever it was built, there it had to stay. If the organ case was in the gallery or over the choir screen, the organist also was in the gallery or over the screen, quite a distance, perhaps, from the choristers and priests for whom, at moments in the liturgy, he furnished an accompaniment.

With the modern electric action the various organs can be placed anywhere, and the console can be moved about at will, since it is connected with the organs by a cable. Yet the old principle is nearly forgotten, that the great organ, the swell, and the choir should be located some distance apart. In few churches today is the organ set out in a case where the pipes can sound freely. The architect usually provides what he calls an organ chamber, into which all but a few pipes and all the mechanism are packed like the filling of a tooth. For decorative purposes a row of pipes, short at each end and rising toward the middle, usually hides the organ chamber, but even these few pipes, the only ones exposed, may be silent dummies, a façade.

Oddly enough, though the organ is hidden and muffled, the tendency now is to fill it with as many stops and mechanical conveniences as possible. The equipment of a modern console is as bewildering as the forest of gadgets and instruments which faces the air pilot in a large plane. There are banks of stops to the right and to the left. Along the highest keyboard there are little tilt-tables which work the couplers. The various manuals, of course, can be hitched up to each other. Though the pedal keyboard has its own large pipes, it can be coupled to any or all of the manuals. More often than not the choir organ, like the swell, is encased in a box with shutters and has its own swell pedal, so that it can produce crescendos and diminuendos. The full force of any manual can be turned on or off by the push of a button. At the right and left of each keyboard there are rows of buttons or pegs, each representing a stop. Under the keyboard are five or six pistons which can be pushed in by the player's thumb. Any combination of stops, set by the buttons or pegs, can be controlled by the appropriate piston. The player, therefore, knowing in advance what changes of stops he will need during a performance, sets a combination for piston No. 1, another for piston No. 2, etc. He can then play the piece without lifting his hands.

The advantage of the several keyboards hardly needs stressing. The organist can play a melody on one manual, with one quality of stop or combination of stops; he can play an accompaniment or a parallel melody with a different combination of stops on another manual; and he can play the bass part on the pedals. He can move suddenly from the great organ to the swell or choir, bringing the sound from a different location, and marking the contrast between the pipes on the various manuals. The keyboards are placed so close together that he can reach two at once with a single hand; if the music is not rapid, and if it is written to permit of such treatment, he can play a four-part passage on three manuals and the pedals, each part having an entirely different tone-color. The fingers of his right hand play one part on the swell, those of his left hand play another part on the choir, and the thumbs manage a third part on the great.

In some large instruments the choir and the swell have a repertory of stops powerful enough for the great organ, but such lavishness is unnecessary, and master organists deplore it; they want each manual to preserve its peculiar character, and for this a comparatively small number of stops will serve. Some of the most beautiful organs in the world with four manuals have altogether fewer than fifty stops. Quite a number of modern instruments, unfortunately, have over a hundred, and those who pay the bill for this colossal mistake count their prodigality as merit. The best organists think of the stops as colors on a painter's palette. They want their colors to be luminous, of the best quality, and they want only the primary colors. If there are more, they must be mixtures of primary colors, and a good organist, like a good painter, likes to do his own mixing. For that reason any approximate duplication of tone color in the stops is a nuisance rather than a help.

This point may not be clear when stated in words, but no listener fails to recognize it when he contrasts a fine organ sufficiently equipped with primary tone-colors, and one of the mammoth instruments in music halls to which the name of organ might well be denied. The monster with a battery of stops imitating other instruments than the organ, with a multitude of what indeed are true organ stops, but which in color resemble each other closely, becomes in a few minutes unpleasantly monotonous. As the organist plays on, the listeners wonder why he doesn't change the registration. As a matter of fact, he does make new combinations, and if you are near enough to the console you can see him busy with the pistons; but the sound remains much the same. A proper organ, on the other hand, is almost foolproof against such monotony. Unless the player refuses to make any change of stops, the contrasts are unmistakable.

The characteristic organ stop is the diapason. Most of the diapason pipes are found in the great organ, but the same quality of tone is the basis for the choir and swell. A diapason pipe on the manuals is cylindrical and made of metal. The tone is produced on the principle of a whistle, the air being directed to an opening in the side of the pipe. The pedal diapason pipes are usually square and are made of wood. If the diapason pipe is open at the end, the length of the pipe must be approximately eight feet to sound the lowest note on the keyboard. An eight-foot stop, therefore, is one that gives the normal pitch. If the pipe is stopped at the end it need be only four feet long to sound the lowest note, but there is a marked difference in the quality of tone. The great organ will contain both open and stopped diapasons.

If the pipes are open, yet only half the normal length, they will sound the octave above the usual pitch. There are a number of four-foot stops on all the manuals. If the organist draws an eight-foot stop and also a four-foot stop, he plays in octaves though he puts down only one note at a time. Since no opportunity for color is wasted on a good organ, the four-foot flute ought to provide a tone quite different from the octave played with the hand on an eight-foot flute. A two-foot stop is one that sounds two octaves above the note played.

What has been said about harmonics and overtones in a previous chapter will be found helpful in understanding all organ stops, and essential for understanding the stops called mixtures. The overtones of organ pipes are strong, as the listener can feel from the heavy, enveloping vibration. Very early in the evolution of the instrument it was thought an advantage to reënforce the overtones by providing a stop in which each note would play simultaneously two or three pipes, sounding not only the tonic but the fifth, and perhaps the third. The addition of a mixture to several diapason stops produces an effect of undoubted brilliance which most people admire, but some others do not. I am one of those who do not. Since the organ harmonics are already strong, the ideal to be sought in any note, I believe, is clear tone. A mixture produces a grand blare, in which the notes are smudged. No one, of course, would use a mixture in playing a fugue, where the voices must be distinguished. Even in chord passages, where a massive effect is sought, I like to hear the notes with some distinctness. Large concert-hall organs, however, of the kind to which I've already paid my compliments, are full of mixtures. It's as though you made your meal of pepper and seasoned it with a little meat.

By changing the shape of the organ pipe, the essential diapason tone can be modified completely. The diapason family of stops are as easy to tell apart as the violin, the viola, the 'cello, and the double-bass.

The main contrast to the diapasons is furnished by another family of stops called the reeds. In a reed pipe the tone is made by a flat metal strip fastened at one end and vibrating freely in an opening cut in the side of the pipe. Roughly, the difference between a reed tone and a diapason tone is the difference between the sound of a clarinet and that of a horn.

The great organ contains the larger diapasons and the stronger reed stops. Pianissimo effects are not sought on that manual. The choir organ contains lighter diapasons and reeds, some of the stops being very soft. Though the use of the swell is extended in large organs to the choir, it may be doubted whether the advantage of crescendos and diminuendos is enough to offset the loss of tone which results from encasing the pipes in a swell-box. To put the great organ in a box, in any shelter which could interfere with its freedom of tone, would be to take away its character.

The swell organ contains the lighest diapason or flute stops and a variety of delicate reeds. The tremolo effect on a three-manual organ should be obtainable only on the swell. If the choir organ has it too, nothing will prevent the organist from using it. The solo organ is what its name implies; it contains stops useful for melodies, it contains a tremolo, and is encased in a swell-box. The merit of the great organ and the choir is that their tones are unobstructed by any enclosure. They need room in plenty and the choir should be separate from the great, preferably above it. The merit of the swell organ and the solo organ is that on either manual a tone can be diminished until it is inaudible. Any organ which can't make its pianissimo fade out is far short of perfection.

The pedal keyboard has long been extremely important. Johann Sebastian Bach in his great fugues expected the organist to play with his feet the same themes that were played by the hands, and in modern times the best performers exhibit astonishing pedal virtuosity. The usefulness of this keyboard will be understood if we remember how occupied, and more than occupied, the player usually is with the organ mechanism, in spite of inventions for arranging the stops in advance and bringing them on or taking them off by means of push-buttons and pistons. There are many moments when one hand must leave the keyboard, but so long as the pedals supply the bass, one hand can be spared temporarily without making a gap in the chord. Most pedal stops are of course deep and loud, but there ought to be a few soft ones, and if there aren't, the pedals can be coupled to whatever manual the hands are using, and even on the most delicate stops the bass can be played with the feet.

A word should be said about wind pressure. Our organs are now blown by an engine of some kind, usually by an electric motor and a fan. It is a great advance in humanitarianism that we no longer ask a human being to pump by hand. The largest organs in the old days called for more than one pumper, but even in the smallest instrument it was a back-breaking job to keep the bellows full. Quiet passages were a God-send. But in the shift from the hand-blown to the mechanically filled bellows there was one great loss; in most organs the wind pressure was increased, the tone became louder, perhaps more brilliant, frequently a little shrill. The quality of the diapasons was ruined. Should we ever have occasion to visit an old church which still blows its organ on low pressure, we'd recognize in a few minutes an important difference between a true organ and an orchestra. The fortissimo of the organ with all its diapasons seems as loud as the fortissimo of the band, but it's a different kind of loudness. It envelopes rather than stuns us. A voice can quite easily he heard through the massive sound. It is altogether rich and luscious. If the organist wishes to build up a climax through successive chords, he goes deeper and deeper for more tone instead of adding shrillness at the top. But there are few such organs now in use. The old ones are equipped with modern action and mechanical wind supply, and richness of tone has been sacrificed to noise.

The organ is the only one of the three self-sufficient instruments which can compete with the orchestra. A large concert-hall organ can reproduce the tone quality of all the orchestral instruments except the kettledrums, and it has many tone qualities not found in an orchestra, chief of them being the diapason quality. Theoretically, therefore, the organ has a larger color palette. But no audience admits this superiority. If we have the choice between a symphony concert and an organ recital, we are sure which program will offer the wider variety of tone color, of rhythm, of mood. In spite of its extraordinary possibilities the organ is and always will be a limited instrument, for the obvious reason that it is played by a single individual who has only two hands and two feet. He can't call on all the resources of his instrument at once. He can play many instruments in unison by pulling out the right stops, but the unison, unfortunately, will be too perfect to suggest the concerted effort of eighty or ninety artists. When the first-violin section of an orchestra is playing in unison, the men read the same music but no two desks play a note mathematically the same way; there are personal variations in the pitch, in the vibrato, and in the bowing, even though all the bows move up and down together. From the composite result of so many individualities comes the peculiar vitality and excitement of orchestral music. From the organ we get many stops but only one personality.

The organ may be said to contain strings, woodwinds, and brass. The effect of percussion cannot be produced on the organ; it may be suggested in a staccato passage but it isn't the real thing, and though we recognize what is being imitated, we are not stirred, as we would be by drum or cymbals.

Since the organ is played by one performer, it is naturally compared with the piano. Most organists are fairly good pianists, and most pianists have at some time played the organ, but very few musicians are supreme on both instruments. It's a matter of temperament. The born organist is at home with the mechanism which comes between him and the music he produces. The born pianist wants the minimum of mechanism; he envies the violinist, whose instrument seems almost a part of himself. Enthusiastic organists will tell you that the mechanism doesn't get in the way, doesn't slow up the performance, doesn't call for a degree of cerebral exertion which could possibly interfere with the spontaneity of the emotion, and when they play, if they are skilful, they can almost convince you. Almost, but perhaps not quite.

The organ is a stately and solemn instrument, it has its moments of gaiety, but of dignified gaiety. In a large room, and it should be heard nowhere else, it fills space in a peculiar way with what may properly be called waves of sound. Instinctively and correctly we say the organ "rolls." A good organ rolls but never roars. As an instrument it was developed in the service of the church, and it still evokes, even in other places, the atmosphere of altars and lofty arches, of rituals, of worship.

THE PIANO

THE PIANO is a harp played by a keyboard. The strings of a harp are plucked by the fingers, and some of the early keyboard harps preserved the plucking system and the consequent harp sound. In the piano, however, the tone is made by striking the string. The piano is therefore a percussion instrument. Paradoxically it has been developed to conceal the initial thump and glorify the resulting vibration. Its mechanism, as beautiful and delicate as the works of a watch, cannot be described here in detail. Roughly, the piano key liberates a hammer mechanism, the hammer, cushioned in felt, flies up and strikes the string, and instantaneously falls back to rest. The vibrations started by the quick blow and reënforced by a sounding-board continue for a remarkably long time. Over the strings a row of felt-covered dampers are lifted singly by each key, and remain off the strings so long as the key is held down. In a rapid passage these dampers, falling at the release of the key, stop the vibrations much more rapidly than in the harp, where the dampening is done by the palm of the hand. All the piano dampers can be raised simultaneously by a pedal.

The strings in a piano may stretch perpendicularly as in the original harp, or horizontally. We keep the perpendicular position in upright pianos, the horizontal in squares and grands. The advantage of the horizontal position is great, since the mechanism can make full use of gravitation. In the upright the hammers must strike horizontally. These paragraphs have in mind the modern grand piano.

Early pianos were made with wooden frames, variously reinforced but unable to sustain great tension. They got out of tune as quickly as a harp, perhaps more quickly. The pioneer pianists were constantly tuning their instruments, and prolonged performances were interrupted, either to tighten the strings, or to let the player move over to a fresh instrument. The piano keyboard, even with its first crude mechanism, had an immense advantage over the organ, to make up at least in part for the organ's superiority in various tone-colors; by striking one note harder than another, the pianist could make a voice or part stand out. Naturally the pianists soon learned to strike the keys hard, and the harder they struck the quicker they put the strings out of tune. Franz Liszt was a sad threat to the most stalwart instrument. He had the bright idea to make the piano sound like an orchestra. An orchestra, however, not only is permitted some overt tuning between pieces, but it can correct its pitch surreptitiously as it goes along. If Liszt put a string out of tune at the beginning of the piece, there it stayed, like a sore tooth, till the end was reached.

Piano makers became ambitious to invent an instrument which would remain approximately in tune until the end of the concert. Most of us haven't the keenness of ear to notice that even the finest pianos today are less nearly in tune at the end of the evening than they were at the beginning. But it should be said in passing that our fine pianos are now extremely sensitive; a slight change in temperature disturbs their pitch, so that an instrument freshly tuned before the concert may go perceptibly off the moment the doors are opened to let in the audience from the street.

In the process of evolving a concert-proof piano, a steel frame was substituted for the wooden. The metal strings were made longer and heavier and stretched far tighter. The strings in the bass were reënforced and made very heavy indeed. To get the maximum tone, two strings are now assigned to the lowest octave and a half, and three strings to all the other notes. For great brilliance in concert performance two of the three strings are put in perfect accord, the third string being tuned slightly higher.

The hammer strikes all three strings at once. Of the three pedals, the one to the left, the so-called soft pedal, shifts the keyboard so that the hammers strike only two of the three strings. The difference in tone volume is very slight, and there is practically no difference in quality. The pianist has such command of dynamics that he could do without the soft pedal. It would be another matter if the hammers could be shifted so as to strike only one string; the tone quality would then be changed.

The soft pedal is at the left. The pedal at the right, sometimes called the loud pedal, is the one which lifts all the dampers simultaneously. The pianist uses it constantly. It is his chief aid in developing the harmonic possibilities of a tone, and in making his instrument sing. The middle pedal, a fairly modern invention, sustains one note or a group of notes while leaving the dampers free to act on all the others. The player, to avail himself of this sustaining device, must put down the note or notes before he uses the pedal. He need not play the note; it's enough to get the key down. Once the sustaining pedal is applied, the note or notes held down will respond when struck as though the damper had been lifted. A player can therefore fix, as it were, a note or a chord at one end of the keyboard and perform a crisp unpedaled passage at the other. It's as near as the pianist can come to having three hands.

When the felts on the end of the hammers have been played on for some time, they become packed down and hard, and the tone, consequently, is metallic and over-brilliant. The piano tuner or "voicer" remedies this condition by brushing or picking the felt surface until the tone is mellow again. Some concert pianists prefer the harder tone because it is louder and they think it carries farther, but in smaller rooms, as in any ordinary home, it sounds unpleasant. Softer felts and mellowness can be justified even in concert work. Since loudness in any music is relative, massive climaxes were produced a hundred years ago on pianos which were gentle, not to say feeble. But perhaps as we have suggested before in this book, a kind of megalomania has overtaken all forms of music; we like large orchestras, some of us like loudness, and most of us think well of pianos which have, among other qualities, great power. To help the power along, the top of a grand piano can be lifted and held up by a stick.

The piano is only one member of the keyboard family, but it has practically exterminated all its relatives. We are accustomed to say that the pianist has an enormous literature to draw from—by which we mean that he can begin his recital with Scarlatti or Bach, go on to Haydn, Mozart, Beethoven, or Chopin, and end up if he chooses with Prokofiev, but to say that these different kinds of music belong equally to the piano is to stretch the truth. The clavichord and the harpsichord were not pianos, and they had no resemblance to each other. The instrument for which Haydn wrote sonatas was not the instrument for which Chopin wrote ballades and scherzos, and Chopin's piano would have collapsed promptly under an attack of Prokofiev. Specialists still play clavichord music on the clavichord, harpsichord music on the harpsichord, and early nineteenth-century music on early nineteenth-century pianos, when such can be found, and the effect is convincing, since music sounds well on the instrument for which it is written. If it were possible to give a program of some Bach on a clavichord, some Handel on a harpsichord, some Mendelssohn and some Debussy on pianos, a sharp difference would be felt between the early instruments, a diminishing difference between the later. The variety of technique employed and of tone obtained would impress us. In a recital today the performer tries to indicate the character of each composer, he plays, as we say, in the proper "style"; but he plays on only one instrument, the triumphant piano which however magnificent in itself has swallowed up its predecessors.

In recent years piano-makers have given attention to extremely small grands, and they have revived the old square piano in a diminutive model. The reasons for this tendency are not musical. A very small grand piano is inferior as an instrument to a larger one, and the miniature squares, though they are softer than the grands, cannot equal them in tone. Small pianos are in demand because the average living-room is small, and so is the average pocketbook. Many pianists would gladly make the harpsichord their instrument if harpsichords could be obtained at a moderate price, but they are hard to obtain at all, and they cost as much as a concert grand. The clavichord is a delicious instrument but its tone is extremely small. In an intimate room its softest effects are audible, but in an auditorium it cannot be heard. Public concert halls were unknown when Bach wrote his *Well-Tempered Clavier.*

The influence of the piano, then, is enormous. Since it is the instrument through which all of us make our approach to music, it conditions our ideas of what music is or should be. The keyboard stretches the scale out from low notes in the left hand to high notes in the right. An extremely high or low note is for a pianist something to reach for. It implies a muscular effort. A singer who is also a pianist will always strain a little, we may fear, at high notes or low ones. On the violin a higher or lower note means simply a different position on a different string, and the strings are approximately only a half-inch apart, and the arm is stretched least in the higher position. On the keyboard a tremolo is played, let's say on a major third, by striking the notes alternately. On the violin the notes are played together, and the tremolo is supplied not by the fingers but by the wrist of the right hand. Before a composer can think in the idiom of the orchestra he must forget the piano. Yet in the preliminary study of orchestral scores a piano is used for convenience. It accompanies opera singers in their early rehearsals. It is used in performance to piece out orchestral scores where some of the instruments happen to be lacking. The piano is music's man of all work, its rescue squad, its towing car. Though the growth of the art in colorful directions calls for the full orchestra to express great music adequately, yet the piano refuses to be left behind. It is on hand when anything breaks down. It suffers thumbtacks in its hammer pads that it may sound like a harpsichord in the recitative accompaniments of a Mozart opera. It obligingly imitates, on request, the harp and the bells, the banjo, the music box, and the drum. For soft stretches it can at least suggest the organ; Liszt has made it do so in his numerous *Ave Marias*. Its tone palette, however, extends little beyond a mixture of black and white. To know music only through the piano is as though we studied painting only through engravings. It's a bad sign that so many composers write their ideas first in piano score, orchestrating later, in some cases much later. Their ideas are piano ideas. If they came as flute ideas or as trumpet ideas, they would be so written from the first.

The history of piano technique is curious, and it's far from finished. With the different types of keyboard instrument there were always no doubt some highly original individuals who took sensible shortcuts and helped themselves out with all their fingers, including the thumb. They didn't hesitate to pass the thumb under the fingers, or the fingers over each other. These, I repeat, were bold and exceptional folk. Even today far too many piano players, supposed to be well taught, would gape in surprise at the fingering of Sebastian Bach and Chopin. The little finger is weak and the thumb is clumsy; until they are both developed by special exercises they seem far less useful than the three middle fingers. In the days of the clavichord, the harpsichord, even the early piano, the three middle fingers did most of the work. The exercises of Cramer, Clementi, and other nineteenth-century pedagogues, have for one of their purposes the equalization of all the fingers. Theoretically every part of the hand should be as good as any other part, but nature does nothing for this ideal; any pianist, if he has free choice, will trill with whatever fingers are easiest for him. If necessary, however, he now plays a trill in any part of his hand, and the thumb, once thought so superfluous that it dangled from the keyboard to keep out of the way, has become so important to virtuoso performance that one great player of my acquaintance wishes he could replace his little fingers with extra thumbs, that the hands might move in either direction with equal facility and power.

Yet the limited technique of former days persists in the timid fingering still taught in many places and still published in most piano editions. In the first instruction of my childhood it was a cardinal point that the thumb should never be used on a black note, and that the fingers should never be passed over each other, only over the thumb. Thumb and little finger already had been promoted into good society, but the hand, to be respectable, must maintain at all times what was called its "natural" position— that is, the thumb was to be laid straight on the key, the fingers should be arched until the tips rested in a straight line parallel to the black keys, from the end of the thumb to the little finger—or since the little finger is unfortunately short, the straight line might be spoiled by drawing in the little finger until it rested perpendicularly on the key. With this ideal position always in mind, the fingers and thumb were to be used hammer-fashion, straight up and down. Some departure from the ideal was unavoidable in arpeggios, and thumbs had to be used on black keys in octave playing, but these exceptions were regarded as misfortunes, about which the less said the better.

Since the thumb is the strongest finger, experienced performers now rely on it for force and security. In a loud melody, if a jump is called for at a distance of an octave or more from one black note to another, the thumb will be used. If two fortissimo notes occur on any keys, and if the hands are not otherwise busy, both thumbs will be used. Where there is an advantage in doing so, a pianist will apply the fingering of white keys to the black, he will pass any finger over or under any other finger if the contortion is convenient—and he will call it no more a contortion than the passing of the thumb under the hand. Furthermore, he will not feel bound to play with the right hand all the notes written for that hand, or with the left hand all the notes set down in the bass clef. He will play all the notes, of course, but he will divide them in the way most convenient for him.

Fingering is not the only department of piano playing which has advanced further than pedagogues sometimes admit. The piano is basically a percussion instrument, and therefore richer than the organ in staccato or other percussive effects. On the other hand its notes, once struck, die out, however the fading may be delayed. It is customary to say that no crescendo can be applied to a piano tone once it has been sounded, and literally this is true, but a note after it has been struck can be reënforced. Here the piano has a large superiority over the harpsichord and the clavichord. The reënforcing is done by starting sympathetic vibrations in the same note in a lower octave, whether or not the lower note is played. If we play the chord of C major in our left hand and a melodic theme in our right, whenever the theme touches C, E, or G, the sound will be enriched by the vibrations already set up in those tones. If we sound E with the right hand and play a melodic passage with the left, every time an E is struck down below, the E held in the right hand gets a longer life. An accompaniment in the left hand which constantly reiterates a sustained note in the right, delays the fading of that note. If there is no accompaniment the upper note can be reënforced, though less effectively, by pressing down, without playing, the same note in a lower octave. A simple experiment demonstrates the principle. Put down, without playing, middle C. Play and hold for a moment the octave above. Release that key, and listen to the sound of middle C.

A fine piano stays in tune so long that some of us apparently expect it to stay in tune forever. We'll have it tuned only so often, and if like a bad child it asks to be tuned more frequently, we just won't humor it. Pianos are sturdy instruments and with proper care remain for many years in superb condition, but just because the care required is not great, we sometimes give our piano no care at all. Usually it can do well enough in a private home on one tuning every three months, but if it is much played on, it will need attention more often. In a severe season, after sharp changes of weather and temperature, it must be retuned at once. The simple but neglected rule is this—in mercy to others if not to ourselves, we should never play on an instrument which is out of tune.

The purpose of this chapter has been to describe the contribution of each instrument, and also its limitations. I make a special effort to state fairly the liabilities which may be charged against the piano, just because, through sheer love of it, I'm tempted rather to sing its praise. Violins, woodwinds, and brass have variety of color and many other charms; clavichords and harpsichords had qualities which music could not well afford to lose, but the piano superseded them because of its superiority. I think it is today the noblest of musical instruments, and as I have indicated, I believe it is influencing the development even of orchestral music.

I believe also that it hasn't yet attained its potential perfection. We dare not imagine better violins than Cremona gave the world, but even the loveliest piano suggests further improvements in tone and in action. Perhaps the rate of progress from now on will be slow, since so much has already been achieved.

There is no rosy prospect that a good piano will ever be cheap. The cost is in the skill of the craftsmen who make it, in the value of the carefully selected materials, and in the length of time some of the material needs for seasoning. During a period of depression one of the great piano companies continued to manufacture, even though finished pianos jammed their warehouses. Had their craftsmen gone to other employment or remained idle, it would have taken years to reassemble or revive their skills. If the skills had once been lost, they might never have been recovered. The secret of piano-making, like the formulas of the old violin masters, might have slipped from us.

Part Two

Chapter six:

A CAREER IN MUSIC

1 MANY YOUNG MUSICIANS, and some older ones, are asking today whether there is such a thing as a career for them in the United States. After music has been composed it of course needs a performance, and to perform music there must be many kinds of artists, players or singers, with various instruments or combinations of instruments. All these artists must have been well taught. There are therefore many teachers of music. The music itself must be published and when it is performed at last there are—though some musicians think there should not be—critics. Any career in music therefore involves a large number of people. Or to put it in practical terms, any one career makes possible and perhaps profitable, several other careers. We should glance at each of these musical careers in turn, since they are all different in some detail, but first we may consider the musical career in general.

The older musicians who ask whether there is such a thing as a career are frequently competent performers, who, having missed the rewards of the concert platform, naturally believe that there is not yet in this country an audience appreciative of true art. Or they may be orchestral players worried by the inroads of the sound picture and the radio. The younger enquirers have probably heard of the disturbing case of Susie This or John That, who, having been hailed as the local genius in the home town, made progress under a famous teacher in a large city, gave an initial recital of which the critics spoke kindly—and since then has been able to find nothing to do, except to teach the children of the neighbors at two or three dollars an hour.

Sometimes the question is raised with a backward glance at the fabulous tours of distinguished artists in other days. Now, we are told, the radio and the phonograph are driving the true virtuoso from the platform. Only a few men and women still concertize on any large scale, with profit to themselves or their managers. The great day of music, by implication, is past.

However the question is put, it raises certain difficulties which it would be stupid to ignore. Yet when a young student or an old musician asks whether there is a career for him in America, it is not unfair to ask in return what he means by a career. To some extent he means a money profit. He would not put it so bluntly, but what he wants to know—and why isn't it a proper thing for him to want to know?—is whether a musician can earn a living comparable to that of the lawyer, the doctor, or the professional in any other field.

Accepting the question in these terms, and with full sympathy for a fellow citizen in his natural ambition to support a home and a family, and to provide for them and for himself the things essential to a cultured life, we still might ask what kind of musician he wishes to be. Is he looking for the career of a Franz Liszt, or of a Richard Wagner—or for the career of a Johann Sebastian Bach? I ask the question this way because Liszt and Wagner, though they were both superb craftsmen in all branches of music, had chiefly the temperament of the virtuoso. Neither was content with a quiet life. Both needed a large audience. Bach on the other hand, though a virtuoso performer on the violin, on the clavichord and most of all on the organ, was distinguished for his complete and all-round practice of the art of music. One thinks of him as preëminently a craftsman.

If Liszt and Wagner are the ideal, as in most cases they will be, then the answer is simple—there is probably no such career for the musician in the United States, nor anywhere else. If on the other hand he would be content to lead the life of a Sebastian Bach, then the United States offers him, in this writer's opinion, a greater career at the present moment than any other country in the world.

Of course, no parallel in talent is implied between the average person who asks this question and the three great musicians just named; it is only the types of career which are compared. One can fancy that the musician will reply with a smile that he'd be glad to lead Sebastian Bach's life on any terms, if he only had the genius. But the distinction between the two types of career is sound, even if we leave out the question of genius and stick to those elementary matters, economic and practical, implied in the original question. Liszt and Wagner were the virtuoso type of artist, achieving success by a sort of tour-de-force in a field which they created for themselves. To perform this tour-de-force one would need their astonishing personality and their almost unique musical gifts, and even then, their kind of success could be achieved only by extraordinary conditions, as in the case of Liszt, or by the aid of well-disposed patrons, as in the case of Wagner. The career of the virtuoso was invented little more than a hundred years ago, and if it seems now on the decline, there is little cause for regret. Because we have been hypnotized by the virtuoso ideal, many young musicians confound it with the higher standards of their art. They think to be anything different from the great players and singers is to be something inferior. To accept steady employment in music without spectacular individual appearances, they consider an abandonment of their higher selves.

On the other hand, Sebastian Bach was a craftsman. That, first of all; and afterwards a supreme artist. The works of genius which have made him immortal were the natural flowering of his craftsmanship without thought of concert-hall applause, and certainly with no economic result in the increase of his salary. He was a craftsman in the sense that he expected to supply music to society wherever music was wanted. Like every true craftsman, he allowed society to say what form this demand should take. If a violinist was needed in a court orchestra, he played the violin. For most of his life he was, what our young music students would hate themselves for being, a church organist and choir-master. He made his living by playing, by training choirs, and by teaching. His superb compositions he furnished gratis for the pleasure of his family at their reunions, or for the glory of God in the church services. In other words, he earned his living as a craftsman, but his creative genius was without price. In the history of art, in all its branches, no saner career has yet been found. It can be followed by anyone in the United States today who has competent training, and who is willing to be, not a virtuoso, but a craftsman.

This distinction between the craftsman and the virtuoso is worth emphasizing. The future of art among us depends upon which ideal we give ourselves to. In the happiest period of Greek sculpture, as again in the thirteenth century, and at other times when the artist has enjoyed a sane relation to society, the craftsman's ideal prevailed. The sculptor carved the stone where carving was needed, the musician played or sang where or when he was wanted. It rested with him, however, whether he should remain a mere workman, or whether he should perform his task with that addition of joy and personality which is genius. The reward of this addition, so far as he was concerned, was the pleasure he had in his work. It rarely added to his wages, and not often to his fame.

In literature Shakespeare is perhaps the last and greatest illustration of this type. He followed the craftsman's career as actor and as mender of old plays, perhaps also as dramatist, furnishing new material for his company. Apparently he supported himself on his salary as actor and playmender, and by the investments of his savings in the theatre itself. But for whatever makes Lear or Macbeth immortal, he received no salary whatever. Those who wonder that the death entry in the parish church refers to him simply as a gentleman, without mention of his genius, over-look the fact that from the medieval point of view, the point of view of the craftsman, what we now call his genius was only his excellence in his daily task. To attempt to read into his life the spiritual conflicts and agonies of the virtuoso, was always absurd, and will continue to prove fruitless.

The Renaissance which, according to most histories of art, conferred an inestimable benefit upon us by the rediscovery of Greek art, did us also great harm by the manner in which that art was restored to the world. To the Greeks, art was a normal thing. In the Renaissance, Greek art was reintroduced to western Europe as something not normal at all, something remote, almost supernatural. What was recovered from the ancient world was in a sense only debris—statues or fragments of statues which once had been designed for a harmonious whole, but which were now isolated and enjoyed for themselves alone. This isolation made the original creator seem an individualist, a single spirit, yearning for self-expression. As a matter of fact, he had been extraordinarily social-minded, with the same ability to coöperate in a public work which came to perfection again in the cathedral builders. We don't know the names of the remarkable archi-tects and sculptors who worked on the famous buildings of ancient Athens, but we do know that architect, stone-cutter and mason thought of them-selves as collaborators, joining forces to produce a unified effect. In the Middle Ages the same collaboration was illustrated not only in the won-derful cathedrals but in many other public buildings and monuments, and though the name of some one artist like Giotto may attach to the completed masterpiece, we understand that a crowd of superb craftsmen did the work in detail under his direction. It is not far-fetched to see a parallel between this noble ideal of collaboration and the team-play of the modern orchestra, where all the players are masters of their instruments but all submerge themselves for one effect under the conductor's direction. The conductor may be and usually is of the virtuoso temperament, but if the orchestra player allowed himself to be too much of a virtuoso he would probably lose his job.

The first Renaissance collections started the tradition of our modern museums by bringing together, for man's admiration, this isolated debris. Naturally the craftsman of unusual talent, seeing the honor accorded to these ancient fragments, felt that he too could produce isolated debris, if he tried hard enough. Thereupon the artist ceased everywhere to collaborate in the creation of beauty for social and public purposes, and applied himself rather to the making of fragments, for which some patrons would pay an arbitrary but high price, and which would then be preserved in a museum.

The clash of these two ideals was of course illustrated often in the same individual—in those who had been trained in the best traditions of craftsmanship, and yet were fascinated by the new individualistic philosophy. Of this conflict Michelangelo is the chief example. A craftsman, to begin with, first a stone-cutter and afterwards a sculptor, he showed at more than one point in his career the growing ambition to create statues for their own sake, fragments gorgeous but from the standpoint of the wider social need, insignificant. The painter today who complains that there is no career for him in the United States, is probably perpetrating in his studio canvases, embarrassingly large, which he hopes to sell to collectors or museums. The wishes of the collector are rarely consulted in advance. He is supposed to be waiting in a receptive mood for anything the genius of the painter may dictate. If you offered this painter a commission to decorate a space on your wall, seven feet by three, the offer would probably offend his pure ideals—he might curse out your bourgeois idea of art, which confounds his inspiration with the merely useful technique of the interior decorator. Michelangelo was annoyed too, when the Pope required him to decorate the ceiling of the Sistine chapel. His annoyance, perhaps, indicated how modern he had become; the masterpiece he actually accomplished indicates how much he preserved of the craftsman's ideal, which transfigures a commission for daily work into a thing of permanent beauty.

The musician today, in America as elsewhere, has been made unhappy by this conflict of ideals. The young man or woman who is told, first by the family and then by more competent critics, that he or she has talent, begins to dream at once of a public career which will give free play to temperament and individuality, and which will result in wealth and other forms of independence. But after his studies are completed, the young man discovers that the world is full of competitors, most of them as well equipped as himself. The market, he will say, is overcrowded. The solution usually offered is either that more people should go to concerts, and more concerts should be given, or that fewer people should be taught music at all. The young artist usually holds to the first view, the brain-fatigued critics usually suggest the second.

If the young musician by chance succeeds, however, he finds himself leading a life of which, as a human being, he ought to be critical. He finds himself a nomad, racing from city to city over the face of the globe, seeking audiences as yet unexhausted, himself never enjoying sufficient acquaintance with his home, and without leisure for sufficient study or practice.

It is quite true that in the cities, where the virtuoso struggles for a chance to appear, there seem to be at times almost as many performers as there are persons in a possible audience. Yet in the country at large there is a music-hunger, for the most part unsatisfied. In many towns of the United States, as of other countries, no excellent musician resides, no excellent teacher, no friend and guide of the art. The ambition for a virtuoso career, moreover, strips the country of any talent which it automatically produces. The promising student from some Western state, let us say, who has been encouraged by the neighbors to follow a concert career, is in a sense a product of the community, at least a product of its sympathy for music. In hundreds or thousands of instances, the neighbors actually contribute to the students' musical training, in the hope that this investment of faith and money will somehow return to enrich their lives. If the student once gets to a large city, however, it is at present almost impossible to blast him out of it. He would much prefer to compete hopelessly with Artur Rubinstein and Horowitz, with Kreisler and Heifetz, than to be the best musician in his state, the inspiration of future artists in the place of his birth.

If someone tells him he has a voice, especially if he is a tenor, nothing will satisfy him but a career in opera. He sees in himself another Caruso. Even assuming that he has an unusual voice, the fact which he refuses to notice and which his teachers perhaps neglect to point out, is that there are not enough opera houses in the world to take in all the tenors, let alone the geniuses in other registers. He knows that there are opera enthusiasts in great number, and them he is willing to consider as intelligent, but he passes harsh judgment on the honest souls who confess they don't enjoy an entertainment not one word of which they can understand. If he learns to sing Verdi in Italian, he can find no excuse for his fellow-countrymen who insist upon being sung to in a language they know. He deplores their lack of culture, forgetting that the American audience who ask for opera in the vernacular are asking only for what every European country demands and gets. He probably overlooks the fact that the kind of opera we'd like in this country is sprightlier, of a quicker tempo, of a stronger dramatic appeal, than the old masterpieces which only by much pious encouragement on the part of music patrons and by the genuine enthusiasm of a few experts have been kept alive.

I should be sorry to seem here to be slighting opera or expressing a lack of sympathy with it. Some of the greatest music we have was composed in this form. On the other hand, the texts or programs to which great opera music has been composed are in more than one instance extremely dated and in some cases, even when they were new, they were silly. When we express a love of opera we usually explain that it is the music we love. Moreover, we notice that few operas are now composed of a quality comparable to the old, and that the attempts at opera now made are for the most part highly imitative, as though there could be no such thing as an up-to-date opera written in the idiom of our day on a subject which in our day is vital. It is enough to notice this phenomenon here; it deserves fuller discussion in another place.

If the young student is not a performer but a composer, in almost every case he will devote his efforts to composition in the old forms—that is, in forms which once answered a need, but which now correspond to no need at all. However it may shock the traditional musician to be reminded of it, it is a plain fact that the larger symphonic forms, as well as opera, have developed to a point where they can be performed only at great expense and under rare conditions. To be properly heard, they presuppose concert halls of a sort that few cities can afford to maintain, since they are useful for few other purposes. There are in the United States, at the present moment, any number of composers who have failed of recognition and will continue to fail, because, like the virtuoso artist of the Renaissance, they insist on rivaling the debris of former times. They absolutely refuse to furnish music for the occasions in our life when the public demands it, or on a scale commensurate with our resources.

If, however, we returned to the craftsman ideal, this talent and more could be used. The young student who is sent from a small community to a large city to complete his musical education, ought first of all to go back from where he came. That is the one spot on earth which is prepared to give him a warm welcome. His neighbors will be proud of him, and will give him freely, at least at the beginning of his career, the benefit of every doubt. He is their local genius. His business is to justify their confidence.

Since he will wish to play or sing for them, he will do so, if he is sensible, on those occasions when they wish to listen to him. Perhaps he would prefer to give a stilted and rigid program in a large hall, a program which would begin with Bach or Beethoven, and end with a Hungarian Rhapsody or a Stravinsky Study. But if his neighbors prefer to listen to their music at a church sociable, then he's something of a fool if he lets what he calls his professional ideals prevent him from giving to the church sociable a musical importance.

He can earn his living by teaching. Among virtuosos, for some reason, teaching has a bad name. They are often reluctant to teach for money. If they take pupils at all, they like to do so only in the case of an outstanding talent, some child to whom, without loss of prestige, they can hand on the torch. Yet in art, whether music, literature, or painting, there are enormous spiritual compensations, as well as an income, to be had from teaching of the finer sort. The musician who is competent in technique and at home in the works of the masters can improve his own powers as he imparts instruction to his pupils. He need listen to no bad music, since he knows better than to give bad music to beginners. If his pupils are so advanced that they perform the music which he puts on his own programs, it becomes an enormous advantage to him to teach; he doesn't have to worry about memorizing his repertoire, since he hears it played over almost daily. He may, if he will, enjoy the satisfaction of building up a tradition in his community, of directing the taste of his fellows, of controlling some important parts of the development of their lives. If he is willing to teach those students who, though talented, are not likely to become virtuosos, or even professionals, he can do his share toward training the future audiences of America. He can have time for his own practicing, even for composing—that is, if he is willing to work as systematically and as steadily as Sebastian Bach, or as César Franck, who also did not think it beneath his dignity to give music lessons, even to the predestined amateur. To be sure, many modern musicians have pitied Franck for what they call the drudgery of his life, but this pity was suggested by the virtuoso point of view. Franck's place would hardly be higher in modern music, if he had had time to compose more. It was not leisure which accounted for the enormous production of Sebastian Bach, and if César Franck had been totally withdrawn from what to the virtuoso seem the humble occupations of his craft, perhaps he would have had less rather than more of that humaneness and of that spirituality which make him precious to us.

The demand for the church organist is universal, and the quality of the supply is none too high. So far, the difficulty has largely been that the well-trained musician is unwilling to accept a modest but genuine opportunity, and develop it into larger things. The church organist in even a small town comes naturally in touch with those who like to sing. If he has the vision he can organize choral groups, quite outside of his Sunday tasks, but in a natural sequence to them. He can start an interest in good singing, which will, of course, take time. He may have to devote his life to it. In most cases the young musician hopes for results more immediate, and certainly more spectacular, but the true opportunity for the artist lies rather in just such a slow building up of music around him. This means that his organ playing and choir drilling will be supplemented by teaching, either instrumental or vocal. If his time is fully occupied, it will hardly be more so than that of any lawyer or business man with ambition to get on. In my youth I once heard Edward MacDowell say—what came with particular force from him, an artist who arrived too early for his true public—that leaving genius aside, any talented musician could make as much money as any business man of equal talent, if he would work as hard and as systematically. Of course, the virtuoso ideal has brought with it great leniency toward what is called temperament—the over-indulgence of one's sensibilities and irritabilities. The craftsman, however, finds nothing incongruous between art and sanity, and a sane musician who lives as normally, with as much regular sleep and exercise as his neighbor, can do as much work for as many hours a day, without impairing his natural gifts.

Somewhat parallel to the opportunity of the church organist, and perhaps even greater, is the opportunity now enjoyed by the teacher of music in the public schools. In no part of our social system is there a greater need or a more immediate welcome for the well-trained musician. Those of us who have witnessed only half-hearted incompetent attempts to teach music to children, may not realize that in the best school systems of the country the school orchestra, the chamber-music unit, and the school chorus, are fast becoming essential elements in American education. To some extent the interest in the school orchestra is as yet forced and artificial; it has been fostered by state and inter-state competitions. Local pride often supports this activity in the school program as a sporting rather than a musical event. It is pleasant to have one's high-school orchestra carry off the prize, just as it is agreeable to know that the school has a winning football team. In some places the school orchestra returns at the end of the summer, like the football team, a few weeks in advance, in order to make an advantageous start.

But whatever humor there may be in this situation, the youngsters who play in the orchestra are genuine lovers of music, and during school age the musical interest of the American population is extraordinarily high. It will be our business during the next fifty years to readjust our educational system so as not to stamp out, as we now do, the childhood interest in the art. Just now the high school's opportunity is to maintain this interest through the upper years of the school course. The number of competent teachers, however, available for this work is at present too small. If the communities look on their orchestra or their choral society as a sort of athletic team, and judge its value less by the performances than by the results in victories, at least this good comes of their attitude, that for victory in the orchestra you must have a competent conductor, as for the football team you must have a competent coach. During the next few years there will probably be a large demand for energetic and capable musicians who are willing to prepare themselves for work in the school systems. In addition to the musical training, they will need less a course in pedagogy than a general acquaintance with the school system itself, with the machine into which the music training must fit. And even more important than this acquaintance with the school system, will be the temperament of the craftsman, the disposition to serve society through those channels which seem to society itself most important.

The best high schools are so large and their activities so engrossing that not many musicians have energy enough to do good work in the school music department and to serve the community in additional ways outside. Yet in some cases such an extension of the school work is possible, and everywhere it is now desirable. The majority of school children still do not go to college, perhaps the majority never will go. What the colleges may do, to permit young America to continue its childhood interest in the arts, is a separate problem; but the average child, on leaving the high school, usually leaves also its last opportunity to practice the arts. What we need in almost every town is someone to carry on into early manhood and womanhood the musical activities which the graduates usually abandon. The violin player who was happy in the school orchestra needs another organization to play in. It makes little difference whether aid comes from the teacher of school music, or from some local organist, or from the private teacher. The opportunity is there, for whatever musician has the necessary imagination and skill.

These opportunities all look to the education of the amateur. Again it must be admitted that the average professional, to whom these opportunities will be open, has usually been trained to think it unworthy to teach any but professionals, and if possible, geniuses. Yet it is an obvious truism that since the virtuoso has been the ideal of the musical world, the educational theory of music has been upside down. We have tried to teach the geniuses in the hope that some benefit might leak down into the mass. If ever we produce great art that way, it will be for the first time in history. Until now, professional art and great virtuoso accomplishment have always risen upon a broad and competent amateur sympathy. Every musician who now does his share toward spreading a love of good music and the ability to take part in it creditably, will be making not only a career for himself, but possible careers, many times more interesting, for the musicians of the future.

It is perhaps too soon to estimate the effect of radio upon the musical career. Personally, the present writer has not the slightest doubt that the radio is doing more to foster a love of music in the average American than anything else that has occurred in the art. At the present moment, to be sure, the radio, like the sound pictures, has disarranged the traditional functioning of certain kinds of musical career, and this change has brought inconvenience, perhaps suffering. Yet in the long run there will be a satisfactory readjustment, and meanwhile the benefit to the majority of the people seems unquestionable. In cities such as New York, musicians debate the radio as though the choice were between listening to a great orchestra in a concert hall, and hearing it over the air, with the consequent loss of beauty, power and tone. This question is relatively unimportant. For the majority of Americans the choice is between hearing that orchestra over the air, and never hearing an orchestra at all.

It is an old effect of contact with art that when you see or hear a perfect performance, you wish you could do it yourself. For the majority of human beings the wish dies of its own weight, but some proportion of us will always try to practice the art which we have recently enjoyed. If the radio has interfered with the tours of concert artists, it has also excited in thousands of people the wish to make music themselves. Often, let us add, with meagre results—but that only because there was no adequate guidance or instruction near at hand. Similarly, the hearing of fine orchestras over the air leads to a natural desire to hear some orchestra, as it were, face to face. It may turn out that the radio will have been responsible for the establishment of orchestras in many communities which do not now have them. It may dawn upon our public that a good orchestra may be maintained at less than the terrific cost now involved in such organizations in the large cities. An audience interested genuinely in the music, rather than in a virtuoso performance, will be content with a conductor who is a sound musician, even though as yet he lacks a great name, and with players who are competent, even though their skill is not phenomenal. Before long many cities may follow the example of Baltimore, which through the aid of what is after all a modest subvention from the taxpayers, has established an admirable Civic Orchestra, and enjoys, at a price which anyone can meet, an annual series of concerts which would do credit to organizations far less modest. Anyone who has seen the Baltimore audience listening with rapt attention to great music, will have no fears as to what the radio will do to the taste of the country at large.

In what has been said of the teacher, the implication has been that public performances are more or less incidental to the musician's life. The implication need not be pressed too far. Obviously the proportion of concert work and teaching will vary with the individual and with the locality. Such a variation is found in all parts of the world. But it is sound doctrine to say that public performances should be far more spontaneous, far more an overflow of energies normally directed elsewhere, than they now are in the concert world. There is something very artificial in a system which compels artists to make contracts a year in advance for public appearances before audiences whom they do not personally know, and in conditions which they cannot foresee. The chances are overwhelming that they will not be in just the mood to play those particular works at that place and at that moment. We have all had occasion, however, to remember priceless evenings when among a small group of friends some artist has played spontaneously for his and their delight. Such rare moments seem comparable to the happy moods in which the stone-carvers on the medieval cathedrals were inspired to express in the face of a saint, or in some Biblical scene, some vital contact with the life about them. In an ideal society, and in such a musical career as we ought to work for, the public performances of our best players would have this spontaneity. But they can have it only if the playing supplements their work as craftsmen.

The same principle might be suggested for the composer. When the musician was a craftsman, he was both composer and performer. Now many of our virtuosos cannot compose, and the majority of composers can't play. If the young student asks what musical career is open in America for a gifted composer, he would not think us kind if we replied in self-defense that for those who do nothing but compose we hope there will be no career. Yet if the young musicians in the United States and Europe who are devoting their entire time to composition could secure a hearing for all their work, the audiences would perish beneath the inundation. There would hardly be time to listen twice, even to the offerings of each season. What is to be gained by exclusive composing?

If in what we have said of the teacher's life we have implied that the composing should be done with his surplus energy and in his extra hours, we still are keeping in mind the example of an artist like Sebastian Bach, who thought of the theory and practice of music as one thing, of composition as an essential aspect of singing and playing. Allowing for the titanic resources of Bach's nature, and admitting that most musicians, after they have done a hard day's work teaching and practicing, would have little energy left for composition, we still hesitate to say that the result would be unfortunate. Those only would compose who had the greatest vitality, and whose inspiration could not be kept down. It is from their type only that important work has come, in any age.

The temptation is as strong for the composer as for the player to resent such a doctrine, and to set up against it the virtuoso ideal. To compose well, he will say, one needs solitude, peace, consecration. Yet the field is open for any talented musician who cares to use a little time each week writing for those occasions in our modern life in which music is demanded. He might even compose for us operas of a practical kind, with librettos in English. The Little Theatre movement in this country has been practically dissociated from music, not because the audiences which have supported the Little Theatre do not care for this other art, but because no operas or musical comedies exist on a scale which the small theatre can handle, or on subjects which would interest the American audience. If the young composer who now wastes his talents writing operas which can never be produced, would inquire how large an orchestra the little theatres can accommodate, and how many singers they can afford to pay, and would compose operas to this scale, he might inaugurate a new kind of musical entertainment, and certainly he would find immediately a considerable and appreciative audience.

If the composer is alert to all our modern demands for good music, he knows there is a career for him in motion pictures. Every film needs music. The day has gone by when the studios are content to play arrangements of famous music; they know the advantage of music written specifically to enhance the effect of the scene in the story. Many composers brought up in the older traditions of the art look upon the motion picture field as an opportunity too popular, and as they would think, too vulgar for them to enter. In my opinion nothing could be more absurd than this attitude. The composers already engaged in writing for pictures are of a very high order of talent and training. The demand is so great that their employment is fairly constant and their reward measured in salary is more than respectable. But motion pictures offer no opportunity to an egotist. If the composer wishes to be recognized by the audience as the particular genius who invented those lovely sounds, if what he really wants is the personal kind of applause which will bring him out on the stage to take a bow, then he should leave pictures alone. His music probably accompanies a very dramatic scene, the audience may not be paying close attention to his melodies. They certainly won't stop the show to ask his name.

A less lucrative opportunity in America today, but one likely to bring personal prestige in the old tradition, can be found in music for high schools. The young people in our public-school system have unusual opportunities to develop their musical talents, they hear good singing and playing from touring artists who now realize the importance of the high-school audience, and fortunately the good music they hear makes them wish themselves to sing or play. When they can, they like to produce musical shows for the benefit of their fellow students and their parents. In many high schools the older children acquit themselves creditably in the production of simple operas, not too difficult for their voices nor for the school orchestra. But there are few operas of this description. Far-sighted composers would seize the opportunity; some are already creating a kind of entertainment which will run continuously for forty-five or fifty minutes, which is approximately the length of the assembly period. These operas are not divided into acts, for the reason that all the children, including the youngest, are accustomed to motion pictures, and if the curtain should come down, they would think the show over and go home. The composer of opera for adults would be fortunate in any one season to have his work performed in America ten or twenty times. The composer of high-school operas for children, assuming that his work pleases, might easily have from two hundred to four hundred performances a winter.

It is customary, of course, to turn up one's nose a little at the music of the Broadway shows. Whether or not he is willing to admit virtue in jazz, the average well-trained composer inherits from his virtuoso tradition a feeling that his genius should operate only in a formal opera house, sponsored, if not by royalty, at least by the rich, or in sedate and refined circles, where chamber music is understood, or in the reverent concert hall. To such a musician it is inconceivable that his mission may well be to lift the current musical entertainment nearer to the level of great art. Personally, the present writer feels that in the musical comedies of Broadway, in such an entertainment, for example, as *Show Boat,* or in such music drama as *Porgy and Bess,* we have come nearer to the solution of a genuine American form of art than in anything yet composed by native talent in drama or in opera. If in any respect the music of such entertainment falls short of what it might be, the responsibility rests neither with the public nor with the producers, but with the talented composers who decline to study what is here needed, and to supply that need. To look disdainfully on the taste of the average man has always been in art as in other matters a dangerous form of snobbery. It has been fortunate for music that men of the greatest genius a century and more ago did not despise the court dances then popular. Those dances would mean nothing to us now, if Couperin, Rameau, Bach, had not written in their quaint measures certain imperishable suites. Had Chopin despised the popular dances of the romantic period, we should not now have his waltzes and his mazurkas. To write mazurkas today, however, is an anachronism. The comparable task for modern composers is to compose fox-trots and tangos which musically will be important.

The career of the virtuoso brought with it the career of the critic. If one's life is to be spent in a competition, however friendly, with other performers, then one needs the satisfaction of an umpire to say who is which, and which is ahead. Whether there is a permanent career for the music critic, may be questioned. The verdict of practicing artists on the performance of their fellows is usually illuminating. The service of the professional music critic is most often of an historical character. He helps to educate the audience by furnishing information about the music on the program, and by estimating the performance on the basis of the tradition. His lot is not a happy one, and much of his best work fails of appreciation, largely for the sound reason that an audience which has enjoyed a performance has got out of it all it wants, and an audience which hasn't enjoyed itself is usually willing to let the matter drop, provided it doesn't have to go again.

In America the music critic is horribly overworked. No large newspaper cares to be without its critic, yet practically no newspaper gives him enough assistance to cover all the performances and to pronounce mature judgment. As a consequence, few critics can attend more than the academic kind of performance—operas, concerts, recitals. If there should be a musical show of distinction, the over-worked critic could hardly get to hear it, and if you asked him to cover the music of moving picture houses as well as that of the musical shows, he would probably expire on the spot. We have therefore no good means at present of surveying the whole musical movement at any one time.

A visitor from another planet surveying the number of musical activities in our country and understanding that every concertizing musician must travel many thousands of miles, would have no difficulty in grasping the theory of the artist-bureau or agency. It is a great convenience for the music committee to know where to write if they wish to engage Jascha Heifetz or Josef Hofmann. But Heifetz and Hofmann are already well-known; where are you going to find the next generation of artists, full of promise but as yet too young to have made their name? This is the weakest spot in our organization of the musical career. Agencies or bureaus are little interested in the youngster, however promising, who hasn't yet enough reputation to bring in a large fee. Amateur organizations do what they can to assist the beginner to his first performances, but they accomplish very little. The women's clubs in all the states are in the habit of inviting lecturers to speak before them at a fee which though less than that of the great concert artists, is still adequate for traveling expenses and for something over. If these clubs or other groups would put on their programs each year a number of promising musicians from their own state or locality, at the same fees they now pay the lecturers, they could vary and enrich their own entertainment and greatly advance the cause of good music. To some extent they already do this, but unfortunately they do it in the spirit of missionary work, somewhat as though they were patronizing a young artist who hadn't yet earned the right to their support. The fact is that the love of music among the ladies has a lot of snobbism in it, and although they may be really fond of Mozart or Beethoven, they are never quite sure the masterpieces are worth listening to unless they are performed by a worldwide reputation.

We ought to have in every state of the Union at least one focal point for the musical interests of the community. At present a few cities, and chiefly on the Atlantic seaboard, attract too many of the young students and artists. For music in general we ought to develop a state pride. It is no small loss to any community when the talents which it has produced have gone off elsewhere, and an expenditure of money on the part of each state, which would result in keeping its gifted children at home, would yield profit a hundredfold.

American music would be advanced more than anyone can measure if each state established a small opera house, to be paid for out of its tax rates, and to be administered in the interests of its music talent. Such a house ought to produce not so much the older operas, and certainly not the large and costly ones, but modern works expressing the drift of our own taste and the needs of our own spirit. In such a house the best orchestral players in the state should find employment, and the singers and composers their careers. The tickets, as in Europe, should be so cheap that the entire community could enjoy the performances.

These two suggestions may seem unrelated to general considerations of the musician's career, but they follow from what has been said of the musician as craftsman. If the young student can envisage his career less as a spectacular triumph on the platform than as a life-long labor in the interests of one of the most sociable of the arts, we might soon have a greater demand for good music in such groups as the women's clubs, and a clearer need for houses where the whole community can find musical entertainment, not only in every state but in every city. When music is defined not as the expression of the individual, but as the social need of us all, the too-often criticized public will show a prodigal hospitality to the art.

Chapter seven:

THE PERFORMER

1   IF YOU SING, people say you are musical. If
you play an instrument, they say you are a
musician. In general the word musician will mean to your neighbors
a performer, and by performer they will understand soloist. A performer
is one who renders the music created by the composer, and to the public
he is more important than the composer; the song or the piece is more
often than not associated with the person who performs it just as the
play is associated with the actor rather than with the dramatist.

These popular misconceptions or inadequacies are worth noticing because even musicians themselves are influenced by them. The young
person who looks for a musical career probably hopes to be a soloist.
The audience at the Philharmonic concert are only too likely to regard
the conductor with more respect than the players, as though he were
necessarily the better musician. And if there is a soloist on the program,
they will undoubtedly think him a better artist than those in the orchestra accompanying him. Because of this prejudice, the soloist is paid more
for playing a few minutes than his colleagues in the orchestra for playing
several hours. The social and economic implications of the musical career
reach far.

Solo performers are most often pianists or violinists. They can give
recitals without the help of an orchestra, and the pianist has the advantage of the violinist because he needs no accompaniment at all. Let us
include with the violinist the viola players and the 'cellists. If they seldom
reach solo rank, the reasons are not necessarily musical. The public likes

best the violin, next the 'cello, next the viola, and least of all the double bass, though there have been and still are soloists on that instrument.

The advantage of the pianist lies not only in the fact that he can manage the whole performance himself, but also in the enormous repertoire he can draw from. Many of his audience have played or tried to play his simpler pieces. He begins with bonds of sympathy between him and his hearers. This advantage is offset by the size and weight of his instrument. He can't carry it around like a violin. He must depend on the manufacturer of his favorite kind of piano to get an instrument to the hall at the proper time and to have it fresh tuned. The manufacturer accomplishes this complicated service through his various agencies or coöperating music stores. If there should be a demand for a pianist in some out-of-the-way place where no agency or music store is located, then the piano must be sent in the baggage car of a train, an extremely expensive and laborious operation.

The solo artist, whether instrumentalist or vocalist, must be willing to travel. Paganini invented the touring career a little more than a hundred years ago, and what he did for violinists, Liszt at once imitated for pianists. How much advantage either brought to his profession may be questioned. In ancient times there were strolling minstrels; the touring virtuoso is only a modernized version of that unfortunate creature. The minstrels were homeless wanderers; the modern virtuoso rarely sees his home unless he is something of a failure as a performer, and therefore lacks engagements.

These engagements are made by the performer's agent, who receives a high percentage of the profits and therefore has every inducement to ask a large fee. Before the season begins, the agent enters his stable of performing artists on as many programs as possible, and after the season is launched, he devotes attention to the travel arrangements and to the general furtherance of the artist's comfort. The engagements are booked and the programs decided upon well in advance. When at last the performer fills his date, he may not be in the best mood to play the program he selected months before, but he carries out his contract as well as he can.

The life of the virtuoso, the performing soloist, is therefore an extremely hard one. It is possible only for men and women of strong constitution. If they are all-round musicians, they resent so much playing, so much repetition of pieces, even though those pieces are masterpieces. They regret also the lack of opportunity to compose or to join other

musicians in performances not of a virtuoso or solo kind. The inducement to become a touring soloist is the amount of money which may
possibly be earned. Only a few musicians, however, are of such compelling and continuous appeal that they can keep on playing to crowded
houses year after year and decade after decade.

In the picture of the touring soloist we include singers, but they do
not properly belong there. Very few singers of importance do any large
amount of touring. The life is too hard on their health and therefore on
their voice, and they are likely to have much more attractive engagements in opera or in oratorio work. Nowadays the singer seeks first of
all an engagement in opera. Inevitably an opera artist sings over the
radio or gives recitals near the opera house. But those who have the
dramatic talent rarely do so well in songs, the musical material which
is proper for the concert hall.

In one respect, a very important one, Paganini and Liszt, who set the
fashion of virtuoso solo concerts, differed from all their imitators and
followers. They were both composers. Liszt was one of the most completely equipped musicians the world has known. It is true that some
great performers today are also composers—Fritz Kreisler, for example,
and to an exceptional degree, the lamented Rachmaninoff. But in general the modern performer is a performer and little else. He may be at
home in all branches of music but he concentrates on his recitals and
trains for them as an athlete for a race. His technique must be prodigious; he must practice constantly; his repertoire must be very large. So
long as he does nothing but perform, he makes himself only a more human
and more stimulating kind of phonograph record. But since it is he who
probably made the record, it might be wondered why he need play those
particular pieces again since we can put him on the phonograph any time.
This particular question suggests obvious answers which we needn't stop
over.

A larger question is why the solo performers confine themselves rather
exclusively to the music of the past, and why their programs follow a
conventional pattern. Whether they are singers or instrumentalists, they
usually begin with early music, probably of the eighteenth century, and
work their way down. A piano recitalist, for example, will start with
Bach, will go on to Mozart and Beethoven, with perhaps a glance at
Haydn, then splurge on Chopin or Schumann or Brahms, will then go
modern in Debussy or Ravel and become quite up-to-date with the
Russian composers or the contemporary English and American.

This routine program, peculiar to our time, is defensible on economic rather than artistic grounds. Perhaps the management fears we wouldn't pay so high a price for our ticket if we didn't get a good deal of music for our money. I can think of no other reason why the performing soloist should always play a long program, or why it is impossible in the concert hall to hear one masterpiece unless we are willing to listen at the same time to two hours' worth of other masterpieces. There is no musical reason why programs should be chronologically arranged, or otherwise should serve as a lesson in history. No doubt you have seen imaginary pictures of great musicians playing to an intimate company of their friends—Beethoven at his piano, or Chopin. Musicians today, as in every other age, play or sing to each other in private in exactly this way, and they agree now as they always have agreed that the masterpiece communicated intimately enjoys the fortune that any composer could wish for his work. If music is a language, and says something to those who understand it, then to arrange recital programs so that half a dozen masterpieces are heard consecutively, is just as indefensible as to insist that no orator can make a speech unless he is allowed or compelled to make six speeches.

Even if the touring artists invented some new and better kind of program, they would be troubled by one question which perhaps will never be answered. What music should they play? The classics, of course, but there are so many classics now that no performer could cover the ground even though he ignored all the music written in the last fifty years. Contemporary music should certainly be played if the performer is to be more than a phonograph record—if he is to justify his claim to be the composer's interpreter. Composers have every right to bring their compositions, as far as they can, to the attention of pianists, violinists, singers and conductors. It would seem logical for the performers to divide their attention between the great things of the past and the promising new things. But in what proportion should we divide the program? The performance is paid for by the audience, and the audience everywhere overwhelmingly demands the famous pieces which they have heard before, or which they know by name and want to hear. This situation is true with opera audiences as with concert-goers. There is so much marvelous music for the piano that great artists would probably be glad to leave off their programs even so lovely a sonata as the Beethoven *Pathétique*. Perhaps they would prefer to play the great sonata of Liszt, or a Prokofiev concerto. But practically all the young and the middle-aged in the audience, if they ever took piano lessons, had a try at Beethoven's *Pathétique,* and they want to hear it properly done. The performer is under pressure to give his audience what they want, so long as they want music of the first quality. Who can say that the young generation hearing its first splendid performance of the music, hasn't the right to hear the *Pathétique,* or at the opera to hear *Trovatore?* Very well, the solo performer says, I must play the *Pathétique* for them this season and afterwards I will go on to other matters. In the same spirit of sacrificing service the operatic manager puts *Trovatore* on his schedule instead of *Pelléas and Melisande,* or Richard Strauss's *Salome.* More likely than not, the audience will pack the house to hear the old things, and beyond doubt there will be another installment of the younger generation next season clamoring in its turn to hear *Trovatore* or Beethoven's *Pathétique.*

All the great performers play as much modern or contemporary music as the audiences will permit them, and the needs of the audience are so sound that their demand for the older things must be listened to. But we evidently have here a problem which will grow in seriousness and for which some solution must be found. I used to hope that after enough recordings of the masterpieces had been made, people would listen to the famous old things on their phonographs and go to the living interpreters for an introduction to the new and the modern. Now I confess there seems little likelihood that music-lovers will accept such an arrangement. Listening to masterpieces on the phonograph record incites in them an overwhelming desire to hear the same music played by living artists. If the record has been made by a living conductor, they grow so fond of it that they sometimes travel hundreds of miles to hear the music rendered by the same conductor and the same players in the flesh.

Personally I am not greatly disturbed by such a problem as this, because I remember that music flourished, perhaps was at its best, before solo artists or orchestras gave concerts. Johann Sebastian Bach was not a solo performer in our modern sense, and though he played the violin and was accustomed to perform in orchestras, and used the orchestra of his time in some of his major compositions, he never heard of anything like our modern Philharmonic concerts. The recital and the symphony have added prodigiously to the musical pleasures of the world, and beyond measure to the potentialities of the musical career, but in their present state they have made the profession a bit lop-sided and they have created some bottlenecks, especially for the composer. I doubt very much if it is good even for a supreme performer to do nothing but perform. The musician who cannot or does not compose is in my opinion handicapped in his performance. Anton Rubinstein or Liszt or Chopin, or preëminently Beethoven and Bach, were so essentially creative geniuses that according to all testimony their performances had a quality of inspiration, almost of improvisation, such as we never hear nowadays. Our virtuoso performer is meticulously letter-perfect. He can thank his stars if enough of the composer is left in him to keep his perfection from being mechanical.

The men and women in the orchestras or in the first-grade bands must be good musicians, and usually they are great artists, but they are not soloists, and therefore they do not enjoy the individual popularity which they deserve. The player in a symphony or opera orchestra is handicapped, so far as I can see, in only one thing, that he must play over and over again so many of the masterpieces all his life. He has few opportunities to play new music. In every other respect his career follows the good tradition of Bach. He probably has opportunities to play with his fellow artists in chamber music; he is sure to have many pupils, especially if he occupies the first desk in any section of the orchestra, and he has opportunities to do solo work on occasion, with his own orchestra or with other orchestras, sometimes in recitals. It is from the ranks of the symphony or opera orchestras that most conductors emerge; having played orchestral music and having become sensitive to someone else's conducting, they have learned the art as it were automatically, and when accident or opportunity puts the baton in their hand, they already have the confidence of their colleagues. Some conductors, it is true, have never been orchestra players. A few, very few, but altogether too many, have never been players of any kind.

Nowadays the conductors are solo performers of the most virtuoso character. Musically this is in many respects a misfortune, and perhaps it is only a passing phase, but symphony audiences go primarily to hear so-and-so conduct such-and-such masterpieces and the attention is not on the masterpieces. To be sure, a first-rate conductor must have many talents, some of them not shared by other musicians. He must have not only a thorough musical education, an interpretive talent of the first order and a personal gift for leadership which will insure coöperation from the players, but he must have a genius for mixing the tones, for suppressing the brass or the woodwinds, or for balancing the strings against some other section. The composer can write down only the notes with a few indications of tempo and of dynamics; just what the right balance should be between the different instruments, the conductor must decide. For this decision a certain rare talent is required, an instinct so immediate and so sure, that a really great conductor is understood and recognized only by good musicians, and even though the conductor has this talent or instinct, his admirers in the audience are less likely to praise him for it, than for some minor and negligible quality.

The immense attention given to conductors nowadays compares with the sentimental adulation poured upon the early virtuoso performers. It is rarely based on musical grounds, and it carries a serious threat to the art. In the United States symphony orchestras have been supported not by the government but by private philanthropy. Much can be said for this arrangement; unfortunately much can be said against it. Where music or any art is supported by a government out of the taxpayers' money, there is danger of political interference and favoritism; where symphonies are supported by private generosity, there is little political interference, but an enormous amount of artistic ignorance and incompetence on the part of those who subscribe or collect the funds. The history of the choice and appointment of conductors to our leading orchestras would be a riotous record if anyone were allowed to publish it. Once the conductor is appointed, his tenure of office depends to some extent on his ability to please or flatter the members of the directing board, chiefly the ladies of that curious body. I know of no instance where the fortunes of a symphony society are controlled by professional musicians. The advice of the competent is doubtless asked in the selection of conductors, but after it has been asked, it quite often is not followed. I realize that I am pointing out the weakness in groups of admirable fellow-citizens, genuine lovers of music, to whose efforts we owe the existence of our great orchestras; yet we may be grateful without laying away our brains in camphor. The ladies and gentlemen on these boards still have an idea that a European musician is superior to an American, that he should have the first opportunities at the best positions and that he should receive the highest salary. Of course all Americans or their forefathers are or were immigrants, and most of us came from Europe, but in the amiable conviction of these boards, the European who is last off the boat must be a better musician than one who got here earlier.

The ladies and gentlemen of these boards are quite willing to pay the conductor with the European background a staggeringly large sum of money—fifty thousand dollars or more. Twenty thousand dollars for twenty weeks of conducting is for the European musician so mean a recompense that he will beg his directors, his intimate friends, to keep the figure a secret for the protection of his artistic reputation. In Europe he got no such salary. In many instances a young European conductor in a provincial opera house, earning three thousand dollars a year, has come to America for the gracious purpose of accepting an annual thirty or forty thousand.

The musicians' union in recent decades has been steadily increasing salary demands for the orchestra players. Though I know that increased budgets make the existence of orchestras and opera companies very, very difficult, I can see no justice in holding down the salaries of the orchestra players so long as conductors and solo artists are paid so much. An opera singer expects to make a fortune, and the most popular of them do make large fortunes. That they often end their lives in less than wealth is a commment on what they did with the money, not on how much money they received. Some conductors now earn even more than the great opera singers of the golden age, and the boards who direct the symphony orchestras, the ladies and gentlemen who give their time generously towards raising the necessary funds, are extremely unwilling to let the public know how much even in these bad times their conductor receives. They are especially reluctant to publish such figures side by side with the report of what they pay the orchestra. They are afraid the union would immediately make further demands. I suspect that the union would, yet I think the figures should be published. A great artist in any field should receive more than a lesser artist, but a conductor, just because he is a conductor, is not necessarily a great artist. There is plenty of conducting talent in this country which could prove itself if it had a chance. If our orchestras and our opera companies were supported by public funds there would be disadvantages of many kinds, but perhaps this one advantage, that the choice of conductor and of singers might be made by a jury of musicians, in terms of the musical ability necessary for the post.

If I seem to be indicting one class of music-lovers, those engaged in supporting the larger forms of music, let me add that the American people everywhere share some of the blame. In this country we have small regard for competence in any field, and in music we don't know what competence is. If a church in France or Germany, or any other country on the Continent, needs a new organist, a jury of distinguished organists is usually chosen to select the candidate. In this country the choice is made by the pastor, and in a Protestant church, by the pastor assisted by the music committee of his vestry or his elders. Only by the special mercy of God does any one of these gentlemen know the slightest thing about organs or organ playing or choir training. What they select they will stubbornly admire in loyalty to their own judgment.

I spoke in passing of chamber music. This name is given to the music played in an intimate room by a small group of instruments, a string quartet, a quartet of three string instruments and a piano, or music in some other combination of instruments, the one invariable characteristic of chamber music being that only one instrument plays each part. There is of course a first and second violin, as in the orchestra, but each makes a distinct contribution. Most musicians agree that in chamber music is found the finest illustration of their art. The fact that each part is played by a single instrument insures a high degree of personality in the performances, yet the fact that the instruments are playing together protects the music from the excessive individualism of virtuoso playing. To be a good performer of chamber music is not easy; some brilliant soloists lack the gift for it.

To perfect the team work which chamber music requires, the players must practice together constantly. There is little hope that their concert success will justify the expenditure of so much time, since few audiences appreciate the refinements of this art. Chamber music therefore is never well paid for and those who persist at it must be devoted artists, playing more for love of the music than for any material return.

A small group of singers, a quartet for example, has the same fortune and the same kind of reward as the chamber music group. In fact, string quartets are modeled upon the part-singing once in vogue in the fifteenth and sixteenth centuries. The technical possibilities of the violin surpass those of the voice, but otherwise this instrument and the human organ show the same capacity for song. A quartet of voices can be musically as important as a quartet of violins, but only on the same condition of team play, possible by constant practice. From time to time a vocal quartet does appear in concert, but these intervals as time goes on are spaced further and further apart.

All music, we are told, rests upon the human voice. In our time, unfortunately, this is not true. We ought to begin our study of music, each one of us, with lesssons in singing, but instead we start out with the piano or the violin or some wind instrument, and having absorbed the prejudice that the voice is hardly in the same class with man-made instruments, we rarely recover the respect we should have for singing and singers.

The singer's career now is chiefly on the stage and over the radio. Musical shows pay well and grand opera pays extremely well, but there aren't enough performances of it. Yet the singer will try for grand opera in the hope that once arrived there, he will be invited to act a singing part in a motion picture, to sing over the radio, occasionally to sing in concerts. The opera star who receives a thousand dollars a performance can command a fee of three thousand for a concert, and five thousand for a radio appearance.

Are these details mercenary? You can't study the position of music in our society today without attending to mercenary details. The singer has encountered them during the years of study. There are many superb vocal teachers whose ethical standard is of the highest, but there are also a number who have made of vocal teaching an out-and-out racket. The predatory type of singing teacher flourished until recently in Italy, in the neighborhood of the Scala and other opera houses. They preyed upon foolish young Americans by promising an audition with leading managers after a certain number of months of study—and after the payment of certain fees. Such scalawags of course had no influence with any responsible management, and their promises were as worthless as their instruction, but it was inevitable that where a good voice might lead to an opera career and to great financial rewards, a certain number of harpies would settle down on each prospect for what they could get.

If a singer is not mercenary, not cynical, we ought to be surprised. No other artist attempts a career so uncertain, so full of disappointments. Even the best teachers in the world, the most competent and the most honorable, cannot guarantee that their methods will work equally well with all their pupils. The difference will be created by personality and temperament. The singer, alone among musicians, is himself the instrument he performs on. If the pianist has a headache or has missed some of his sleep, his piano at least remains in tune, but the voice is subject to the singer's mood. Men singers vary less than women. Not even the greatest of women artists can absolutely count on themselves to the extent that a violinist or pianist can. Indeed, many of the greatest encounter disastrous periods in their career when their voice fails them entirely, and they must rest until it is restored.

Even when they are in excellent condition, their opportunities to perform are few. Even if they are well established in grand opera the number of times they will appear each season is not large. Their concert appearances will be hardly more numerous. They may on occasion do solo work with oratorio or other choruses. The truth is that if you like to sing, and hope to sing often, you'd be wiser to join the chorus of the opera than to study for stardom. If there once were very different conditions in the musical world, if instrumental music was once less highly esteemed than vocal, it was in days when there were fewer wonderful instruments and more well-trained voices. In Shakespeare's time and for many years afterwards, the great music of the world was performed by singers. There were as yet no orchestras in the modern sense, no pianos, and only the rudimentary beginnings of the organ. Intimate singing could be accompanied by some simple form of clavier or by the lute or even by the violin, but large groups of singers performed unaccompanied, since no accompaniment at that time would have been loud enough.

In Elizabethan times part-singing was carried to remarkable perfection in Italy and in England, for the same reason in both countries, that there were many good voices and comparatively few instruments. Choral works of a more majestic kind were composed by the great masters in the eighteenth and nineteenth centuries, usually for accompaniment by orchestra. To sing elaborate music *a capella,* or unaccompanied, gradually became difficult. In modern times only a few picked choruses of extremely able musicians have devoted themselves to unaccompanied singing. But is unaccompanied singing so difficult, after all? Have we perhaps allowed the instruments to hypnotize us?

In the public schools we have made great progress in vocal instruction, so that it is no longer extraordinary to find a good chorus in secondary and high schools, or several choruses if the school is large. These groups have enjoyed good ear training; they can sing unaccompanied and keep on the pitch. It is no longer startling to hear schoolchildren sing Palestrina or some other polyphonic composer. With the right approach, therefore, the average person can probably sing well and without the aid of any instrument, but to secure the proper approach we must escape from the spell which the highly perfected instruments of our time exert upon us.

The school choruses are excelled by some of the college or university choirs. It is by no miracle that they attain what amounts at times to approximate perfection. We all should enjoy singing if we were properly taught—that is, if we could sing the high notes without undue effort and if we had a conductor capable of securing from the voices a unified effect. The music departments of schools and colleges provide such teachers and such conductors. Since the young people sing in school and college, it might be expected that the singing habit would last over into mature life and that choral music would once more be popular and important. I have no explanation to offer why this is not the case. A few choral groups persist but usually on very unstable terms. The Westminster Choir School, an endowed institution, trains its singers not only for participation in choir music but for leadership in other choral groups. This school is unique, however, and until its influence spreads and the fine teaching in public schools creates a demand for further instruction such as the Westminster Choir gives, we might as well admit that music for the voice has lost the popularity it once enjoyed, and that the career of the singer is therefore less promising than that of the instrumentalist.

In this account of the relation of music to society, we must not forget the church choir, earliest source of all music, and still offering in my opinion remarkable opportunities to a true craftsman in the art. From primitive times there has been a demand for music in religious ceremonies. For centuries church singers have had an important career, the choirmaster another important career, and the organist still another, unless choirmaster and organist were the same person. Since the average church is not rich, choirs and organists are paid little, and for that reason the short-sighted look elsewhere for employment, yet the church still offers one of the best doorways to an all-round mastery of the art. If the organist or choirmaster is a composer, he can write music for his choir; and in few other musical posts can he find such opportunity for immediate performance of his work. If he is a dynamic personality he will persuade his choir to join other singers in a choral concert, himself of course conducting. He may even compose for his choir a small opera and perform it before his fellow townsfolk, usually for some public charity. Those who complain that they have no chance to try out their wings in the various musical forms, forget what they might have done as a by-product of choir work, had their energy been equal to their ambition.

If the choirmaster is also the organist, he need not content himself with the mediocre performing which satisfies the average congregation. No one will object if he plays the organ well. Assuming that he is willing to practice, he can give recitals of great interest. If the quality of his playing is admired, he will be asked to appear in other places. If to all this he adds the ability to train voices, there is nothing to prevent him from becoming the leading vocal teacher in his community.

The church musician, in other words, has this unique advantage, that his immediate audience is guaranteed in the congregation which employs him. If his choir training and his playing satisfy this audience, they become automatically his friendly agents, advertising him by their praise wherever they go. His initial salary for the church music is small, but his post is a highly honorable one and it leads to opportunities, if he will seize them. Unfortunately, however, this prospect does not appeal to most young musicians. They will serve as choirmaster and organist temporarily, while they are establishing themselves, but as soon as possible they will hurry on toward the ordinary virtuoso career. They care little for the craftsman's relation to the community; they wish to be touring soloists.

In three major fields the performance of music faces in our time serious problems which have been already glanced at, but which should be considered now more closely. Symphony orchestras and opera companies are maintained at terrific cost and their budgets always show a deficit. These are the two chief outlets for music in its major form; the recital career is a third. The touring virtuoso now is disappearing, for the reason that only too often his recitals, like the symphony concerts, are given at a loss. The problem in these three cases is of distribution. The audience is there, the artists are ready, but they find it hard to meet.

The modern symphony orchestra contains from eighty-five to slightly more than a hundred players. Their salaries, fixed by the musicians' union, vary with the price asked for the tickets; at a concert where the top admission is five dollars, the players receive more per hour than where the top is three dollars. In no case are musicians of this kind overpaid, since they have spent years in perfecting their art, and the artistic rivalry of the leading orchestras makes it impossible for any player to hold his position unless he is remarkably skilful. But the total of these salaries, however well deserved, is staggering. Any first-rate symphony must be prepared to pay its players, not including its conductors, two or three hundred thousand dollars. Its annual deficit will run from twenty-five to seventy-five thousand. Few auditoriums contain more than thirty-five hundred seats. If the orchestra, then, gives twenty concerts a year, and if its total budget is five hundred thousand dollars, and if the number of seats available for each performance is only thirty-five hundred, each ticket, to meet expenses, must cost over seven dollars. Such a price is of course prohibitive. If some seats were as low as a dollar or a dollar and a half, others would have to sell for twelve or fourteen dollars.

The same conditions in an exaggerated form make the opera problem, and in a simpler form the concert problem. Theatres and concert halls pay high taxes, and they must rent for a sum usually beyond the intake at the box office. When recitalists give a performance, they invite many of their colleagues, and even without such invitations, they may fill the hall, but they are not likely to meet expenses. Accepting this situation, most of them support themselves by teaching, and give occasional concerts as a luxury.

The situation which troubles the symphony orchestras and the opera companies can to some extent be remedied by building larger halls, but there is a limit to such extension. The amplification of sound by mechanical means makes it possible for orchestras to perform before twenty or thirty thousand people, and with an audience of such size an engagement would be profitable, even though each ticket cost only a small sum. But we like to watch a performance as well as to hear it, and sight cannot be amplified. On the operatic stage it is essential that some at least of the facial expression should be seen. The only practical solution therefore is to reach a large audience by giving many more performances at reduced prices, and this solution is an economic absurdity so long as music is supported solely by private benefactions. Some day music in all its professional forms will be subsidized by the state, and the citizen will get a return for his taxes in the low price of the tickets. This government subsidy might take several forms, one of which in my opinion should be the exemption from taxation of all concert halls and opera houses. The recital career would revive if artists could find an inexpensive hall. We have too few halls. There is no inducement to build them so long as high taxes interfere with their use.

All that has been said here applies to the professional performance of music, the one exception being the reference to choral singing in schools and colleges. I have made no attempt to disguise the fact that the career of the professional performer is hardly in a flourishing condition. Fortunately there are other aspects of music than virtuoso performance, or even of performance on a large scale before a large audience. Music is above all an intimate art, though from what we hear in the modern concert hall or stadium we might think otherwise. If the soloist does not flourish as once he did, if the *lieder* singer is not sufficiently appreciated or encouraged, if chamber music has to be a labor of love, perhaps we have got ourselves into these predicaments by developing a sort of musical megalomania, best illustrated in the tremendous spectacle of Wagnerian opera, but having other illustrations as well.

Some of us hope that the balance may be restored, and that moderation and sanity once more will characterize our musical ideals. The chamber quartet or the small chamber orchestra can render almost everything that music has to say; the solo instruments are adequate for the music that belongs to them; the piano in its larger sizes is more than adequate. If composers in their orchestral inspirations crave massive effects, they can secure them with fewer players than we now are accustomed to see on the symphonic platform. The virtuoso mania and the cult of loudness have reigned only during the last century, and it may be that both diseases have almost run their course. We may learn again what used to be well known, that the quality of music is not improved by doubling the size of the band.

One great benefit, however, the virtuoso era will leave to us. The solo performers of the last century developed technique to a point undreamed of before, and they worked out sure methods of imparting that technique. Anyone who studies music at all, any child who takes lessons merely to obey its parents, can now be taught by methods so scientific that the difference between beginner and expert is merely that of talent, of persistence and maturity. The amateur need no longer be imposed upon with the wrong kind of exercise and with inferior pieces. The small child need learn nothing which the virtuoso could not play sincerely and with self-respect.

2   FOR EVERY PROFESSIONAL MUSICIAN, there are at least a dozen amateurs. In concert halls they are found among the audience, but in less august places they meet for performances of their own. Sometimes the quality of these performances is good, sometimes less good, but the amateur, good or bad, cannot be left out of the musical picture. By his good-will he keeps the profession alive, and in some respects and at certain times he even contributes to the advancement of the art.

There are two kinds of amateur. There is the poorly trained, ineptenthusiast who likes music indiscriminately, and who listens as clumsily as he performs. Among artists he is a pest, but he associates chiefly with other amateurs of his own kind, who derive pleasure from simultaneous assaults on each other's eardrums. Lacking the application to study and practice, they usually avoid instruments and specialize in song. Their chief service to the art is this, that though unable to tell bad singing from good, they think John Charles Thomas is in the same class with themselves and in the spirit of comradeship attend the concert to encourage him. Encouragement is a good thing no matter where it comes from.

The amateur of whom I wish to speak differs from the professional only in that he does not earn his living through music. Since he is not a traveling virtuoso, he practices less than the professional soloist, but often he plays or sings almost as well. The difference lies in this, that the professional, through routine, becomes steadier than the amateur, who may be superb when he is in form but at other moments may disappoint himself. The professional, musicians say, has more margin to allow for shrinkage. Yet the amateur, if he were not mortified by his occasional lapses, might claim that the routine which guarantees stability to the professional may be shrinkage of another kind. The amateur is likely to play with more enthusiasm and spirit than the professional just because he can't play so much. The ideal, as all great artists know, would be to combine the spontaneous temper of the amateur with the discipline of the professional.

Before the invention of the phonograph record and the radio, the amateur got himself—or more often herself—a bad name by a performance before helpless visitors and friends. In a home where the daughters had taken music lessons they would be called upon to exhibit their accomplishments whenever the neighbors dropped in for the evening. In America the children were more often than not badly taught and the performance was to them as well as to the listeners an affliction. In France the children were often very well taught indeed, but the pleasure of listening to them was small, because in most cases they played against their will. In England there seemed no unwillingness to perform, which on the whole was a great pity; the children passed from the nervous incompetence which might be expected of their age, to a well-poised mature incompetence which was terrifying. Forty or fifty years ago there seemed to be as many male amateurs in England as female. The men loved to sing, and their sisters or wives accompanied them. The sisters or wives in many cases also sang, and there was always danger of a duet, probably one of Mendelssohn's. In the United States at that time the piano playing was done chiefly by girls, the violin playing by boys, but both girls and boys for the most part abandoned their music as soon as possible, and there were few mature amateurs such as made an English evening formidable.

Now on both sides of the ocean the radio and the phonograph have pretty well shamed the incompetent amateur into silence. When first-rate performances can be turned on at will, or the great singers of the past can be heard again as often as we please, not even the musical amateur is sufficiently egotistical to compete. But the effect of bringing matchless performances into the home through the radio and through records has not been to suppress true talent. The shameless amateur has been pushed out, but the competent amateur has moved in. Expert performance of any art or craft always stimulates to some degree the desire of emulation. We are imitative creatures in childhood, and we remain imitative in a very good sense as long as we live. Those who have talent are encouraged by a fine musical performance to perform the same music themselves, approximating the professional fineness as closely as possible.

This development indicates, I believe, the future of all the arts in our common life. Centuries ago it was unusual anywhere for a majority of the citizens to read and write. Where illiteracy was general in those ancient times, or where it exists today, the person who can write becomes the local scribe, the letter writer and letter reader, the wise man of the community. When everyone learns to read and write, the scribe may seem to have lost his place in the world, yet an entirely new profession arises, authorship. The progress of the average person from illiteracy to literacy is accompanied by a parallel advance from mere letter scribbling to novel writing or playwriting or some other advanced form of literary composition.

Music is a language which more and more people understand and use. My confident belief is that the professional musician, like the professional scribe, tends to disappear, but in his place will rise the great artist to whom the amateur can listen with deeper appreciation because all amateurs will be excellent performers. The new methods by which the professional virtuoso is trained are equally effective in training the amateur musician. If the progress which we are now making continues for another decade or two, every amateur who performs at all will do so with a technical skill which twenty years ago was possible only for professionals. When that time comes, however, we shall ask of the professional far more than technical skill; to say anything of value to us, he must have imagination and vision and the other kinds of spiritual height and depth. To ask at all for public support, he will be obliged to bring such an interpretation to the music as has come only from the supremely great—from Bach or Liszt or Rubinstein or the giants of our own day.

The millennium I here describe is perhaps no millennium at all. The day has gone by when only the professional musician can perform well. Most of us know dozens of men and women in public or private life who would be called professional musicians if they did not earn their living in some other field than music. There are amateur singers of both sexes who have enjoyed the best of training and who have sung in public frequently enough to be at home on any platform. There are business men and bankers now carrying some of the heaviest responsibilities of the world, who rise an hour or so earlier each day in order to get in a little practice on their instruments. One of the three or four best flute players I know—and I know some of the most famous professionals—is a hydraulic engineer now serving his country with his extraordinary scientific equipment. I knew him first as the instigator or inspirer of a remarkable amateur orchestra in which he played the first flute. When his presence and example attracted other flute players to the orchestra, he shifted over to the string section and sat among the 'cellos at the first desk. Few men in the United States have his knowledge of acoustics, of the whole science of music, and few have his emotional and imaginative equipment, the endowment of the artist which makes his playing beautiful.

To such men as he, chamber music has a particularly strong appeal. The late Henry Holt, the publisher, was a 'cellist both skilful and indefatigable. His taste in music was perhaps a little narrow but it couldn't be said to be mean. He spent a good many hours toward the close of his life playing the Beethoven quartets, and he liked best the later ones, which he declared were the most beautiful music in the world. Sweeping statements are dangerous yet something can be said for this opinion of his. In any case, the kind of amateur who can play and fanatically enjoy that music is not the kind of amateur whom the radio and the records drove out.

Amateur singers of professional quality find their pleasure, of course, in choral groups or choirs. Some of them disclose skill in conducting; others go in for musicology and become experts in the editions and the texts of great music. Though it is still altogether too true that the men and women on the governing board of large musical enterprises are not always competent musicians, yet the prospect is very bright for a host of well-trained amateurs from whom future boards can be drawn.

In our high schools, along with the choral groups, there are excellent orchestras. For the most part the children in orchestras and choruses do not intend to be professionals, but their competence in the art and their love of it is so great that they continue to play in college orchestras, or they sing in college glee clubs, which nowadays are entirely musical organizations; or if they don't go to college at all, they organize amateur orchestras and choruses in their home town and continue the enthusiastic pursuit of their hobby.

For reasons not difficult to explain, the accomplished amateur sometimes has a repertoire more interesting than the professional. I don't say that the professional's repertoire is not likely to be the best selection of the best pieces; I do say it is liable to be somewhat stereotyped and narrow. There is an immense amount of music; no pianist plays even a large proportion of all piano music, no violinist has control of more than a small part of the violin repertoire, and the great songs which singers on the concert stage do not get around to learn, are beyond counting. The amateur, however, feeling no compulsion to acquire the stereotyped repertoire, is free to browse. I have heard from amateur violinists sonatas which once were well-known but which the professional ceased to play fifty or sixty years ago. It is only from amateurs that I have heard all the songs of Schubert. It is only from amateurs that I have heard all the compositions of Chopin. Some pianists do play all of Chopin's piano pieces in a series of titanic recitals. But Chopin also wrote songs; also he left us a famous 'cello sonata.

Besides the volumes of songs on which a large part of Schubert's fame rests, the Viennese composer wrote frequently, in the most impromptu and amateur spirit, music for groups of his friends who wished to perform together, some of them being singers. I have never yet heard certain of these casual masterpieces performed by professionals. Doubtless they are given some time, somewhere else in the world, but in my own country I know of no professional performance of the *Nachtgesang im Walde,* Op. 139b, or of the serenade, *Zögernd leise,* Op. 135. The first is for four men's voices and four horns; the second, for the birthday party of a young girl, was written for alto solo and female chorus, the words being by Grillparzer. In either case professionals would see difficulty in preparing a performance, since it is hard to secure four horn players and a good male quartet, still harder perhaps to find the right alto soloist and the right chorus of women. Amateurs, being more numerous and not necessarily less skilful, can effect these combinations more easily.

It is by the increase in the number of amateurs that music will one day establish itself among the great languages given to mankind. Every art is a language, each neatly fitted to say what can't be said otherwise, and until we all have command of all the languages the human race will remain only partly articulate. It is not enough for a few to speak the tongues; complete communication is the privilege of us all. The story of the tower of Babel seems essentially true, but perhaps the ancient chronicler missed the point and got his story confused. To say or imply that the tower builders all spoke one language when they started, but suddenly branched off each into a separate tongue, is to assert a miracle hard to believe and perhaps not worth believing, since it conveys little which bears on any experience we know. But it would be both plausible and sadly illuminating to say that the race began speaking all the tongues needed for the complete expression of life, and afterwards, whether gradually or suddenly, specialized in a few of these tongues, or in only one of them. From that moment they could not altogether understand each other. Certain things can be said in words; other kinds of truth or emotion in music; other kinds in painting or sculpture, or dancing. To have one language in common is not enough; we must have all. The musician and the non-musician may speak the same language of words, and yet fail to understand each other. The progress of music encourages us, even though there are other arts besides, and our race has a long way to go before it recovers all the tongues. The amateur with his zeal and his curiosity is perhaps leading the way.

Chapter eight:

THE TEACHER

1   THESE PERFORMERS of whom we have spoken, and the composers of whom in a later chapter we shall speak, learned their art to some extent from other musicians, yet to call someone a music teacher is not considered high praise. For most of us the music teacher is a person who gives lessons to reluctant children. The music teacher, as the public think of him, rarely plays in public and rarely composes, or if he does, we wish he didn't.

I describe the poorest kind of teacher, since the type is numerous. Such persons have a hard life, with little return for their effort, and with no future. What they are doing is firmly integrated neither with society nor with art. Their history can be guessed at. They may have studied music themselves, with something less than thoroughness and with no intention of earning their living by it. When accident or misfortune compelled them to take inventory of their resources, they decided to make what they could of limited talent and imperfect training. They teach children to play scales and to do five-finger exercises, and as quickly as possible they teach them to play pieces—not easy passages from great music, not the two-part inventions which Johann Sebastian Bach wrote to instruct one of his sons, but modern pieces of a kind ground out in quantity, called "teaching material"—insignificant tunes for the right hand, unimaginative thumpings for the left. It is inconceivable that this teaching material should ever be used for concert or recital purposes, or that anyone with a natural talent could find pleasure in performing it.

It is invented for the incompetence of the teacher rather than for the instruction of the pupil.

The unfortunate creature I here pillory gives lessons in solitude. He, or more frequently she, would be embarrassed if an accomplished musician heard either her instruction or the performance that results from it. Very rarely indeed—I might say never—does she teach her pupil how to practice. For half an hour at a time, or for longer periods, the victim plays the pieces over, hoping to play them well at last by playing them badly a number of times. She may give a child the impression, since she probably has it herself, that practicing limbers up the fingers, the wrist, and the arm, and that the performer's skill resides in muscles and joints. The fact is, of course, that musical skill, both technical and interpretive, is located strictly in the head and heart, and practice should train us in those regions. A good teacher increases not only our ability to say something but also our store of things to say.

The child practicing in almost complete isolation can be heard from various parts of the house as it romps through the easy passages and crashes at last against a difficult one. It returns to the beginning, takes a fresh start and once more bogs down. Then having got its mad up, by sheer will power it comes at the hurdle a third time and goes over triumphantly, no doubt feeling encouraged. What has been accomplished, however, merely guarantees permanent inability to play that piece. At each repetition, whether in practice or in more public performance, we cut a mental groove or channel; we make it easy to do again what we have just done. To play the piece twice wrong and once right is worse than not playing it at all, for the grooves cut by the mistakes must be obliterated before the music can be played correctly. To practice the piece twice right and twice wrong, is to establish a strong chance that in public we shall play it wrong, since in public we must make allowance for tension or nervousness. But to play the piece three times right and no times wrong, gives us a practical certainty of going through it without failure. The virtuoso artist whose impeccable skill dazzles us, takes as great care to avoid playing wrong notes as to play the right ones. He tries to keep the brain grooves absolutely straight and clean. If in the excitement of a performance he strikes a wrong note, whether or not the audience has heard it, he is worried. He will practice the piece carefully after the performance in order to repair the damage he did to the brain grooves.

This is what an inferior music teacher doesn't teach, but all good teachers do. The beginner with talent will progress faster if he does enough practicing than if he does too little, but whatever distance he goes in the art, the instruction he receives and the habits he forms should be correct. They can't be unless he knows how and how long he should practice. He must practice enough, but not too much. The limit is set by the capacity of the brain to pay strict attention and to absorb. Fingers never get tired, nor does the body if we keep the right posture, but for the brain there is a point of saturation. To get in as much practice as possible before that point is reached, we must learn to save time and to concentrate.

Time is saved by a knowledge of harmony and counterpoint. A poor teacher attends only to the notes on the page; a good teacher, from the first lessons, teaches the theory as well as the practice. Unless the child knows the vocabulary and the grammar of the musical language, it can't know what it is trying to say through its fingers.

If children would rather play by ear than study a piece, the reason probably is that they know the music which is in their heart but don't know the music which is on the page. They have not been properly taught. You may yourself remember the childhood inconvenience of picking the notes off the page one by one, of getting them at last into some mental order and then of forcing them out through arm and elbow to the finger tips. By that curious process, no one can learn to play. If, however, you can first hear the music, performance will be easy. The singer who hears the note before he sings it will have little difficulty in sounding it true; the piano player reaching for fast octaves, is likely to miss them so long as he hears the tone only after he has hit it; if he hears it first, his hand will fall on the difficult stretch every time.

I remind you of these fundamentals in order to describe bad teaching in reverse, which is the only constructive way to consider it. The largest number of music teachers are inadequately equipped. First-rate teachers do their best to raise the standard of instruction in their art, either by reforming those that can be reformed, or by suppressing them, or by educating the public to know good music teachers from the other kind. Some of the distinguishing marks I have here given. There are three rules, however, which when applied broadly, and with common sense, are a helpful guide.

In the first place, those who teach music should also perform it. They should play in public, not necessarily on the concert platform but at least before their friends and at frequent intervals before other musicians. If your child's music teacher drops in of an evening and excuses himself or herself from playing on the ground that teaching takes too much time for practice, my advice is to get your child another teacher. There are two reasons for this severe sounding judgment. Your small boy probably plays baseball with more enthusiasm than he practices the piano. Perhaps he has a greater inner urge toward baseball, but I venture to say that the ball players he has seen rank higher in their art than the piano players he has heard. Anything superlative in our experience we are likely to imitate or wish we could imitate. The average human being, listening to really fine music, wishes that he could perform it himself. If while the wish is on him a competent teacher shows him how to perform it, or at least how to take the first steps toward performing it, he will not be a reluctant pupil. When you engage a teacher for your child, therefore, pick someone who enjoys performing what he teaches.

Even if the teacher is highly competent and in former years played frequently in public, there is some loss if the habit of performance is abandoned. Music is an art which makes great demands on the performer's nerves, whether the performer is a child or a mature virtuoso. The voice must be managed differently in small rooms and in large ones, in resonant halls and in those in which the acoustics are poor. To make the proper effect, a piano piece must be played more deliberately in an immense hall than in your living-room. Furthermore, in every piece of music there are opportunities or pitfalls which you discover only in performance. Have you ever noticed that the experienced pianist at the end of the andante, having created a poetic mood in his audience, preserves it as long as possible? He won't lift his hands from the last chord until the vibrations of the strings have stopped. Even then by sitting absolutely motionless and keeping his fingers on the keys, he will create for you the illusion that the tones still sound even after the strings are silent. Don't make the mistake of saying that he does this merely "for effect." Of course that's what he does it for, but the whole performance is for effect. He wants to cast a spell on you, a spell of beauty, and often the spell becomes most poignantly strong in that long moment when he is motionless but your heart is not. The piano teacher should know how to train your child not to spoil a good performance with a final thump, or to jump off the piano stool before the hearers have drawn the utmost beauty from the last notes. But to teach this phase of the art, the teacher must practice it, and must remain in practice. A good musician, having recently performed a piece himself, usually has some new advice to give, some wisdom which he gathered as he played.

The teacher, then, should be a performer, and should play in public. He or she, if really competent, will arrange opportunities for the pupils also to play in public—that is, to play before other children and before strangers. The child who practices and takes lessons in private, will have the kind of nervous system which is adequate for performance in private, but when an aunt or an uncle visits the home and there is a request to hear the latest piece, the child will almost certainly break down, since the presence of aunt or uncle calls for nerves which haven't been exercised. All children like to perform, and they like to excel before other children. The great music teachers of the world are so aware of this truth that as often as possible they give their instruction to each pupil in the presence of the others. Some of the pupils may be advanced, some just beginning, but it makes no difference. They all hear a large number of pieces which they themselves do not yet play. The more advanced hear again what they studied in former years. They all acquire the habit of performing without nervousness—certainly with solicitude for the perfection they are aiming at, but with no fear. If you had the opportunity to play when you were young for Hofmann and Rachmaninoff and Godowsky and Lhevinne, would you ever again be afraid to play before any audience? The advantage here suggested is secured for all children by constant performance in the presence of their contemporaries or before their elders. In many communities several music teachers bring their pupils together frequently, but a single teacher can get the same result by letting the pupils play for each other once a week, or by teaching them in each other's presence.

The third mark of a good music teacher, assuming the virtues already mentioned, is the disposition to teach principles rather than imitation. The very fact that a fine performer induces a certain envy or emulation, leads to this pitfall, that the beginner will try not only to acquire the teacher's technical skill but to reproduce literally the teacher's interpretation. It is altogether too easy for a master of technique to say, do this as I do. If you are choosing a teacher for your child, ask to hear his pupils. Even though they all play well, be on your guard if they all play alike, especially if they all play like him. You wouldn't think much of the teacher of literary composition whose students all wrote on the same subjects in exactly the same sentences, word for word. It is a common saying among the masters of the art that no greater misfortune can overtake us than this, to acquire more technique than is needed, to be able to say more than we have to say.

2 MUSIC TEACHING of the kind I have been speaking about deserves more thought than we usually give to it. If instruction in any subject is given on a large scale by many teachers, and if the results are not what they should be, we all suffer the consequences. The leading musicians, I repeat, do their best to raise the standard of private instruction, but only to a slight degree can they change widespread habits, or the venerable traditions which now make it easy for the solitary teacher to be a poor teacher. An attempt to understand these conditions and this tradition is more than worthwhile.

Western music as we know it is a young art. The ancients of course had their music, and the Orient today cultivates an art which has a long continuous history, but in the western world there is a large gap between the music of Greece, let us say, and earliest examples of medieval music which remain to us. Only in recent times have we paid much attention to those vestiges of the Middle Ages. Our musical performances have a repertoire which reaches back only to the sixteenth century. We have this advantage at least from our ignorance, that since the period of musical history which we know is brief, we can grasp easily its social characteristics as they develop.

Music in Palestrina's time, like painting and the other arts during the Renaissance, was thought of as a craft. The autobiography of Benevenuto Cellini, with certain personal expurgations or softenings, would serve well enough for the life of any musical genius in his time. The musical genius might be a performer, a composer or a manufacturer of instruments, or he might pursue all three of these careers, but in any case, like Cellini, he learned his art from some older craftsman, and having emerged from his apprenticeship he sought and obtained commissions in his own right and at once attached to himself youngsters wishing to learn, who served an apprenticeship to him as he had served to an older man. The craft was handed down complete from generation to generation, the teacher serving not only as instructor but also as employer, also as guardian, also as sponsor before the members of the craft and their patrons. Part of the wisdom which the craftsman handed down was his accumulated experience with patrons and clients; the apprentice could learn not only how to produce a masterwork but in what market to dispose of it.

This craftsman relation of teacher and pupil persisted into the nineteenth century, and some features of it are still discernable today. The surviving pupils of Liszt carry on his tradition, enriching it, of course, with the contributions of their own genius. They recall with pride his thoughtfulness and tact in finding opportunities for them in the profession, and in speaking a good word for them long ago, when they were young and unknown. The master did this for his pupils out of a sense of duty; if he had another motive it was the wish to keep alive in the world and to maintain at points of influence the essential doctrines he felt he could bequeath to his fellow artists. The pupils would continue this jealous care for their disciples, giving a friendly hand in dozens of ways until the youngster proved himself self-sufficient—or in tragic cases proved himself undeserving.

Leschetizky was an illustration of what I've called the master-apprentice tradition; Leopold Auer was another; Isidor Philipp, fortunately still living, is one of the last. Philipp differs from early illustrations, from Liszt for example, in having taught in a great conservatory. The master who gave instruction in his Weimar home did not give courses in harmony or counterpoint, or in the theory of music. Many of his passing remarks illuminated those subjects, but systematic instruction in these essentials he expected his pupils to find elsewhere.

To transpose the methods of Liszt in his private home to the methods of the small music teacher today is a reduction to absurdity, yet in the absurdity there is a parallel. Too often the music teacher expects the pupil to learn harmony and counterpoint, if at all, from someone else. Consequently, the pupil doesn't learn these subjects. Since the pupil we are now speaking of is only a beginner, the teacher feels little concern over the later career of the child—which is fortunate since this kind of teacher is in no position in the profession to extend a helping hand, not even one joint of one finger of one hand.

I pause to say a word, not of apology but of regret, that I make these statements. They are usually not made. Writers on music either think the incompetent teacher can be ignored and should be, or they keep silent because their hearts are tender. My heart is tender too, but my adventures in musical education have taught me two facts which few of my colleagues dwell upon; the number of incompetent teachers is astoundingly large, and since they would not stay in business if they hadn't at least a few pupils, the number of their victims is still larger. My tender heart aches for the pupils. In the large cities there are many first-rate teachers, and there are first-rate teachers in many towns, but our country contains

many, many places, either cities or towns or villages, in which there is
not a single competent music teacher. I am second to none in admiring
our musical progress; I know it would not be possible without the devotion and talent of many good teachers. But I also know that bad teachers
flourish in still greater number. In some sort of fashion they make a living
out of the gullible public at the expense of youth, and to no small degree
they keep the country as a whole from understanding music and enjoying
it. The law doesn't permit the practice of medicine without proper training in advance; we shouldn't permit the teaching of music without some
guarantee of proficiency.

I may be wrong in my reading of history, but I think the modern conception of music education was inaugurated by Mendelssohn when he
founded the conservatory at Leipzig. There were of course earlier conservatories, but the program of education which he announced and set in
motion is followed everywhere today where adequate equipment is available. Though he did not say so in just these words, he felt that the advantages of the medieval guild apprenticeship could and should be continued
in the changed social conditions of our time. What the apprentice learned
was the total craft; he was to become not simply a sculptor, a painter, or
a violinist in the sense that he could model a statue, produce a canvas or
play a tune, but he was to be proficient in every branch of his art. The
great Bach was not primarily a manufacturer of musical instruments, yet
his advice was sought in the planning of organs, his opinion was desired
in the purchase of a clavichord or a piano, he was a fine judge of a violin
from the maker's standpoint, besides being a fine violin player, and he
wrote an extraordinarily famous set of preludes and fugues to illustrate
a new method of tuning the keyed instruments. Mendelssohn was a
pioneer in the modern rediscovery of Bach. Musical education, he believed, should train more such craftsmen, if Heaven would only send the
talent.

Those who entered the Leipzig conservatory, therefore, might intend to
excel as pianists or singers or violinists, but they would be composers
also; they would learn the whole theory of their craft; they would know
something about the voice if they were instrumentalists, and something
about instruments if they were vocalists, and they would know how to
conduct. Mendelssohn himself was a piano virtuoso, an organ virtuoso,
a skilful player of stringed instruments, a very respectable singer and a
superb composer. While he directed the conservatory he continued to
compose, to conduct and to perform in public. At the school he let other

masters only less notable than himself teach most of the branches in which he excelled, but he had his class in composition and of course his class in piano playing.

Today, as a result of the educational impetus which he gave, there are many conservatories in the world, and with the best of them not even the best private teacher can compete. Incidentally these schools train pianists, violinists, vocal soloists; their ideal is to train musicians. Having in one place facilities for teaching every branch of the art, they naturally attract among the students specialists in each of these branches, and naturally the youngster who wishes to be a specialist is to a certain extent reluctant to accept the complete education of which in his green condition he cannot see the need. But in a conservatory, reluctant though he may be, he cannot escape the broadening influences. The singer makes friends with the piano player, with the horn player, with the violinist. Though each would prefer to talk about his or her specialty and about nothing else, the others insist on having their say too, and in the end they all break even. Through their egotistical enthusiasms, they educate each other.

Between the well-equipped conservatory and the host of rather incompetent music teachers, there is a wide gap. In this large area good private teachers are found, occasionally very fine private teachers. They would not disagree with the statement that the best musical education is now found in conservatories. They wish, as all wise musicians do, that we had many more conservatories. A town that boasts a business school should have a music school also. Wherever there is a high school there should be on some proportionate scale a conservatory staffed by teachers as well trained as those who teach science, mathematics or languages. But since we are as yet far from this goal, energetic private teachers here and there join forces to produce an approximation of a conservatory; a piano teacher, for example, associates himself with a violin teacher, a singing teacher, and a teacher of composition, and together the four put on their pupils what pressure they can to study more than one aspect of music, and to perform on joint programs. Even where this venture toward a conservatory has not yet been made, there is a tendency among parents to organize or to import lectures and discussions about the history of music. In most public schools the music department, starting with performance, tends to round out its instruction so as to include theory and history. In all this development, great aid comes to us over the best musical programs of the radio.

A true picture, then, of music teaching today includes these three panels or sections. The best-equipped conservatories set the pace for the art and maintain the tradition. They are as it were at the top of the pyramid. They are elevated but few. Next comes the large body of individual music teachers who are well taught and competent and whose only handicap is that they are separated or even solitary. It is hard for them to make a mass attack on our ignorance, but they are aided enormously by their colleagues in the public-school system and in the music departments of colleges. I believe they will more and more become incorporated into the public-school system, as the appreciation of music grows and as instruction in the art is recognized as the right of the talented.

Below the conservatories and the well-equipped individual teachers, come the large mass of those whom I have called, truthfully but mercilessly, the incompetent. The harm which poor teaching does is so great that we can hardly be excused if we shut our eyes to it, or dismiss it with facile optimism. It is not likely to disappear until music-lovers of all kinds protest against it at every opportunity.

The advantage of the conservatory, or of the group of teachers who occupy themselves in various branches of music, is obvious when we remember that only the pianist or the organist can perform alone. All the instruments of the orchestral family must have an accompaniment, and so of course must the voice. In conservatories, the piano students usually accompany the violinists and the singers, making possible adequate practice in the sonatas, and in the concertos for which piano accompaniments have been arranged. The advantage is as great for the pianist as for the string player, since piano-violin sonatas are concerted pieces, a kind of duet, and even in ordinary accompaniments the pianist learns to collaborate, an art in which through so much solo playing he is too often deficient. All this holds true equally for the piano and voice, and of course for trios, quartets and larger groups in which the piano has a part. From what has been said in the early portion of this book, the reader, let us hope, is aware that the piano by itself does not represent all of the art of music, nor does it represent at all some of the tonal possibilities of the string or wind instruments. If the object of music teaching is to produce a musician, one who understands the whole art, then the isolated teachers, even the very competent ones, are at a disadvantage. Pupils and teachers learn from each other, teachers from other teachers, pupils from other pupils. This truth should be understood by parents before they provide musical instruction for their children. Even the best teachers are unlikely to stir in a pupil the enthusiasm which may be roused by association with other children learning the same art.

I wish there were space here to develop this idea fully; few things in education seem to me more important. Where we study any subject in a group, we and the other members of the group acquire a common set of ideas, a common fund of interest to talk about. Studying mathematics with a group, we acquire a way of thinking and a special language in which to articulate and discuss that way of thought. The group who study music together acquire also a special language, and a subject matter which, as Pater said, is or should be indistinguishable from the language which expresses it. No one can master a language in solitude; we learn to talk by talking. Indeed, when we think of the large proportion of music study which is pursued in solitude or isolation without exchange of ideas, without an audience, with neither the approval nor the disapproval of our fellows, it is remarkable that the love of music persists, and that men and women so taught do sometimes acquire a moderate ability to practice the art.

Since conductors are performers, they need like any other performers a training in technique and much routine in the presence of an audience. Conductors often instruct or coach promising aspirants, but any such teaching in private must be theoretical, and its value is small unless practical experience precedes or supplements it. Many, perhaps most, conductors begin as players in the orchestra and learn the language of the baton in order to obey it. An amateur trying to get a band or a chorus started will make frantic signals, will sometimes count out a measure in advance to set the tempo, may—if his incompetence is deplorable—stamp with his foot or shout, as though the musicians were a herd of animals to be scared into motion. The master conductor and the players under him understand that the first beat of the measure is indicated by a clear downward motion, and the last beat by an equally clear lift of the baton. If there are three beats, the middle is indicated by a horizontal movement either right or left. If there are four beats, the second and third are indicated by a horizontal motion from left to right or from right to left. The conductor starts the orchestra by giving them the beat which precedes the one on which they enter. Through practice he can impart directions and the orchestra can grasp them so easily that the audience hardly detects the preliminary beat or any other.

An amateur conductor, the type which inclines to beat in time with the foot, will of course wave both arms. The master conductor controls the tempo and starts and stops the performance with his right hand; he uses his left to control expression, to call for more sound or less, to encourage each section of the orchestra in the particular effects desired at any moment.

These are no more than syllables in the conducting language, but even they can be learned only by practice. It is not easy to stand before an orchestra and beat time intelligently. The novice is always amazed at the confusion he produces. Of course a good assemblage of veterans can play by themselves, and they can help the novice out by ignoring completely his various gestures, but if they courteously attribute to his signals the usual meaning, and obey them, the result will be quite awful. The novice is sure to make signals he doesn't intend, or signals of which he has not yet learned the purpose.

Where many students come together in large music schools, aspiring conductors have golden opportunities. They can either persuade their fellows to play under their awkward leadership, or they can practice the technique of the baton out of sight of a quartet or a quintet, yet within hearing. This form of discipline lets the players do the conducting and compels the baton to follow; it's a tricky kind of exercise, a very difficult one, but rewarding.

The teaching of music, in other words, is most likely to succeed where it is most coöperative in spirit and in fact. I doubt if any musician would challenge the statement that his is the most social of the arts. Paintings are enjoyed by individuals; even in museums the great convases are visited rarely by crowds, usually by one person at a time. Sculpture and architecture and whatever other space arts there may be, wait for their appreciators to come in whatever numbers are convenient, one by one, two by two, or ten by ten. Even dancing can be thoroughly enjoyed by a very small audience, but a play cannot, and still less can music. A dramatist even of long experience dares not estimate the value of a work until it is tried out before a full house. Before a thousand people it makes one effect; before five hundred another; before one hundred, still another. In the performance of music, as of a play, the artist on the platform is affected by the audience. He may play better before a small audience, but the size, whatever it is, is not a matter of indifference to him. The music may be intended for an intimate room or for a large auditorium, but in either case it is at its best when the audience is of the expected size. No student has acquired much insight into the art until by experience he learns this relation of the music to the hall, and the relation of his own temperament and his own powers to the various kinds of music, large scale or intimate. None of this can he learn from the strictly private teacher.

3   FOR A MOMENT I'd like to take again the point of view of that visitor from another planet, of anyone, real or imaginary, who looks at our world of music for the first time. If I have represented correctly the frame in which the art is taught, he would see that musicians organize in different ways to impart technical proficiency, the general trend now being toward education in groups in schools or conservatories. He might conclude that the influence of the individual teacher is diminishing.

I believe the contrary is true, yet it is hard to justify this conclusion by more than an encouraging experience here and there. It is wisest to record simply our strong hope. No matter how elaborate the equipment, education depends finally on the individual teacher, and, since great teachers are always rare, only a rash optimist would say that our musical world, with all its endowments and facilities, is particularly rich in Leschetizkys or Garcias or Leopold Auers. What we can say, however, is that the best musicians, whether they teach in conservatories or privately, agree in certain ideals for their profession, and that these ideals are characteristic of our time.

The leaders in music see room for improvement in the social status of their profession, but they recognize that much they complain of has been brought on by the behavior of the egotistical. Much but not all. If artists have been regarded for centuries as little better than vagabonds, if Shakespeare and Molière and their fellow actors were licensed like dogs before they were permitted to run loose in public, if a master musician like Haydn was a retainer in a nobleman's household, an aristocrat of the servants' hall, the cruel attitude must have had wider explanations than individual conduct. Those explanations are known and have been thoroughly traced in histories of the medieval stage, but they do not concern us here. Society's attitude toward artists has changed. Liszt and his contemporaries won from reluctant conservatism a decent respect for the musical profession, especially for the virtuoso artist.

But we are aware also that Liszt and some of the virtuoso performers since his time gave conservative society new reasons for distrusting the musical character as such. Far-sighted teachers of music now try to impart to their pupils a sense of responsibility, not only to maintain and defend the dignity of their craft, but to demonstrate by their own lives that musicians are as healthy-minded as other men.

No doubt genius will always find its own way of working; no doubt those who concentrate on any creative art may be a little untidy in their housekeeping; no doubt the sincere informality of an intellectual Bohemia will always attract gifted minds. Yet it is unfortunate that society still thinks of musicians as spoiled children, and that some music patrons continue to spoil them. Those who value the spiritual wealth which music stores up for the race, would if possible instil in their pupils a professional sense of honor, such devotion and integrity as we expect of lawyers and doctors.

The typical weakness of the musical temperament is not perhaps what general opinion ascribes to it. Many people think musicians are poor business men, but the average of business ability is as high among them as among those of any other profession. Musicians are thought to be impractical in public affairs, but as a matter of fact they excel as diplomats and as politicians. Their true weakness lies in the apparent independence of their talent from character. I must be careful here not to malign men and women whom I highly esteem; some of the noblest characters in the world today are musicians. But they would agree with me that this perplexing phenomenon exists, that there are and always have been instances of musical genius joined to character so weak that it seems not to exist. The division between Wagner the artist and Wagner the man, remains inexplicable and terrible, and the same can be said of Debussy. A composer may be entirely undependable in human relations, he may be financially irresponsible, not to say dishonest, he may be incurably lazy, and he may prove himself a habitual liar, yet at the same time in his art he may work indefatigably and with unflagging conscience.

This amputation of talent from character has been variously accounted for, but never, I think, to anyone's satisfaction. Music may be so self-sufficient a language and so self-contained a world that those who are at home in it are not to be reached by normal duties and standards. But if this were so, which I do not believe, the necessity would only be the greater to draw musicians back into the normal path of life, and to establish contacts for them with other men. It is not good for an art to bring on its practitioners the reputation of eccentrics. Too many great musicians have led irregular and unhappy lives, and far too many have made others suffer.

The best teachers of music bring these facts to the attention of their pupils, not in plain statements to discourage them from the profession, but by various hints and suggestions and chiefly by example, holding before them an ideal which if carried out would answer fears and criticisms. Though public opinion nowadays distinguishes promptly between individual artists whose talent is stronger than their character, and the excellent musicians who are also excellent men, yet there persists even among music-lovers what must be called frankly a fear of music. The idea has long been abroad that an art which can be successfully practiced apart from the ordinary standards of life is not a heathy art to follow. Serious philosophers, adopting this view reluctantly, have given reasons for it which are not lightly cast aside. The musician stirs emotions in his hearers; he not only expresses his own feelings and aspirations, but he increases their strength by expression; he lives in a welter of beauty, and unless he preserves a wholesome balance he is easily persuaded that the process of exciting emotion in others and of increasing it in himself is the whole duty of man. The intellectual effort necessary for the creation and the performance of music calls for a special use of the mind, aiding in only a slight degree other kinds of intellectual effort. To follow any profession exclusively is narrowing, but to be a musician and nothing else is in some sense dangerous to the individual and to society.

It is against the threat of this opinion that the teacher of music tries to fortify his pupils. Having imparted the mysteries of the craft, he hopes in addition to instil and strengthen such a broad humanism that in time the suspicion of music will have little to feed on. He calls to the attention of the young the handicap of those artists who are over-specialized, and the advantage which the broad-minded derive from knowledge of other things than music. It is true, he insists, that music next to words is our most complete language, and in some respects it is more self-sufficient than words, but even in music what we wish to express is life, and the musician who knows life broadly has something to say. Against the ideal of over-specialization he sets the truth that those who meet the problems of normal experience bravely, become more appealing in their art, speak to a greater number of their fellows, seem more mature and more deserving of an audience. Those who are victors in the struggle develop strength, but so also do those who are not victors; provided only that the conflict was genuine and of a kind which all men must face, the artist finds his material equally in victory or defeat, in success or in sorrow.

But this ideal will not be advanced necessarily by the virtuoso performer. Virtuosity of performance as an end in itself is little in harmony with the search for more wisdom, for more sanity, for more universal truth.

4 WE MUST RECOGNIZE how widespread is the fear of music before we can understand one problem which handicaps the teaching of music today. I have spoken of the teachers in conservatories or music schools, of the talented and able private teachers, and of the private teachers who are neither able nor competent. I have mentioned the need of protection against the incompetent teacher, and have referred in passing to the efforts made by great artists to standardize teaching, at least to the point where the incompetent can be rendered harmless.

But we have music instruction in our public-school system, and all public-school teachers are standardized. Those who wish to join the music department in grammar or high school must take courses prescribed by the educational authorities of the state in which they wish to teach. Like lawyers and doctors, they can't practice their profession unless they hold the proper certificate.

If we were to explain to the visitor from another planet this much and no more about music teaching in public schools, he might conclude that here we had achieved an ideal condition; the private music teacher may be incompetent, but the public-school teacher must certainly be good, a very fine type indeed. If, however, the visitor looked into the system before he spread too much enthusiasm on it, he would probably be amazed that the teachers of music in public schools are as good as they are. The authorities who set the requirements for teaching certificates apparently hope that whatever else the teachers know, they will know as little as possible about their subject. A large part of their preparation is in matters which have nothing whatever to do with music, and their strictly musical courses have more to do with theory than with practice, so that in many states a teaching degree in music can be secured with a smaller ability to perform, to conduct, to play, or sing, than many of the children already possess. Candidates for teaching jobs recognize the fact that in honesty and fairness to their pupils they must know much more music than the educational authorities require. They therefore ignore the requirements, adopt higher standards of their own, earn the degree without which they can't teach, and on the side pick up enough music to make their teaching worth while.

I treat the mess very gently; it is worse than I imply. My own state of New York for many years has issued a bulletin of information about the courses required for the teaching certificate, laying stress on the non-musical subjects, English, mathematics, science, language, history, civics and miscellaneous courses classed as elective. Each one of these courses well taught would be beneficial to anyone, but the teacher of music should know music, and though mathematics, science and history are valuable supplements to a musical education, they are not a substitute for it. A thoughtful educator, furthermore, might question the value of any number of so-called cultural studies pursued superficially.

But whatever we think of the non-musical requirements, there are more serious questions about the music courses. Our traditional education is through lectures and recitations, not through experiment and practice. The candidate for a teaching certificate in music must give twice as many hours to the theoretical study of music as to actual music making—what is called by the pedagogues "applied music." Now, applied music is what a musician would call music. It is also what the children in the schools would call music. If the candidate for the teaching certificate is successful, he or she will give courses in the history of music, in elementary harmony and counterpoint. Though children like to compose, these courses in theory will not necessarily teach them to do so; the teacher himself, or herself, may not have learned how to put theory to use. In addition to theoretical courses, the music department organizes of course an orchestra or band, and in some instances chamber-music groups or operatic performances. The teacher must know how to conduct, how to train the voice, how to play the various instruments. There is indeed some gesture in normal schools toward a kind of instruction in singing and in the orchestral instruments, but the result so far is meagre indeed. How meagre the educational authorities expect it to be, they indicate in their description of "performance standards." Candidates for the music certificate should, they say, present evidence that they can read and play on the piano simple accompaniments of hymns and folk songs; that they can sing with tone quality and artistic interpretation; that they can read at sight a composition of moderate difficulty such as hymn and folk tunes.

The abilities here prescribed are insufficient for the performance of school music, and in the matter of singing there is apparently no requirement that the teacher shall know the proper care of a child's voice. Almost all children, both boys and girls, can sing when they are young; few can sing later. Either they ruin their voices through their own ignorance, using them improperly, or the school teacher ruins them through improper instruction.

I repeat, the teachers in the public schools out of self-respect provide themselves with a better equipment than the authorities require. But why don't the authorities require it? To conduct a chorus properly, or to conduct an orchestra, a teacher needs not only thorough training but long experience in dealing with various kinds of voices, soprano, contralto, tenor or bass, and in dealing with these voices in various stages of development. To conduct an orchestra properly, the teacher should be able to demonstrate the correct way of playing any passage on any instrument. The country is full of veteran singers or veteran orchestral players, who could easily meet these severe requirements. From a rich variety of professional performance, they have mastered the whole field; they knew more about the theory of music before they cut their eye teeth than a graduate of a normal school could possibly find out from the instruction there received. But in most cases the veteran professional has never taken the required course in civics or what-not, and without the proper certificate, he can't join the school faculty.

I don't wish to exaggerate; I am not suggesting that the school orchestra must necessarily be conducted by an artist with the equipment to lead a philharmonic orchestra. I am, however, emphasizing the fact that many a conductor in the United States who now presides brilliantly over a first-rate symphonic group, wouldn't be allowed to teach in our schools, not even if he wished to. He might be turned down by the instructor in English for his spelling, or he might be deficient in commercial geography.

Why do the educational authorities select their music teachers on non-musical grounds?

The answer brings us back to that prejudice against artists, and especially to that fear of music of which we have spoken. When music was first introduced into the modern school, it was shoved in by public demand, not welcomed cordially among the traditional humanities. Those in authority were not sure what the effect on the students would be, what influence musicians might have. Mathematicians, historians and linguists they were used to, and though some mathematicians here and there were eccentric, and some linguists, especially foreigners, were occasionally uncertain in their domestic relations, still, on the whole, their behavior compared well with that of the average mortal. But how about musicians? The members of the board of regents, a few decades ago, were familiar with musicians at a distance, in the concert hall, but they didn't hobnob with them, they rarely asked them to dine, they suspected them wholesale of extreme unconventionality. If musicians, then, must be admitted to the teaching staff, prudence suggested that they should be as little like other musicians as possible, and as much like other teachers. The state requirements for the training of its music teachers still serves this aim, to encourage a resemblance between music teachers and other teachers, and to prevent the music teacher as far as possible from being a musician.

Knowledge of music and musicians spreads so rapidly among us that these old prejudices will soon, we hope, diminish, but they will disappear only if the ground for them ceases to exist, and there is no use denying that to some extent the grounds still do exist. Some conductors, opera singers, virtuoso artists, composers, still behave like spoiled children, and the public knows of their antics. Yet the proportion of those artists who are fine personalities and thoroughly respected citizens, grows steadily, and much effort is spent by the best teachers to make this wholesome proportion grow more rapidly.

The theoretical studies required of the prospective teacher deserve further comment. Theory is essential even for those chiefly concerned in the performance of an art, but a musician does not separate performance from theory; that bifurcation is achieved by educational philosophers who look askance on all performance. When Sebastian Bach composed the Two-part Inventions for one of his sons, he explained that they were designed to impart not only the technique but the principles of composition. Today no good teacher tries to show a pupil how to play a piece without first explaining how the piece is put together. Why do the educational authorities think so well of theory and so comparatively little of the ability to perform? This question, alas, can be asked of other subjects besides music. Why are college degrees given for composition courses in which nobody learns to write, in which nobody is expected to learn to write, in which nobody including the teacher wants to write? The theoretical approach to life is fatally attractive. Give us a seat on the sidelines, and most of us are willing to let others take part in the game and manage the show.

In recent years there has been a rapid spread of the subject called musicology. A musicologist occupies himself with the historical and theoretical aspects of the art. He is a bibliographer; he is at home in the science of acoustics; he understands the construction of the various instruments. In some cases, in addition to all this learning, he is also a musician, able to create or to perform. But it can easily be imagined that his erudition took time to assemble, and if he is a musician at all, he is probably not a very good one. Some of the most learned are extremely bad musicians.

What shall we do with musicologists? Or if they continue to multiply, what are they likely to do to us? True scholarship is precious for itself and for the service it renders in all branches of culture, but scholarship is not art, and mere information is not scholarship. A scholarly textbook of harmony, for example, would be very brief. Most textbooks contain unnecessary information and hair-splitting definitions, which serve to keep the student occupied for two or three class periods a week throughout an entire term. It takes a scholar, and a conscientious one at that, to know the essentials of his subject and to put nothing else into his textbook.

But even with a scholarly grasp of harmony, we should not yet be an artist; music must have a performance; either we bring the notes to life or someone else must do it for us. Even the phonograph record must first be made by a performer before we can turn it on at will. The scholarship of the musicologist we can admire, yet at the same time regret that anyone with a talent for music should be anything but a musician.

5 It is simpler for a school to organize instruction in the theory of music than in the performance of it. If normal and public schools exaggerate the proportion of theory courses, the explanation, in part at least, is inertia. Administrative officers can provide instruction in theory for fairly large groups of children all of the same age, and they can reasonably expect to graduate their pupils on a pre-arranged date. This orderly procedure makes its appeal to any over-burdened schedule-maker, and those who do the planning in education are usually over-burdened. The trustees or regents, inspecting the activities of their institution, are reassured to observe that music instruction proceeds at the same pace and by the same methods as instruction in other subjects.

But the public schools do teach boys and girls how to sing and how to play instruments, and in some places this training in performance is of high quality, from every point of view intelligent and efficient. Where this happy condition occurs, however, the teaching schedule is quite as complicated as in a professional conservatory. Every music student presents the teacher with a special problem. The violin players may be of the same age but they are not likely to resemble each other in the degree of their musical maturity. They all should study harmony and counterpoint, but even if their talents are equal, their aptitude for theory will vary greatly; some of the youngest will have picked up an impressive knowledge of counterpoint before anyone thinks of giving them a lesson in the subject, and others, though older, may still be fumbling with elementary harmony. If you have ten pupils of the same ability in violin playing, and send them all to the theory class, the teacher may find that he is conducting an ungraded school, in which each pupil is a class by himself.

The study of certain instruments, particularly the violin and the piano, should begin as soon as possible. Where the talent is precocious any instrument can be taken up at an early age, but the piano and the string instruments call for a technique so elaborate that unless it is mastered in extreme youth it will not be mastered completely. The voice, however, develops late, and much of a singer's training must be postponed, yet children sing while their voices are still childish, and unless they sing correctly there will be no voice to train when they grow up. Moreover, a singer should be as good a musician as a violinist or pianist, with as thorough a knowledge of harmony and counterpoint, with ability to play the piano, and with an understanding of the instruments in the orchestra.

A thorough educator in music, therefore, will know at what age each kind of talent should begin training, what should be done for the child voice even if the child does not expect to be a professional singer, what especially should be done for a child voice which shows promise of great development, and what studies the future singer should follow while waiting for the voice to mature. Only an extremely competent person can be wise in all these matters, but instances of such competence multiply; in the public schools, as in the conservatories, more and more musicians combine knowledge of their subject with tact in handling pupils. If ever temperament is difficult, it is in the young, especially in gifted singers who, knowing that they have a voice which people enjoy hearing, usually can see no reason why their career should wait till the muscles of the throat grow up, or why, during the waiting period, they should practice scales on the piano when heaven so obviously intended them to open an uneducated head and make a noise like a bird.

Chapter nine

THE COMPOSER

1   THE CAREER of the composer in our day is
                peculiar and unpredictable. It may be brilliant,
or perplexing, or tragic. It is too often solitary. In the eighteenth and
earlier centuries a musician would combine in a single personality creation, performance, and teaching. Performers are still teachers, but some
of them would rather not be. Some performers—Rachmaninoff was a
notable example—are composers but not teachers. More often than not
composers are a little condescending toward performers, in spite of the
fact that they want a performance, and a good one at that, for their own
works. If they do anything besides composing, they teach composition,
and if they are distinguished composers they attract talented disciples,
but they rarely enjoy teaching. If they had their way they would do
nothing but compose.

All composers lead much the same career, whether they write symphonies, songs, grand operas, Broadway shows, or dance music. They all
need the same equipment, though not all have it. They face the same
difficulties and they are eligible for the same rewards. They should be
well-rounded musicians, whether or not they perform or teach, and in
many branches of their art great competence is expected of them. Those
who compose for the piano and the voice must know the technique of
piano playing and of singing; those who compose for the orchestra must
know the resources and the limitations of the instruments; those who
write music for the dance or for any other program must know what aid
from music the program desires. The broad scope of the composer's

specialty justifies him to some extent nowadays in devoting all his time to it. Yet the fact that he usually is, by preference, a specialist, makes his career more than a little eccentric, and often very unhappy. Music-lovers are called upon to aid performers, but often to rescue composers.

If the composer were engaged in a business rather than an art, he could write to satisfy a known demand. The maker of hats or shoes knows what the customers have liked before and will probably like again, or he knows what they disliked; he has only himself to blame if he doesn't improve his product and adjust it to the market. But in art the customer never asks for anything; he can't tell what he wants till he gets it, and the better he is satisfied, the less he will tolerate duplicates or imitations. One Chopin or one Wagner is enough.

Doubtless some composers try to succeed by calculation, reckoning success in money, but the effort is vain. Whether or not he wishes to do so, the composer who would make his mark must be sincere. He has nothing certain to build on but himself. If he writes down to his audience he misses the audience and merely writes down. A musical show which succeeds pays better than a symphony, but there is no formula for success in either kind. The composer of symphonies follows the bent of his talent, and so does the composer of shows, and just as many, many symphonies should never have been written, the number of shows which die every year before or after they are staged is beyond computation. To compose in any style is to run a great risk, but an authentic talent refuses to be warned off, one of the signs of talent being an awe-inspiring stubbornness. More than other musicians a composer, especially if he does nothing but compose, is likely to be fanatically devoted, impractical, exasperating, and attractive.

If composers as a class are distinguished from other mortals by excessive temperament or by undue awareness of their own worth, they have plenty of excuse. The world never asks in advance for any creative art, least of all for new music, and when the composer arrives uninvited, which is the only way he can arrive, the world draws a deep sigh. There are so many composers already! Not that the world doesn't appreciate composers. On the contrary. Composers are so highly appreciated that we wish to hear their compositions over and over again. So deeply are the best composers respected, that we talk about them until the titles of their masterpieces are known among the very young and in remote places where performing artists do not often come. When the solo virtuoso or the symphony orchestra does appear, the demand is for those masterpieces which are already known by name. No one can say that composers lack success, but obviously the most successful composers are the dead ones. The genius at our elbow, waiting in line for his turn, has grounds for fearing his work will not be heard immediately, and even though he is not a genius, he may as well think he is, since the test of performance is indefinitely postponed.

The composer, therefore, competes not only with his contemporaries but with the best of the past. Yet he alone could, under the proper conditions, speak for the hour we live in. He is right in thinking that we should find our expression in music, as we find it in literature. He is right also in thinking that every age is in a sense misrepresented by its music, if only a few composers are heard. The lucky ones may not be the best. Until all are considered, no one can say what is our musical thought. The living composer finds little satisfaction in the truth that if he really is a genius, and if his manuscripts are not destroyed by accident, he may come to his own as Sebastian Bach did, long after he is buried.

Many explanations are offered of the relation which the composer today has got into, toward his art and his profession, but none of them is completely satisfying, my own no more than any other. It seems significant that those composers who create traditional types of music have departed furthest from the old pattern of the musician's career. They either are specialists or they wish to be, and since they detach themselves as much as possible from all performing activities, they must ask someone else to produce their works. There are exceptions, of course; Rachmaninoff was composer, performer, conductor; and so is Percy Grainger. But the ability of these and a few others to interpret their own compositions hardly alters the fact that the highbrow composer has a marked tendency to withdraw from all musical activities except composing.

The popular kind of composer, however, the kind considered lowbrow by the traditional, still practices his craft in the manner of Haydn or Bach. He composes for the conditions in which he performs, and he is willing to let society name the conditions. Haydn was employed as a band-master to furnish music in a nobleman's establishment. Where would he get the music? In those days there was no local music store or lending library. He was expected to compose the music himself, and being a true composer, he saw in the obligation an opportunity. He wrote his symphonies for the particular players at his disposal and for the rooms in which he knew the music would be heard, much as Bach wrote his cantatas for his choir and his organ music for the instrument in his church. No doubt he and Haydn, like Mozart and Beethoven and all other creative artists, longed for resources which were not at their disposal, but they created for the resources which they had, and they kept the performance of their music in their own hands.

This is precisely what Shakespeare and Molière did. Both dramatists wrote their plays for their own company and for their own theatre. They did not need a producer; they were their own producers. The playwright nowadays, like the contemporary "serious" composer, must ask some other person to stage his work, being from almost every point of view incapable of doing it for himself. Yet the jazz composers who more often than not lead jazz bands or perform in them, have no difficulty at all in submitting their compositions to the world. Keeping alive the wise traditions of their craft, they work in all branches of it so far as they can, and they think of performance and composition as inseparable aspects of music-making.

If we step out of a strictly musical discussion to cite parallels in literature, in painting, or in sculpture, it is only to drive home the truth that over-specialization in any art results in embarrassment for the artist. The painter who does nothing but murals or nothing but portraits is fortunate so long as the demand for murals or portraits is brisk, but if another kind of painting is wanted, he will be neglected, and a specialist of the desired kind will get the commission. All painters and all sculptors nowadays are handicapped to the extent that their work is not integrated in a decorative or architectural scheme.

The wish to specialize can easily be understood, since specialization provides the opportunity to do most what we do best, and the more we do it, the more we are likely to excel. But this is like overworking a strong muscle to avoid developing a weak one. The composer who seeks an Ivory Tower in which to meditate his dreams is dodging the very disciplines of life which would keep him in touch with his fellow men for whom he presumes to speak. In proportion as he withdraws from life, he withdraws from both his subject matter and his audience. His compositions, no matter how adroit, will repeat himself or will re-work the ideas of his predecessors.

2 How DOES A composer spend his time? How does he earn his living? The questions are closely related, but not necessarily so. Some composers are partly or entirely endowed, either because they have inherited money, or because some musical organization or some patron of music from time to time commissions them. Since the lot of a composer is difficult at best, any kind of aid may be thought of as a blessing, yet if we consider his interests in a larger way, it seems unfortunate that the composer does not earn his living as normally as other men. Kindness is not the same thing as justice, and gifts to keep him alive certainly do not serve to demonstrate that his place in society is secure.

I speak, of course, of the composer with the training and the disposition to produce larger works, symphonic or operatic, or solo works for the concert stage. The composer of musical shows, of dance music, of background for motion pictures, integrates himself with the conscious needs of his people, and according to his talents he has his reward. Those in the popular field whose talent and equipment equal the talent and equipment of "serious" composers, deserve credit for their wisdom or instinct; they believe, and act on the belief, that the roots of art are in common life, and that all arts have evolved upward by giving to popular needs an answer at once satisfying and noble. The "serious" composer, on the other hand, is usually less eager to satisfy the musical needs of which men are conscious, than to teach them they should need something else. He is no doubt an artist, but he wishes to be also a missionary.

In no department of music is our thinking hazier than in the matters which concern the composer. We know that music must continually be created. We know that imitation of music already created is at no time what we need. We know also that the scope of music has expanded far beyond the resources of any one instrument, or of a few instruments, and that to express the utmost in music, the whole orchestra must collaborate. We therefore are inclined to call that type of composer "serious" who prepares himself to say big things in a big way. We cling to the hope that he will express us, the common people, as faithfully as do the composers of popular songs, and with this addition, that his music, though still recognizable as an expression of us, may be fully competent, magnificent, and lofty. What we usually get, however, are stretches of ingenious but unlovely sound, which we try to like but can't. Toward the popular composer we may be snobbish, but we hum his tunes.

I raise the question how the serious composer spends his time. The answer ought to be simple; he ought to spend it composing, and in rare cases that is what he does. More often, however, he joins other composers in societies for the promotion of their compositions. He gives talks or lectures on music, preferably on his own music, as though an audience once convinced that it is ignorant of music would promptly educate itself —as though from patriotic motives alone Americans would teach themselves to love American music. He consents also to be a guest of honor at lunches, and dinners, and conventions of music clubs, or perhaps he sits around and accepts admiration from more intimate groups.

He can't be composing all the time, of course, but his social relaxations, if he were wise or lucky, would strengthen him for his work. What most a creative artist needs is a stream of inspiration flowing from the roots of life, and he gets that inspiration from human contacts, not necessarily from contacts with fellow musicians. Since the content of music is emotional even beyond the content of other arts, he is helped most by the experiences which not only stir his mind but touch his heart. For a true artist the Ivory Tower is a prison, and any endowment which provides for him solitude and inviolable retreat makes sure in advance that he won't write the music he should; if he isn't too timid by nature to meet life face to face, he'll become so, thanks to a sheltering benefaction.

The serious composer who earns his living year in and year out usually supplements his royalties by teaching theory or composition. Musicians in general assume apparently that a composer, rather than a pianist or violinist or singer, is the right person to teach harmony to the young. It is as though we looked for high-school teachers of grammar among poets, novelists, and dramatists. Harmony as a subject is as close to piano playing as it is to composing, and a pianist in all probability can teach it quite as well as a composer. Of course young composers of great talent will seek advice from older composers of still greater talent, but even here the benefit is limited. Musical and poetical composition have much in common. You can teach versification, but you can't teach how to write poetry. One poet by the mere exchange of ideas can often stimulate another, but you must be already a poet before you can be stimulated. In our schools and colleges today the heads of the music departments are with few exceptions composers, and the more famous they are, the luckier we feel is the institution. Our satisfaction may be justified, but it is not yet clear that these privileges and opportunities are producing composers throughout the country. The students in collegiate music departments are rarely interested in composition, and still more rarely have they a talent for it. Few musicians of great talent go to college at all; they are too much occupied with their music. I doubt if Chopin would have been an important composition teacher. I have the same doubts about Schubert. For Chopin himself, however, as later for César Franck, it was very important that he should be a piano teacher. He was composing for the piano. Schubert's songs profited by the singing he did as boy and man. I can't imagine a more rewarding occupation for an orchestra composer than to play an instrument professionally in the orchestra. There at least he spends his hours in a musical atmosphere, but the composer who teaches in a school or college must attend faculty meetings.

An artist of great vitality will remain creative even in what seem to be unfavorable conditions, yet even he had better not accept conditions less favorable than they need be. The composer who teaches in school and college too seldom, we repeat, finds incipient composers to teach. Also, he himself is not likely to remain a composer. Class work will draught off his energies, but that is not the worst of it; his teaching will exercise his mind in such a way, will create such a mood, that composition will become difficult. His case is not parallel to that of the performer. It is an advantage for a pianist to teach because the constant hearing of music keeps his repertoire fresh. The creative artist, however, does not want to teach his pupils what he himself is composing, still less to acquire their ideas.

I admit that some qualification is here in order; the attempt to state musical theory with clearness, clarifies the subject for the teacher, and up to a certain point a composer, working over class exercises, may even gather light for his own work. Yet I know from experience that the attempt to teach young writers creatively, to avoid all superficial mass instruction and to develop each individual talent in terms of itself, costs a terrific effort. The author or composer will sooner or later ask himself whether his pupils will write better than he, or whether it is in the humility of such a thought that he is teaching them. De Maupassant had Flaubert for tutor and guide in the writing of his earliest stories, and it is generally conceded that Flaubert was in this instance a supreme teacher, and De Maupassant a miraculous pupil. But Flaubert couldn't have stood the strain of teaching a class, not even a class of De Maupassants.

Some composers, seeing the disadvantage of teaching, supplement their royalties by editorial work in a music publishing house, or on a music magazine. The benefit of this course is that they keep in touch with what happens in contemporary music, they have means of knowing the musical taste at the moment, they have news in advance of fresh developments and opportunities. If there is a disadvantage, it lies in the critical habit which editorial work compels. The creative artist should at some moments examine his own work objectively, but not until it is fully imagined, and if he wants to continue his creating, he won't let the critical approach become instinctive with him. The psychological processes are so different that writers and composers should by instinct know better than to interrupt themselves when they are in the vein. Whenever possible, they should finish their first draft on one unbroken impulse, retaining for the moment the casual errors which come from improvising, but keeping also the inspiration, the happy thoughts and the spontaneity. After the first draft is done it is safe to criticize, to revise, to omit, or to rearrange. But if criticism goes hand in hand with the creative mood or follows close on its heels, the writer won't get much further than his first paragraph, and the composer won't finish a page. Self-consciousness or intermittent self-examination, being easier than creation, is liable to become the stronger habit, soon furnishing the artist with sufficient reasons for not creating at all. The number is legion of those composers and writers who have excellent ideas and intend to set them down, but never get around to it. Editorial or critical work, therefore, usually spells sterility for the composer who over any long period of time engages in it.

Two questions which a composer's friends might ask about his career, ought to bother him. Does he create because he thinks he should, or because nature compels him? Does he recognize the frame in which he belongs, or is he imagining himself in another time and place? Unless he raises the first question by way of self-examination, his friends aren't likely to put it to him. But creation of any kind is exhausting, and in art, especially I think in music, continued creation on a large scale is possible only for those who have a prodigious reservoir of energy. Most musicians are at least mildly creative, and at the end of their career, along with their record of performance or teaching, they can show a modest list of pieces, competent and often authentic so far as they go. The average musician, be it added, even though his occasional creations are fairly numerous, would not call himself a composer. On the other hand too many professed composers turn out by their total effort no more than the busy pianist or violinist creates casually. The same truth holds of course for literature. A Balzac, a Dickens, a Tolstoi is in a special sense an intellectual and spiritual giant, a Bach, a Beethoven, a Mozart, or a Schumann is a giant of the same kind, and giants of any kind are extremely rare. It is not extraordinary after all that we have so few composers; the queer thing is that we accept as a composer any person who says he is one, and by only slight additional evidence we are persuaded he deserves special aid, even endowment.

I once thrashed out this problem with a young man who held the opposite view in an extreme form. He wanted to be financed while writing what he knew would be a masterpiece, though he never yet had composed a note. He thought composers should be endowed not in recognition of what they had created but in order that they might create. I suggested that unless the candidate for endowment produced some credentials, we might endow the wrong man. He admitted the chance, but argued that even though we made many mistakes, we should lose nothing in comparison with the stifling of genius through neglect. I disqualified myself as a humane person by saying that potential genius is not genius, and I'd resist the sentimental temptation to pat on the back conceited folk who after prolonged encouragement would still be only potential geniuses. Here I admit there is room for argument; no one has yet discovered a sure way to value the promises of youth, and where there is even the illusion of talent, we'd like to give it a chance. But what we take to be talent in the young is more often youth than talent. The average shrinkage·is terrific, and the moment the shrinking tendency appears we can be sure the bloom is over. It may be that true genius can be killed by lack of encouragement, but if after encouragement there is a slowing up, it's nonsense to talk of genius.

The proper though hard-sounding advice for most composers is that they get busy and practice, and make themselves useful as performing musicians. Or if they are determined at all costs to compose, they might well consider whether they are trying to create the right kind of music. The snobbishness of composers, as I've said before in other terms, is often their undoing. To compose symphonies and sonatas is in music a mark of good breeding. Audiences do submit to symphonies, perhaps from the same resolute worship of the respectable which inspires the composer, but few informal groups get their musical pleasure listening to sonatas. Continued attention to an out-dated form is not a pleasure but a ritual. Be frank with yourself; don't you keep count of the movements of a symphony or a sonata, and don't you feel better when there is only one more to go? The characteristic talent of our day lies in other directions, and if we saw the problem intelligently, we'd esteem even more highly than we do composers like Jerome Kern and George Gershwin who won their standing by creating what was original in themselves instead of acquiring merit through imitation of old forms.

3 WE HAVE SPOKEN of the various ways in which composers earn their living. It's an unrosy subject. Since a writer, if he is successful, can live on royalties from his books, the composer for some time has been wondering why his intellectual capital shouldn't yield more of an income. Until quite recently he has suffered a great injustice, and though the business aspect of his profession is now better organized, there is still room for improvement. A shockingly large number even of popular composers—Stephen Foster is the early and typical example—have lived and died poor, though their music was played and hummed in every house on every street. The royalties on sheet music are small, and if the composition is fairly simple, many of those who play and sing it, get it by heart and neglect to buy a copy. I speak here of popular music, which is supposedly profitable for the composer. But what about piano or orchestral music? If I buy a copy, I can play the piece over and over again as long as I live without investing another cent. If I am a concert performer, I can put the piece on my programs. Perhaps the composer will realize profit indirectly through those in the audience who are moved by my playing to buy a copy for themselves, but this is a thin shield against starvation. A concert, like a play in the theatre, is a performance. The dramatist receives royalties; why shouldn't the musician? Composers of musical shows are in the favorable position of dramatists, and they profit also from the sale of their work in published form, but in general it's fair to say that published music does not yet produce the income it should.

This unbalanced situation became exaggerated in recent years with the development of the radio, which needs for its programs music in quantity. The broadcasting of a piece with no payment to the composer or his publisher was ruinous to both. Radio stations naturally used the music popular at the moment and dinned it into the public ear until no one wished to hear it again, let alone buy a copy of it. The American Society of Composers, Authors, and Publishers, familiarly known as ASCAP, now gives the creative musician and his publisher a large measure of protection by standardizing and collecting performance fees, very much as the Authors' League and the Dramatists' Guild serve the novelist and the playwright.

Yet the composer in many ways still goes unrewarded. Of all the arts music spreads itself most easily, and music lovers see no reason why they shouldn't help themselves to whatever they like. Themes from famous pieces are constantly appropriated by those who can produce no important themes themselves, and if the lifting is done boldly enough, and if the looted composer is already dead and famous no charge of plagiarism is brought. The ethics of the situation become even more twisted when the borrowing is done by a great composer, the equal or perhaps the superior of the man who thought of the theme first. Chopin adapted Polish folk themes to his own uses; Liszt made piano versions of Chopin's songs, of Schubert's songs, of Hungarian dance music, Wagner took ideas from Liszt. Who got the royalties? To whom would the royalties go in parallel cases today? There is no clear and uniform answer.

Since the same problem in some form perplexes all the creative arts, we needn't stress unduly this economic aspect of the composer's career, yet his plight is in some degree peculiar. Writers do not exact from their audience the ultimate pound of flesh, they don't even try to collect on all the uses made of their writings, but they expect and usually receive at least this courtesy, that those who wish to quote or reprint ask permission in advance. But the composer has not yet established himself in popular thought as a person. He is a disembodied source of entertainment and delight.

He might gladly remain so if he could only live without food. To create beauty and then charge for it, at so much a look or a hearing, or so much a copy, is to him as well as to others a disagreeable procedure, since it compels him to set a price on his work, and he rightly feels that good work ought not to be measured in money. I wish we could follow the example of the great Athenian Greeks, who composed their immortal dramas for no pay at all, considering all creation in art, not as economic investment, but as practice in the grace of life. But merely to mention these facts is to suggest how little an entirely disinterested attitude toward art would now appeal. The modern composer like the modern novelist would give away his work free if the state or some private Mæcenas endowed him. That was not the Greek idea; he created as he breathed, and since he asked no pay and no endowment to breathe, he asked none to create. His living he earned exactly as did those less fortunate men who hadn't the privilege of creating.

Chapter ten

THE PUBLISHER

1 THE VISITOR from Mars, attending a symphonic concert for the first time, might notice the pages of music on the desks before the players, but perhaps he wouldn't ask where these sheets came from, or what becomes of them after the concert. Our own curiosity here is not great. Few of us know anything about the printing and the care of sheet music, yet without a publisher the musical stream would dry up, and without a librarian every orchestra would soon be in trouble.

Printed music receives harder usage than books in a public library. Every time a page is turned, the paper, if not actually torn, is cracked, and eventually it comes apart. If this happens to the music we use at home, imagine what the wear and tear is on the music used by an orchestra in rehearsals as well as performance. A book may be printed on cheap paper and yet last for a long time, but the paper on which music is printed must be strong if it is to last at all, and it must remain white so that the black notes will stand out clear.

Every orchestra has its own library, but this is rarely large enough to include all the music the organization may wish at any time to play. There are lending libraries from which scores and parts can be rented, and friendly organizations lend each other what they have. The cost of score and parts is very great. The market for them is small, since the number of orchestras is limited. If the music wears out, as in time it does, the publisher will sell another copy, but there is no chance that by sales of the music he will recover what it cost to print it.

I speak of orchestral and opera scores because they are the test of a music publisher's chance to survive. Popular music produced in quantity and often on cheap paper, pays well enough, but the finer the quality of the music and the larger the group which performs it, the greater the publishing risk.

Without composers there would be no music to publish; without publishers there could be no performances. This statement needs some qualification, but in a rough way it covers the facts. Musicians, therefore, have reason to be concerned at moments like the present when the publishing of music in Europe, copyrighted music, is interrupted. Publishers have reason to be concerned when good composers are unable to create. The art of music depends on continuous composing, on the continuous printing and reprinting of musical texts, and on the continuous manufacture of musical instruments.

The music publisher usually gets out his own edition of the classics, of those works, that is, which are so old that they are in the public domain. He usually asks some musician of reputation to supervise the edition, to see that it corresponds with the authentic text, to indicate the tempo and the expression, and to make whatever further comment may seem necessary. There is a wide difference of opinion as to how music should be edited, even within this simple plan. Some of us would prefer a faithful reproduction of the original edition, if that was issued under the composer's eyes. Others prefer elaborate commentary, even when carried to the extreme practiced by Busoni. The publisher follows his own ideal, guided as far as possible by public demand, or he lets his editor persuade him.

A music publisher usually retains at least one retail store for the sale not only of his own editions, but of other editions too. He may believe he has brought ou the best text of the classics, but there will always be a different opinion and he must be prepared to satisfy even misguided tastes. He usually sells instruments too, and books on musical subjects. Nowadays he would be strangely neglectful of his opportunity if he didn't sell phonographs and records, even some musical toys. The wide range of merchandise gives him an obvious advantage over the old-fashioned publisher who marketed nothing but music. If the store supplies practically everything a musician could want, not only the music but the instruments to play it on, and whatever is needed to keep the instruments in condition, then the trade is under one roof. The violinist who comes in for a piece of music may buy a set of strings before he goes out.

Thanks to the volume of miscellaneous sales, the publisher can afford to invest in expensive scores which bring no immediate return. He can afford to publish not only the serious, less popular kinds of modern music, but also those classics which sell steadily but not in bulk. If he purveyed nothing but printed music, he could probably afford to print only what at the moment was in demand.

Since the manufacture of phonograph records calls for special skills and equipment, music publishers do not make the recordings they sell, and they classify phonographs and records with musical instruments rather than with printed music. Time may change their point of view. For all practical purposes records are now an essential branch of music publishing. They bring music to those who can't play or sing; to performers they bring the readings of other performers; to the most accomplished artists they bring what no individual by himself could perform, concerted or symphonic music.

In the early days of the phonograph only famous or popular compositions were recorded. Now the recording companies imitate the publisher more and more closely, in selecting novelties even before they have won for themselves a sure audience. So far as he can, the publisher persuades the recording company to put a new composer on the phonograph, and if the company isn't ready for the venture, the publisher may subsidize an album. Publishing and record making, in other words, tend toward an intimate collaboration which may eventually affect the art of music in profound ways. Remember the advance which was stimulated by the development of musical notation, later by the invention of music printing from wooden type or blocks, the lower price made possible by stamping the notes on soft metal, and the still cheaper method of duplicating a master copy by photography. Most people buy music because having heard it they like it. The best way to sell music is to perform it. There's a good argument for bringing out a composition first on a record; if there's a rush to the music store for the text, the publisher will go to press without urging. But if such a procedure is adopted, the record maker will have displaced the publisher as the encourager and arbiter of musical creation.

An important service which the publisher at present renders is the financing of composers in work which may ultimately be profitable, but certainly will not be so immediately. Composers in general might challenge such a statement as this, with its implication that the publisher is to any extent a Mæcenas; writers, perhaps, would deny with equal promptness that the publisher of their books is in any sense their patron. But authors and composers are aided by advance royalties, whether or not they minimize this generosity. Any form of payment in advance is a lending of capital, and so long as no interest is collected on the loan, it's in the nature of a friendly gift. I am not attributing altruism to publishers, whether literary or musical; they are in business for business reasons, and it's prudent of them not only to set up a claim on the future work of author or composer, but also to keep him alive until the work is finished. But the fact, however interpreted, is that creative talent in music is often staked by the publisher. If the compositions sell, the advance royalty is exactly what it is called and no more. If the publisher thinks highly of the composer's genius, though the work doesn't sell, the advance royalty is a philanthropic grant politely disguised. Every important music publisher has a larger investment in fine compositions and in able composers than we are likely to imagine.

It's not surprising then that the publisher has always worked hard to get performances for what he prints, and to collect playing fees for himself and the composer. Playing fees are an old institution in the theatre, where dramatists and operatic composers chiefly earn their money. It is to the publisher of the opera that application for performance is made. In our country ASCAP has extended the scope of playing fees and superintends their collection. On its Board, as in its title, the publisher is represented along with the composer.

In other words, music which in performance gives us the purest and most otherworldly experience, on its practical side is involved with the whole fabric of society, and at the manufacturing end becomes a vast business. How many billion dollars represent the annual turn-over of music as business? No one seems to know precisely, and perhaps the figures can't be obtained, since a great deal of teaching and coaching is casual, without benefit of bookkeeping. But the sum must be large enough to correct the old fashioned opinion that music is merely a supplement to other interests more immediately practical. Music, like all significant enterprises, is a kind of pyramid with a broad economic base and a sublimated apex. As the pyramid rises, the practical element yields gradually to the spiritual, and at all levels musicians can see as an axiom that it is the soul of their art which they serve. The audience enjoys the pure soul of music in a performance. The musician reaches for it always. Only in his ideal, however, can he find it untempered by practical needs.

Books of instruction in music, like other kinds of textbooks, yield a profit, and the spread of musical education in our country has made textbooks very profitable indeed. Almost too much so at times. Good material for teaching purposes can be found in the great composers. The publisher who encourages the concoction of easy or graded pieces to be used in piano instruction, but never, please Heaven, to be heard in serious performance, has something to answer for. But it's another matter with the books on theory. Our ideas of harmony change fast, so do our pedagogical theories. In our textbooks we believe, perhaps correctly, there is constant improvement, at least on the average. My own prejudices may mislead me here; I attach no great importance to textbooks in the arts, where the subject matter can be got at only by practice. A textbook in geometry comes close to being geometry, but a textbook in music hasn't the slightest chance of being music. In musical as in literary compositions there are a few guiding principles, an amazingly small number, which might as well be printed somewhere and kept for reference until the practice of the art has transferred them to our bones. But if the principles are few, the textbook won't be long, and without a fat textbook some teachers wouldn't know how to fill out the class periods for half a year. Of course they could go on and teach music, but it's easier for some of us to teach a textbook.

It's a good thing for the music publisher that he can bring out textbooks in quantity, and in fairness it should be said that nowadays he tries to make them as harmless as possible. They yield a steady income. Needless to say they are marketed in the public-school system, like other textbooks, by a highly competitive salesmanship.

The central position which the publisher occupies in the musical art is indicated by the humble fact that through his offices or his store all the news and gossip of the profession circulate. This is true of the offices and the warerooms of an instrument maker, but the instrument maker perhaps specializes in one instrument, and his news and gossip therefore run chiefly in a single groove. The publisher, however, deals with musicians of all kinds, with pupils as well as teachers, with audience as well as performers. He often sits on the Boards of musical enterprises, and he couldn't escape amateurs if he tried. He is among the first to hear of new talent, of a particularly fine performance, or a particularly unlucky one. For some occult reason he knows everyone's private hopes, scandals, diseases and ambitions. Playing God, he becomes a philosopher. If he lives long enough, he is laden with memories, given to anecdote, and pleasantly melancholy over the giants who are no more.

Chapter eleven

THE CRITIC

1   THERE IS LITTLE point in imagining what the man from Mars would ask about music critics. He probably wouldn't ask a thing. He wouldn't notice their existence unless we called his attention to them. In his ignorance he might think that if he has heard a concert and enjoyed it, there's nothing more to do except remember the pleasure and go again. The music critics themselves wouldn't necessarily object to this simple philosophy; some of them would be the first to say that music criticism as now practiced among us is an accident, if not a mistake. That is my own point of view. Many of our critics are excellent musicians, and I respect their opinions. Others know less about the art, but I like them personally. Still others seem to have a distaste for music and small competence in it. Whether or not I happen to know them, I wish them in mercy another job.

Music critics are usually not critics at all in the true sense. Originally they were umpires. Now they think of themselves as judges, handing down a verdict from a final Court of Appeal. When Paganini and Liszt were astonishing their hearers with new techniques, their supremacy was challenged by rival technicians, who on occasion would arrange a parallel concert or a series of concerts so that the world might decide which was more remarkable. Liszt and Thalberg played such duels. Enthusiasts listened to them both, and of course there were two opinions. The contest needed an umpire. Technicians of established reputation began to write about the performances, balancing the skill of one man against the skill of the other, and listing also the shortcomings. Even for good judges it is always a little easier to point out a slip than a perfection. The umpire chalks up the scores.

Obviously we have no musical criticism of that kind today, since the musical duel has gone out of fashion, and the critic gives even more attention to well-established artists than to beginners. When Toscanini or Koussevitzky conducts, we all know in advance that the performance will be of high quality. What on earth can the critic say about it? Well, he can always praise or he can blame. If he praises, it's because the performance was exactly according to his ideal. If he condemns, it is because his ideal and Toscanini's, or Koussevitzky's, differ, and it is supposed to be of interest to the world to know that he disagrees. Obviously it is too late to do anything about it; the concert has been given, the great conductor's reputation was long ago made; the comment of the music critic is by way of a final verdict, an earthly parallel to the entry the recording angel is making.

Where the performance is very fine, the verdict ought logically to be kind, but many performances are very good indeed, and the critic feels, quite naturally, that monotony should be avoided by all authors. He therefore tries to find a blemish, for seasoning. A few years ago, the morning after Flagstad had sung in one of her great roles, a music critic balanced dithyrambic praise with the remark that some of her notes, at least one or two, sounded "pinched," and she really ought to use her marvelous voice more carefully. And how many times have we been told that Kreisler or Heifetz or someone else who is supposed to know how to play a concert, was not quite in the vein at the beginning, but warmed up later on?

These silly comments are harmless, but they illustrate a queer situation in music, a major annoyance or irritation which contributes to the art no compensating good. So long as criticism is nothing but a verdict, an edict, a good or bad mark, the artist inevitably asks what authority has the critic, how good a musician he is, what was his preparation for his life work, and how did he get the job. The artist sometimes asks also, and with good reason, whether the critic has a sense of humor, and whether he knows anything of human nature. There is no question that performers are sometimes not "in the vein," but critics also may be tired, or they may have a cold, or just before going to the concert they may have had an argument with their wife. Why take it out on the performer, in the public press? It may be that Flagstad wasn't entirely competent to manage her voice, though I always thought she was, but the critic who hints that she wasn't, invites the question whether he is competent to manage it for her. The critic has a right to notice faults which he can correct, and only those faults.

The importance of the Day of Judgment is supposed to lie in the authority and power of the judge. Music criticism is important only when the authority of the critic is known and recognized. Since the criticizing is done chiefly in newspapers, the editors could put the musical world in their debt by announcing in complete detail the professional education and experience of each individual critic. Best of all, they could ask a musician of established name to write up the concerts. Perhaps they do make this attempt, and perhaps their failure ought not to surprise us. Would anyone who really had something to say as performer or composer give up that career in order to criticize others who really have something to say?

The history of some music critics would surprise the innocent newspaper reader. On some papers in the provinces the office boy or someone else in the condition of apprentice may be called upon, in a sudden emergency, to pinch hit in the daily evaluation of an art, and if the pinch hitter happens to be fond of music, he may settle into the career. I have one friend who in extreme youth applied for a job on a newspaper, and since he had no experience in journalism and since there was a vacancy in the music department, the editor tried him out there, where ignorance and inexperience wouldn't be a handicap. He did so well that he was promoted to a sports column.

The larger the paper the critic writes for, the better critic he's supposed to be. The paper contributes his prestige. There are some excellent critics in towns and small cities, but only those who write for metropolitan dailies are quoted.

The newspapers themselves understand this situation, and because they do, the position of the music critic with them is a queer one. Since music is an important art, they feel they should devote a department to it, but they look upon the critic not as a musician and certainly not as a journalist. He never collects any news, since his information is brought to him in the advance programs of concerts and in the publicity of agents, and he knows where the concerts will be. The news seeks him out; all he has to do is submit himself to it. Whatever this process is, a newspaper man wouldn't call it leg-work. Moreover, the criticisms appear after the concert is finished and the audience gone home. It is a post mortem operation, an autopsy, and at best it resembles dissection in this respect, that it tries to deduce principles of life from a cadaver. Perhaps few newspaper men stop to consider—but I know some who do—that their critic is obliged to use words to discuss a quite different language, which is untranslatable, and which can't be produced on paper to illustrate his points.

If the editor finds it difficult to explain to himself what a music critic is, he doesn't worry so much as he should about the hard or impossible life he expects the critic to follow. The abuse I've here been heaping on music critics refers to the lack of standards in their profession, to the consequent unevenness of their preparation, and to the haziness of their aim, but the critics are not responsible for the schedule the newspaper imposes on them. Here they can be blamed only for their willingness to lead a dog's life. In the large cities during the winter season there is at least one concert every afternoon and one in the evening, and of course there may be more than one at any time of day. The critic is supposed to attend all performances and meet the next deadline of his paper. After the matinee he gets ready the criticism which will appear the following morning, an assignment which wouldn't be difficult if he had the evening free, but he attends the evening concert also and gets ready another criticism which also must make the morning edition. The papers of the larger cities employ one leading critic and several assistants, but even so, the staff is not always adequate to cover all the concerts, and critics have been known to keep a taxi at the door so that they could race from the first half of one concert to the second half of another. From the evening performance, especially if it's a long opera, the critic frequently tears himself away in the middle of the last act, or even earlier, in order to get his piece done in time. If he is scrupulous in such matters he will say in his review what part of the concert he attended, but quite often he doesn't say, and the reader assumes that he has heard all that he is criticizing. In the case of symphonic or operatic programs where the conductors, orchestras, and other artists are well known, the wily ones write the body of their review well in advance and rush back to the office only to revise an opinion, or to bring the account into stricter accord with what really happened.

No one bound to such a time-table as this has a fair chance to enjoy what he hears or to give a correct account of it. It's psychologically impossible to surrender yourself to music if you know you must make a deadline. You're not likely to feel the spell if you're holding a stopwatch. It's extremely difficult, if not impossible, to express a worthwhile opinion in an improvised article which cannot be rewritten. It's little short of miraculous that many critics in such conditions do manage to write sympathetically and conscientiously through the whole length of a crowded season. On the other hand, it's not surprising that they sometimes leave the concert or delay their return after an intermission for a leisurely smoke and chat together in the lounge room. To respond to beauty with love and admiration, and to sustain the mood of worship, exhausts the soul. Only creative geniuses of the first rank can keep it up.

The music critic is busy even beyond his schedule. He writes a long article for the Sunday edition of his paper, he contributes to the magazines, and he gives lectures before clubs and schools. Naturally he would be glad to improve himself, and he does read all he can, but his kind of life can't be combined with the quest of scholarship. For specific information for his longer articles and his lectures he depends on the usual encyclopedias, and if he can afford it he hires a secretary, at home in several languages, to do his research for him.

2 IN ALL this activity there may be at times a flash of genuine criticism, but there is no reason why there should be. The umpiring tradition is strong, it finds encouragement in certain mean traits in human nature, in the fault-picking instincts, and it flatters the love of power which lurks in us all. To control the music column of an influential paper, and there to hand out Olympian judgments on the greatest musicians in the world, is a sensation which many of us would enjoy. Olympian utterances do little good, and may do harm, but to think that we earn our living by making them! There is faint hope that music critics themselves will rehabilitate their profession, and the editors who employ them have so far displayed little dissatisfaction with what they get, and small wish for something better.

True criticism is not a man-hunt, nor is it a separating of the sheep from the goats. It may be a judgment, but it is not a final judgment. Criticism properly understood and practiced is indeed a separating of the good from the less good, but it is a progressive separating. It is a function of the creative faculty. The performing artist recognizes it on the rare occasions when it slips into a review; to his joy he reads something which he can put to profitable use in his next performance. Criticism worth writing or reading should always illuminate the art. The audience will get from it reasons for liking the music as much as they did, and reasons for liking it more. After learning from the critic, they will be eager to try out their new knowledge by hearing the concert again. The artist will find in true criticism intelligent recognition of what he is trying to do, and good advice, direct or implied, how to do it better. But if the critic teaches or inspires neither audience nor artist, what he writes is not criticism but unprofitable praise or blame. Most of the verdicts which appear in the newspaper the morning after are a waste of space. If you liked the concert and the critic didn't like it, you must ignore him or he'll discourage you. If you didn't like it and if he agrees with you, you may be glad to have your opinion confirmed, but the concert is a dead loss anyway. On the other hand, if you liked the concert and if the critic liked it too, yet contributes no reason for liking it, you might just as well have written the criticism yourself.

The ideal criticism, the constructive kind, condemns or blames by ignoring. European criticism at its best excels in this polite art of dismissing in silence. The sooner a bad concert is forgotten, the better; if the concert was on the whole good, but if one or two minor slips occurred, the audience promptly forgets the slips in the total pleasure. The wise critic helps the forgetting. He doesn't even add a sentence to the effect that though the slips occurred, they have been forgotten. He collaborates with the audience and with the performer in the effort to create beauty, first in the actual hearing, then in long memory.

The critic with a crowded schedule can't hope to write in this helpful and creative mood; he needs time and reflection. If his present schedule were thrown out the window, a much better one, I think, could easily be invented. I wish we might publish no criticisms immediately after concerts. In the morning paper concerts are advertised for that day or later. It would be an advantage to all of us if the critic told us in advance which are the important items in those programs, and why we should hear them. If the artist is as yet unknown, he might tell us what claims the novice has on our attention. Obviously he wouldn't recommend everything in all concerts nor all the concerts advertised, but he could excite our curiosity with discrimination and prepare us to enjoy. At the end of the week he might well devote his long article to the moments in all the concerts which he has found worthwhile. If some beauty has been revealed which he did not foresee, he might tell us. If success here and there excelled his hopes, it would be encouraging to both audience and performer to know that too. About whatever was disappointing, he would remain silent. By the end of the week he'd gladly forget the rough spots.

This conception of criticism would make of the critic not a judge but a teacher and partner. Liszt at times was such a critic, and so was Schumann, and so are all music-lovers who help their fellows to see more in what they already have begun to admire. These pages try to sketch a portrait of the art in its present incomplete state, but not statically, rather in its condition of constant growth. Our ideas of harmony change and grow, the ear learns to hear more keenly, the mind follows patterns more securely, the performer's career develops, the audience grows, the amateur comes nearer the professional, instruments are improved, the social integration of music in human life advances—and the critic could inspire the advance.

It is too early to hand out marks. The art of music, we hope and believe, has a long way still to go. It expresses the yearnings of the soul, to which certainly we are prepared to set no limits. Composer, performer, and audience are grateful to the rare person when he does appear who can open our senses and kindle our hearts by the contagion of his own intelligent love.

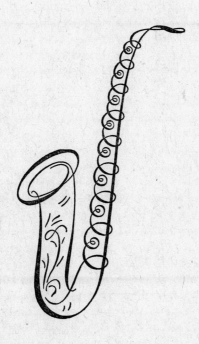

BIBLIOGRAPHY

THE REFERENCES here suggested do not pretend to cover all the subjects touched on in this book. I name merely works which may prove helpful to my readers, assuming that what I say interests them—assuming also that they may not agree with me. I do not myself agree entirely with the authors I here cite, but I have been stimulated by them.

Any student of music knows the standard encyclopedias and other works of reference. It is needless to call the attention of English readers to *Grove's Dictionary of Music and Musicians*. Practically every chapter in this book is to some degree indebted to some article in *Grove's*.

It should be equally unnecessary to emphasize the importance of Cecil Forsyth's *Orchestration*, the best one-volume treatment of the instruments now used in the various kinds of band.

Orchestral scores are most conveniently studied in miniature reproductions, which used to come to us from Germany. Since that supply is cut off, American music publishers have been satisfying the demand, but not at so low a price. I like the miniature scores of E. F. Kalmus, 209 West 57th Street, New York City.

The subject of acoustics can be studied nowadays in many books. I have made clear my opinion that the teaching of harmony should be based far more directly than it yet is on the science of sound. The scientific principles once grasped, we can throw overboard many theoretical rules and warnings, since the traditional doctrines of harmony were developed and promulgated in a period magnificently ignorant of acoustics. An excellent introduction to the subject is *The Psychology of Music*, by James L. Mursell, published by W. W. Norton & Co., New York.

Theories of composition, like the rules of harmony, have been elaborated by some authorities almost beyond belief and quite beyond common sense. For me the classic illustration of theory-spinning is a work published over thirty years ago, unfortunately not available in English, and only with difficulty available now in its original tongue, but it had an influence, perhaps still has in some quarters, and the distinguished name of its author makes it hard to put down. I refer to the *Cours de Composition Musicale,* Vols. I and II, by Vincent d'Indy, published in Paris by Durand et Cie., in 1912. Even if the reader cannot examine this work or doesn't care to, I recommend a short but brilliant comment on it, constituting the first chapter of *Outspoken Essays on Music,* by Camille Saint-Saens, translated by Fred Rothwell, and published in New York by E. P. Dutton & Co. Saint-Saens stood as firmly for simplicity and common sense in music as d'Indy stood for over-definition, for hairsplitting, and for metaphysical logic.

No musician should miss—and very few do—Albert Schweitzer's autobiography, called in the English translation *Out of My Life and Thought,* published by Henry Holt & Co., New York. The comments it contains on music, as on the other subjects which have interested Schweitzer's comprehensive genius, are fascinating. I refer the reader especially to the pages on the editing of Bach's organ works, on the rendering of Bach on modern organs, and on organs and organ-building.

I recommend the various books by Aaron Copland, published by Whittlesey House, New York, particularly *What to Listen for in Music,* and *Our New Music.* Mr. Copland writes with the authority of an accomplished and experienced composer, and also with, what is rare, a broad understanding of the art and profession of music, and of the musical conditions in our country today.

Particularly brilliant as a general estimate of the contemporary art and its practitioners is Virgil Thomson's *The State of Music,* William Morrow and Company, New York. Mr. Thomson enjoys being a little naughty when he composes, and positively wicked when he writes. The cleverness of his book is for some readers a little too dazzling, but they shouldn't let it blind them to solid truth admirably expressed.

From musicologists we have nowadays a stream of scholarly information, some of it new, most of it admirably reorganized. I would suggest, as a useful example, *Music in Western Civilization,* by Paul Henry Lang, W. W. Norton & Co., New York.

I might cite also, with neither false pride nor false modesty, *A Musical Companion,* the work of various English musicians and published originally in England, later edited by me for American use and published by Alfred A. Knopf, New York.

There are numerous handbooks and treatises on the art of conducting. Two classics on the subject, though written long ago, must still be consulted—*Le Chef d'Orchestre,* by Hector Berlioz, 1848, and *Ueber das Dirigiren,* by Richard Wagner, 1869. Both these famous works have been translated.

Paul Bekker's *The Story of the Orchestra,* W. W. Norton & Co., New York, is a helpful study of symphonic development in the nineteenth and twentieth centuries.

The present condition of American orchestras in their relation to American society is admirably studied and presented in *America's Symphony Orchestras and How They Are Supported,* by Margaret Grant and Herman S. Hettinger, W. W. Norton & Co., New York.

The Layman's Music Courses, organized on original principles by Olga Samaroff Stokowski, have had distinguished success in clarifying the subject for the intelligent listener. Madame Stokowski estimates the values of music quite as any other professional artist would, but she stresses the comparatively few essentials and goes straight at them. Her own success as a teacher of brilliant pianists compels attention to her methods. The reader can profitably consult her *The Layman's Music Book,* W. W. Norton & Co., New York.

A standard textbook of the harmonies we are most likely to hear nowadays is *Modern Harmony in Its Theory and Practice,* by Arthur Foote and Walter R. Spalding, published by Arthur P. Schmidt, Boston. Since this work is now almost forty years old, the reader may be surprised that I should agree with its title and call it modern, but at the beginning of this century much of the music which for certain listeners is still too advanced was already composed and known to those who kept abreast of the art. What makes this book particularly stimulating is the quality of the illustrations which the authors selected. They found their examples of modern music in Bach and other established masters, as well as in the so-called innovators of that period. For an alert reader the point is driven home that the modernness of a composer at any date is measured by the extent to which he can hear or imagine the harmonics of a musical sound.

This Modern Music, a Guide for the Bewildered Listener, by John Tasker Howard, Thomas Y. Crowell Co., New York, is a popular up-to-the-minute account of the composers of 1942, the year in which the book appeared. It is stronger in biographical and bibliographical information than in its statement of theoretical principles, but its account of tonality, atonality, tone-clusters, and quarter-tones will be illuminating to beginners.

The Book of Modern Composers, edited by David Ewen, published by Alfred A. Knopf, New York, is a very intelligent collection of studies dealing with some thirty composers who are important today. For each composer there is a short biography, a personal statement of ideals and principles, and a criticism by a known authority. For each composer there is also an individual bibliography, and at the end of the book a general bibliography. There is also a bibliography of selected recordings of principal works.

The following books also are recommended:

Twentieth Century Music, by Marion Bauer, G. P. Putnam's Sons, New York.

Toward a New Music: Music and Electricity, by Carlos Chavez, translated by Herbert Weinstock, W. W. Norton & Co., New York.

New Music Resources, by Henry Cowell, Alfred A. Knopf, New York.

A Survey of Contemporary Music, by Cecil Gray, Oxford University Press, New York.

Sensations of Tone, by Hermann von Helmholtz, Longmans, Green, New York.

Music Here and Now, by Ernst Křenek, W. W. Norton & Co., New York.

Study of Modern Harmony, by Rene Lenornaud, Boston Music Co., Boston.

Science of Musical Sounds, by Dayton C. Miller, Macmillan Co., New York.

Composers in America: Biographical Sketches of Living Composers With a Record of Their Works, 1912-1937, by Claire Reis, Macmillan Co., New York.

INDEX